Selena
Como la Flor

Selena Quintanilla was a vibrant musical performer, wildly popular in the growing field of Tejano music. But her rising star suddenly fell when she was murdered at the age of 23. Now, her life, her work, and her musical legacy have been lovingly documented in *Selena: Como la Flor*.

At the time of her death, Selena was poised to break into the mainstream music scene. But as she enjoyed professional success beyond her wildest dreams, her personal life had more than its share of troubles. There was family tension surrounding her marriage to guitarist Chris Perez. and mounting pressure between her and the manager of her fashion boutiques, Yolanda Saldivar.

Bestselling author Joe Nick Patoski recounts both the ups and downs of Selena's life, as well as her stunning transformation into a sensual Latina superstar. Most of all, he pays tribute to the life of this one-of-a-kind talent and a young life cut short by murder, but one that will never be forgotten.

Selena:
Como la Flor

JOE NICK PATOSKI

Berkley Boulevard Books, New York

THE BERKLEY PUBLISHING GROUP
Published by the Penguin Group
Penguin Group (USA) Inc.
375 Hudson Street, New York, New York 10014, USA

Penguin Group (Canada), 90 Eglinton Avenue East, Suite 700, Toronto, Ontario M4P 2Y3, Canada
(a division of Pearson Penguin Canada Inc.) • Penguin Books Ltd., 80 Strand, London WC2R 0RL,
England • Penguin Group Ireland, 25 St. Stephen's Green, Dublin 2, Ireland (a division of Penguin
Books Ltd.) • Penguin Group (Australia), 250 Camberwell Road, Camberwell, Victoria 3124, Australia
(a division of Pearson Australia Group Pty. Ltd.) • Penguin Books India Pvt. Ltd., 11 Community
Centre, Panchsheel Park, New Delhi—110 017, India • Penguin Group (NZ), 67 Apollo Drive,
Rosedale, Auckland 0632, New Zealand (a division of Pearson New Zealand Ltd.) • Penguin Books
(South Africa) (Pty.) Ltd., 24 Sturdee Avenue, Rosebank, Johannesburg 2196, South Africa

Penguin Books Ltd., Registered Offices: 80 Strand, London WC2R 0RL, England

The author is grateful for permission to include the following previously copyrighted material: Excerpts
from letters in *Brazosport Facts* and *The Corpus Christi Times*. Copyright © 1995. Reprinted by
permission of *The Corpus Christi Times*.

SELENA: COMO LA FLOR

A Berkley Boulevard Book / published by arrangement with Little, Brown and Company, Inc.

PUBLISHING HISTORY
Little, Brown and Company, Inc. hardcover edition / April 1996
Berkley Boulevard edition / March 1997

Copyright © 1996 by Joe Nick Patoski.
Reprinted by arrangement with Little, Brown and Company, Inc.

ISBN: 978-0-425-17124-0

BERKLEY® BOULEVARD
Berkley Boulevard Books are published by The Berkley Publishing Group,
a division of Penguin Group (USA) Inc.,
375 Hudson Street, New York, New York 10014.
BERKLEY® BOULEVARD and its logo are trademarks of
Penguin Group (USA) Inc.

PRINTED IN THE UNITED STATES OF AMERICA

15   14   13   12   11   10   9   8   7   6   5

To Johnny and Henry Molina,
wherever you are

Contents

Selena:
Como la Flor

1
Music and the Muse

T O MOST OF THE DINERS enjoying their chicken flautas at Papa Gayo's, in Lake Jackson, Texas, the sweet little girl with the bubbly personality was part of the Mexican restaurant's entertainment. Papa Gayo's was a family operation, and everyone involved—mom, dad, the kids, the relatives—played a role. The little girl's older brother, A.B., had sanded the tables, her father built the stage, and the little girl, along with A.B. and her sister Suzette, kept everyone amused and entertained.

She stepped up to the microphone tentatively, but once the music started she appeared poised and confident, as if she had been doing this all her life. On cue, she took a deep breath, and then belted out the lines she'd rehearsed:

"*Feeeee*-lings, whoa-ohhhhh-ahhhhh, *feeeee*-lings . . ."

She sang as if the hurt described in the song's lyrics was a hurt she'd felt. Then she sneaked a glance at the man watching her from the side of the stage, waiting for his lips to reveal the slightest hint of an approving smile.

The little girl's name was Selena, and even a stranger could tell she was her father's pride and joy. Behind her, standing only a few feet away on the same stage, her brother and sister played bass and drums in accompaniment. But it was the little girl's booming voice, big and brassy, emotive and evocative, that grabbed diners' attention. Even the mayor, the city manager, and their wives, who were dining together at one table, paused between bites to marvel over the little girl's talent. She played to the restaurant's customers as if they were a crowd of thousands in a concert hall.

The little girl's father, Abraham Quintanilla, had raised her to do just that. Long ago, before anyone else had an inkling of her ability, he believed his little girl possessed a talent, the special something that separated stars from almost-stars like him. It was in her blood.

The restaurant's specialty, Mexican food, was part of the family's heritage. The little girl's mother, Marcella, a sweet, shy lady with an attractive, perennially youthful face, came from Washington State. But like her husband, Abraham, who was born and raised in South Texas, she could trace her roots back to Mexico. Washington harbored many families like Marcella Samora's, people who settled there as part of the mass migration of farm workers from the south. The Quintanilla side of the family could also trace its roots back to the migrants who had crossed the Rio Grande to pick cotton, vegetables, and fruits; they later settled in Corpus Christi, where Abraham, Sr., and his wife, Mary, raised Abraham and his six siblings. Eleven years before the restaurant opened, Abraham had followed the elder Quintanilla to the Brazosport area of Texas, where most of his family was already living.

Though the town of Lake Jackson, where the Quintanillas lived, was two hundred miles from Corpus, it felt a million miles away from there, and at least two million from the Rio Grande, the border separating Texas from Mexico. Abraham and Marcella adopted a thoroughly modern, wholly American outlook on life, working hard, raising their children with a firm hand and strict discipline, and striving for a comfortable lifestyle. Early on, the children were taught to speak English, both at home and at school. It was the best way to get ahead in the world.

Abraham had learned that the hard way: students caught speaking Spanish in Corpus Christi schools when he was a boy were sent to the principal's office and whipped or suspended.

Abraham, his wife and children, and his parents and his brothers and sisters could be identified as Mexicanos by the way they looked and spoke. But having to adapt and assimilate was nothing new to them or people like them; Mexicans in Texas had been adapting and assimilating since before Texas was a state. Lake Jackson was a relatively easy adjustment, even if the population of twenty thousand was ninety percent *gabacho*. At least it wasn't as bad as some of the neighboring communities whose citizens did not welcome people of Mexican heritage and were often downright hostile.

Abraham, Jr., came to the area to be near his parents and his siblings, but it was Dow Chemical, Lake Jackson's major employer, that kept him there, giving him a steady income that paid for a down payment on a house, material goods, and, ultimately, a piece of Papa Gayo's.

Still, no matter how well he and his family fit in, there were always reminders that Abraham was different from most other workers at Dow, whether it was his deep brown skin tone, his prominent nose and chiseled features, or his deep sense of heritage and place. Anglos and Mexicanos shopped side by side at the same stores, ate at the same restaurants, sat next to each other in the movie theaters, and attended the same schools. But at home, they had different value systems and rules, some of which might have struck each other as strange and exotic. The stereotypical Mexicano had a tight-knit extended family, was overly superstitious, Catholic, and spoke only Spanish. The stereotypical Anglo was uptight, the product of a broken home, fundamentalist Christian, and spoke only English. In truth, neither ethnic group fit the stereotype.

The food at Papa Gayo's was the most basic link between the two cultures. For most Anglos, Mexican food was the gateway to appreciating Texas's Other Society. The ingredients—peppers, onions, garlic, cilantro, comino—were Mexican in origin but there were not-so-subtle variations that were distinctly Texan (or Tejano, as the Mexicanos often referred to themselves): in the arroz con pollo (rice with chicken), carne guisada (stew), and chile rellenos (stuffed chili peppers), the cheese was yellow instead of white, and less cilantro and serranos and more jalapeños, comino, and chili powder common in the Mexican interior were used. The dishes were accompanied by handmade flour tortillas instead of the corn variety served in Mexico. In the company of a gleaming mound of beans refried in lard and rice and spiced by a red salsa, the creations were uniquely Tex-Mex.

The implications made little sense to the nine-year-old Selena, raised to sing pop and country songs and the occasional traditional Mexican song to please her father, her family, and the diners. Music transcended cultural differences. Music, and plenty of practice, as she would later reflect. "My dad had this old songbook, and I picked it up and I started making my own melodies. He heard me one day and he started saying, 'No, do it like this.' He was teaching me the melodies and I caught on pretty fast."

Owning a Mexican restaurant wasn't necessarily a life-long dream of Abraham's but, as always, he saw an opportunity and gave it a try. Lake Jackson was a foursquare community where there were no bars, no lounges, and only a handful of restaurants. Not too many folks knew what a tortilla was. So Abraham put some of his savings together with some money from Santos "Jim" Serda, Jr., a coworker and friend of his from church, and opened Papa Gayo's. If the restaurant was successful, he'd never have to look back. Even if it wasn't going to make him a million, the restaurant was a way for Abraham to get back into music. He already knew something no one else did.

On a visit back to Corpus, he stopped in to pay his respects to Johnny Herrera, a record-shop owner who was his mentor. He wanted Herrera to hear Selena, his pride and joy. Herrera, sitting in the company of his wife and mother-in-law, smiled at her and coaxed her over to get a better look. "So she's a chip off the old block," he said, nodding to Abraham. "Let her sing for me."

Herrera set up his portable cassette recorder and aimed the small microphone in Selena's direction. She ran through a bunch of American oldies. She could do them all. Herrera noted that she stayed in tune and didn't miss the beat.

"She's going to be a star." Herrera cackled. Abraham's little girl, little Selena, was going to be a star. But could she sing in Spanish?

"A little bit." Selena smiled. She sang "Con Esta Copa," the old Dinos' Spanish regional hit; songs that Herrera had written. When she finished singing, she looked at her small audience. *"Es bueno?"*

"Sí," they said. *"Muy bien."*

Star. Abraham Quintanilla, Jr., liked the sound of that word. Short, sweet, and to the point. It always came down to language for Abraham. He was a Mexican-American who grew up poor in Corpus Christi, the port of South Texas, where his father supported the family with a variety of jobs, mostly auto-body repair work and painting. Abe, or Junior, as his close relatives called him, grew up in two cultures, part Mexican and part American. He understood their differences through their languages.

In Abraham's childhood home, Spanish was spoken. It was the native tongue of his parents, Abrán and María. Though the father was born in Corpus Christi and the couple would eventually be known as Abraham and Mary, they observed the ways of the old country, from eating beans, rice, and tortillas to celebrating Diez y Seis, Cinco de Mayo, and festivals like the Fiesta de Corpus Christi that were rooted to Catholic holy days. The family moved around Corpus throughout Abraham's youth, residing in a two-room shotgun shack at 620 Virginia Street and in similarly humble dwellings around the west side, the Mexican side of town.

At school, English and only English was spoken. The

children's parents may have been Mexican, but the students were educated as Americans. Abe's roots were Mexican; his future was as a Texan. Yet he was neither Texan, in the Anglo sense of the term, nor Mexican, since Texas-Mexicans were held in a different light than Mexicans from Mexico. The polite term Anglos used for people like him was *Spanish*, although Mexican or Mexican-American sufficed. A term used in Mexico was more accurate: he was Tejano, the Spanish word for Texan.

The world Abraham grew up in was defined by the Catholic Church, which was the glue that held together Mexican-American society; the superstitions and folklore of Mexico, whose influence was as strong as the Church's; and the laws of Anglos, who ran local society and politics.

The confusion about just what a person was or wasn't came with the territory. The southern part of the state where Abe Quintanilla grew up was a neutral zone harboring two distinctly different societies and cultures. Up until the nineteenth century, the Nueces river, which empties into the Corpus Christi Bay, was considered the dividing line between Mexican and Anglo. Mexicanos, or those whose Aztec and Mayan blood had been mixing with Spanish *sangre* since Hernán Cortés landed at Veracruz in 1519, dominated to the south. They had a caste system based on bloodlines: Spanish blood was considered purest, followed by *mestizo*, or mixed blood, and pure *indígena* blood was held in the lowest regard.

In 1810, Mexico declared independence from Spain. Twenty-six years later, rebellious Anglo colonists who called themselves Texians broke away from Mexico. The Rio Grande, 125 miles south of the Nueces, was declared the ultimate boundary twelve years later, on February 2, 1848, when representatives from Mexico and the United States signed the Treaty of Guadalupe Hidalgo, an agreement that ceded all lands north of the river to the United States. The treaty guaranteed Mexican-Americans their civil rights, their right to worship, and the right to retain their culture and language. The Anglos ignored these specifics, though; they instilled English as the dominant language and generally treated Mexicans as inferiors.

In other words, people living in present-day South Texas did not necessarily intend to come to the United States; the United States came to them.

Texans of Anglo descent traditionally looked down on Texans of Mexican descent. Despised, reviled, and disrespected them, in fact. In many parts of the state, Mexican-Americans, though natives by birth and history, were held in contempt along with African-Americans, expressed in signs declaring NO NIGGERS, NO MEXICANS posted in front of public facilities, rest rooms, and water fountains as recently as forty years ago. "Meskins," as Mexican-Americans were sometimes called, may have not been slaves of the white man, but they were on the losing side of the war for Texas's independence, as whites were all too quick to remind them. Much of the hostility officially ceased when segregation laws were repealed in the nineteen fifties and sixties, but in many quarters racism and discrimination persisted.

This was especially irritating for Mexicanos and Mexican-Americans born and raised in Texas. It was bad enough that the Alamo was celebrated as a triumph rather than a defeat. It was bad enough that students of Texana underplayed and demeaned the significance of Texas's oldest families, those having *indígena, mestizo*, and Spanish bloodlines who had occupied the same land since before the viceroy of Spain issued land grants that formalized the existence of Texas real estate. Anglo history books, written from the perspective of victors, portrayed the vanquished as lesser beings, second-class citizens whose contributions were limited to providing the physical labor necessary for agribusiness. That view was a blanket condemnation of the race that migrated north to build missions, irrigate and farm the desert, and bring culture in the forms of music, art, and religion to the wilderness that existed before the first white settlers arrived in the 1820s. Forgotten was the vaquero tradition of Mexico that created the basis for ranching in South Texas, one of the region's most valued institutions.

What applied to John did not apply to Juan. By virtue of living north of the line that had been drawn, Mexicanos had little choice but to suffer quietly under the thumb of the occupying forces, the gringos, who had seized the land that was once theirs. The story of oppression had been told and retold through *corridos*, songs based on true events. This tradition dated back to Medieval Spanish troubadours, who functioned as musical newspapers, spreading the news in rhyming song wherever they went. The antagonists in many *corridos* of the Texas-Mexico borderlands were the hated *Rinches*, the Texas Rangers, who enforced the law on the Texas side and had a tendency to shoot Mexicans first, ask questions later. The heroes of these songs were brave Mexicanos who stood up to the Rangers or managed to escape their wrath.

When Abe was growing up in the nineteen forties, the Anglo-Mexican divide was less pronounced than it was thirty years earlier, when all Mexican-American children attended the Mexican school at Tancahua and Leopard streets no matter what part of the city they lived in or what grade they were in. Back then, the Corpus Christi city directory carried the designations of *C* for colored, *M* for Mexican, and *EM* for English-speaking Mexican. Corpus Christi's high school was integrated only because there was no Mexican high school for students to attend. Educating Mexicans was important, one teacher rationalized, "because it helps make them better servants." Integration of lower grades and inclusion of Mexican-Americans on juries were rights achieved during the forties and fifties through the efforts of the League of United Latin American Citizens, a national organization founded in Corpus in 1929, whose members emphasized that they considered themselves American, not Mexican.

In 1940, Dr. J. A. García won a seat on the Corpus Christi school board and became the first Mexican-American elected to public office.

Mexican-American Corpus Christi changed more rapidly after World War II, following the return of young men who'd been treated as equals by men of all colors from other parts of the United States in the military. After that, they would never again be satisfied with second-class status. Mexicanos in Corpus finally gained a foothold in city government in 1955, when Manuel P. Maldonado, a forty-four-year-old tortilla-factory owner, became the first Mexican-American elected to the city council.

The Mexican-American part of Corpus Christi began in an area downtown known as the Hill. It was the least desirable part of town, since it was away from the water and the cooling sea breeze. The Hill started around Waco Street and followed Leopard Street out toward the San Antonio highway. The Catholic churches, most with ornate facades, columns, detailed sculptures, and red tile roofs, were the community's biggest, most imposing institutions. There was also the Miller High complex, with the football field built into the side of the school, numerous cafés, the Galvan Ballroom upstairs from the Galvan music store, the *panaderías, hierberías*, and *cantinas*—all these things distinguished west side Corpus Christi from the other side of town.

When Abe Quintanilla was fourteen, his parents left the Catholic Church to become Jehovah's Witnesses. It was a decision that changed his family forever. Abraham, Sr., and Mary were among the early pioneers in the exodus of Latin-Americans from the Catholic Church to Protestant religions that was led by the Mormons and Jehovah's Witnesses, who were among the more aggressive groups seeking to convert the Spanish-speaking population through door-to-door missionary work. Junior's parents may have seen the light, but try as he might, Junior could not take the walk that would bring him closer to their God. He was busy answering another calling, one that to him was far more illuminating and personally fulfilling. It was the sound of voices harmonizing, making a kind of music that struck him as the sweetest, smoothest, most soothing form of communication that he'd ever heard. That was the motivation behind joining forces with two other members of the Ray Miller High School Choir to form an informal singing group called the Gumdrops.

But epiphany didn't come until a Y dance in 1957, where he encountered three buddies—Bobby Lira, Seferino Perales, and Lupe Barrera—he knew from Ray Miller High. The three were blending their voices into a unified sound, singing in English and holding the gathering in a state of rapture. The trio had been performing for free at high school dances in Corpus under the name the Dinos. Once Abe caught their act, he was hooked. A few months later, after he'd heard that Lupe Barrera was stepping aside, he approached Bobby and Seff. If they needed a third voice, he would sing with them. Just give him a chance, he said.

Practicing after school and singing at parties, Abe Quintanilla became a Dino, the third voice behind Seff Perales's stirring leads and Bobby Lira's high harmonies that could melt hearts in a New York minute. Perales, the son of a barber, and Lira, a stuttering talker who lost his impediment whenever he sang, gave Abraham reason to dream. This music could take them places.

Their peers sought them out to entertain at their parties and functions, and the Dinos gladly obliged. Singing was fun. It made them popular, especially with the girls. Abe was a solid voice, but his real value to the Dinos did not become apparent until the night they sang at a graduation party and the honored student's father handed them thirty dollars for their efforts. Until then, singing had been its own reward. Now, the boys saw it as a means of putting money in their pockets. The money angle inspired Abe most of all. He decided that henceforth the Dinos should get paid thirty dollars whenever they sang. His ham-fisted attitude troubled Bobby and Seff. What if people didn't want to pay them? They might get mad at the group and never ask them back to a party again. Abe begged to differ. *You* can sing for pleasure, he told them. He'd sing and pocket the cash. His hard-line policy paid off so well that Bobby and Seff were soon suggesting to Abe that he raise their asking price to fifty dollars. Abraham Quintanilla, Jr., was learning the music business fast.

Abe's conversion came at a time in his life when the family was enjoying unprecedented prosperity. The house at 2410 Cloyde where they lived when Junior turned eighteen was a neat wide box on concrete blocks in a neighborhood of well-kept yards, closer to the south side of Corpus, where the Anglos lived, than any of the other places he'd lived. But Junior wasn't around the house much. He was a restless soul, so restless that he dropped out of Ray Miller High to chase his muse.

The Dinos soon expanded, adding pianist Joe Robles and a bass player named Tony Gallardo, then an entire instrumental group called the Jesters that they had met at a talent show at the Melba Theater. Though their passions were initially fueled by mainstream pop harmony groups like the Four Aces and Mills Brothers, they, like teens throughout America, got caught up in the rock-and-roll craze, zeroing in on vocal groups who were driving young people crazy with a street-corner sound call doo-wop, whose pantheon of heroes included the Limelights, Dion and the Belmonts, and Don and Juan.

Before the Dinos, Abe was just another *pachuco* in a *gabacho* world, trying to get by as best he could. His voice put him in the spotlight. He was the center of attention, which gave him a feeling of importance and worth he'd never felt before. It intoxicated him as no alcoholic drink or mind-altering drug could ever do.

The idea of a band of Mexican-Americans raving up doo-wop, a sound born on the streets of the east coast, might have appeared strange to an outsider. But music was a vital part of the South Texas culture. In the beginning, the sound of South Texas was the button accordion and the *bajo sexto*—a twelve-string guitar—playing a polka melody. The instruments and the music came from northern Mexico, where the *ranchera* sound was born, and out of the dance halls of central and southern Texas, where people of German, Polish, Moravian, Bohemian, and other Central European heritages tended to congregate on weekends. The accordions had been imported from Italy and

Germany. The *bajo* was the specialty of a San Antonio luthier named Martin Macías, whose knowledge of his craft came from the guitar-making town of Paracho, in the central plateau of Mexico.

From these ingredients came a style known at *música alegre*, happy music. Bouncy, jaunty, joyful music, it was neither Mexican nor Texan but uniquely Tex-Mex. From the early part of the twentieth century through the fifties, this sound, a less gritty version of the *norteño* music popular south of the Rio Grande, predominated. Dances at ranches across South Texas were scheduled wherever and whenever musicians could be rounded up and a space could be cleared for dancing. For those who spent the rest of the week doing hard labor, it was the sole opportunity for pure recreation. Typically, vaqueros could dance with a woman for fifteen cents—a nickel to the girl, a nickel to the promoter, and a nickel for the band.

After World War II, Mexican-Americans joined Texans of all races in moving off the farm to the city in pursuit of jobs and prosperity, and the urban melting pot brought the culture closer to the American mainstream. English-language music was becoming as much of an influence on South Texas Mexican-Americans as the music from Mexico was. Two trailblazers were Delia Gutiérrez, the daughter of Eugenio Gutiérrez, a bandleader from Weslaco, who covered "Chattanooga Shoe Shine Boy" in Spanish in 1949, and the duo of Carmen y Laura, who did a Spanish version of "Slowpoke," popularized by Cowboy Copas that same year.

During this period, San Antonio become the *Nueva York de la cultura*, where the largest concentration of Mexican-Americans lived. But the creative center was Corpus, the eastern anchor of a geographic triangle that extended forty-five miles west to Alice, a trading center for ranches in the heart of the South Texas brush range, and a hundred miles south to the Rio Grande Valley, on the Texas-Mexico border, where the vast majority of migrant farm workers resided when there were no harvests to follow.

The Rio Grande Valley had been *la música's* historical breeding ground, producing accordion greats Bruno Villareal and Narciso Martínez and trios such as Los Alegres de Teran, musicians whose influences came from northern Mexico. During the thirties and forties, these artists recorded mostly for the white American labels who occasionally sent talent scouts and recording equipment to South Texas to make records.

Shortly after World War II, Armando Marroquín and Paco Betancourt, two visionary entrepreneurs from Alice, opened a recording studio and started the Ideal record label. Betancourt eventually split and took Ideal to the Rio Grande Valley in 1960, where he began recording Freddy Fender, and Marroquín started Discos Nopal in Alice. In 1948, they were joined by Arnaldo Ramírez in McAllen, who built a studio and started the Falcon label, which recorded acts from both sides of the Rio Grande.

Through it all, Corpus remained *la mata*, the seed, where the musical idea and the technology merged to create *orquesta* music. *Orquesta* was the link between old-time Tex-Mex accordion conjuntos and modern Tejano. This wasn't workingman's music played by country bumpkins. This was uptown sophisticated music, black-and-white orchestra music performed by musicians in snazzy matching outfits who read charts and worked out complex arrangements of the same swing tunes people were hearing on the radio. Their cues came from Glenn Miller, Benny Goodman, and other big band ensembles popular elsewhere in the United States during the forties and fifties.

The bands were a mirror of the cultural duality of the people who lived between the Nueces and Rio Grande rivers. They loved American music and appreciated it best by fashioning it into something that was neither American nor Mexican but uniquely their own.

Beto Villa, a handsome man from Falfurrias, between Alice and the Rio Grande Valley, pioneered the concept as the leader of the very first Mexican-American swing band. His material was primarily instrumentals, though he occasionally featured a vocalist named Isidro "El Indio" López, from Corpus Christi. López proved so popular that he eventually headed up his own seventeen-piece orchestra, with four or five trumpets, four or five saxes, guitars, and congas. But rather than cover the Anglo big bands note for note as Villa did, López reworked swing into a Latin sound, largely through the use of saxophone harmonies. López also sang in Spanish. One upbeat, rhythm-charged vocal he recorded in 1955, "Dígale," is often regarded as the first Tejano song.

López inspired a movement among young Texas-Mexicans who were eager to integrate into the Anglo culture while holding on to their own. By embracing big band swing and reinventing it as *orquesta*, both the musicians and their fans made an informal declaration of independence. They were Americans first, but proud of their Mexican heritage too. López's comrades in Corpus included big band leaders Balde Gonzales and Juan "Colorado" García, with whose band López first sang "Dígale," followed by a second generation of local big band leaders, including Johnny Herrera, Johnny Canales, the Galvan Orchestra, and Freddie Martínez. These bands worked Exposition Hall, the Galvan Ballroom, and Domingo Peña's *baile grande* at the coliseum on Monday nights. Chelo Silva, a singing star, kept her home in Corpus. Neco Cuesta, who went on to fame with Lawrence Welk, came out of the scene too.

Another key element in the birth of Tejano was the exposure of young Mexican-American boys and girls to rock and roll; they responded excitedly to the new music. The blame rested squarely on the shoulders of Chuck Berry, Little Richard, Bill Haley, the Clovers, and Joe Turner, performers and recording artists who impressed the teenage Mexicanos in Texas the same way they impressed teens everywhere. But there were some distinctive differences. Many young musicians were not as fluent in English as they were in Spanish when they spoke offstage, but when the light was on and they were performing, it was note-for-note emulation of the black and Italian doo-wops and the white soul bands who inspired them. Not surprisingly, the audience was more responsive to hearing rock music translated into Spanish, though the beat transcended linguistic barriers. The nascent South Texas rock-and-roll scene was hardly a rival to the El Monte scene in Southern California that spawned Ritchie Valens, Cannibal and the Headhunters, and Rosie and the Originals. But taken as a whole, San Antonio, Corpus, and the Rio Grande Valley generated a disproportionate number of regional and national hits, most by Texas acts who were Mexican by parentage and rock and rollers by choice.

South Texas's first rock-and-roll star was a slender guitarist and singer from San Benito named Freddy Fender, who began recording in 1956 for the Falcon label. Fender, whose real name was Baldemar Huerta, grew up around traditional Mexican music but fell in love with the new sound that was sweeping America. "The only one doing rock-and-roll when I started was me," he has since noted. "Everybody else was doing big band swing." He was so good at it that young Mexicano fans in Texas who'd heard his records and went to see him perform were surprised to learn that Fender, otherwise known as El Bebop Kid or the Elvis of the Valley, was one of their own.

Fender wasn't alone for long. A slew of other talented performers who were similarly smitten with rhythm and blues and rock-and-roll music followed, with emphasis on vocal harmonies and big horn arrangements that were inspired by R & B, though easily distinguished with the flat dissonance of mariachis. One such group was Rudy and the Reno Bops, from San Antonio. Fender noted that the Reno Bops were the first South Texas band to apply the soul revue concept to their music. Rudy would come out "dancing like James Brown with girls dancing around him in tight shorts and go-go boots." Little Joe Hernández, a teen from Temple who had apprenticed with David Coronado and the Latinaires, topped everyone in the credibility category when he replaced Coronado as band leader. He didn't just *do* soul, he *had* soul, in the form of

El Charro Negro, a black vocalist from San Angelo named Bobby Butler.

Race-mixing through music was particularly rampant in San Antonio. The Mexican-American rock and soul scene of the fifties and sixties, for example, was heavily influenced by a local hero named Johnny Olenn, a swinging gringo who led a multiethnic band that specialized in Louis Prima–style jive and jump music. Olenn's disciples included a soulful Mexican-American singer who went by the name Sonny Ace and Doug Sahm, a white boy of Lebanese extraction who eventually reached national prominence in the midsixties under the name of Sir Douglas. All of them found common ground in joints like the Ebony Club, a seedy dive where blues and soul were the specialty of the house.

The best-known artist to emerge out of this conflagration was Sunny Ozuna, a handsome, charismatic crooner who led the Sunglows, and then the Sunliners, a big band ensemble known for its R & B sound. Influenced by a local Mexicano blues singer named Randy Garibay, and guided by a promoter and producer from Houston named Huey P. Meaux who had connections to the major labels, Sunny stomped onto the Top 40 in 1962 with his silk 'n' soul take of "Talk to Me," initially popularized by Little Willie John, and followed it with covers of swamp pop classics like Jimmy Clanton's "Just a Dream" and Joe Barry's "I'm a Fool to Care."

Taking a more studied approach was René & René, a San Antonio duo who parlayed the Tex-Mex traditions of dual harmonies and unabashedly sentimental lyrics into a pop sound that put them on Dick Clark's *American Bandstand*, despite the fact that their hits, including their biggest smash, "Lo Mucho que Te Quiero," were sung in both Spanish and English. Some Texas acts, like Doug Sahm's Sir Douglas Quintet, were able to pass themselves off as something different in order to gain access to the Top 40; in Sahm's case, the band's distinctive Tex-Mex backbeat was sold to the public as British rock, which was much in favor at the time, in the forms of "She's

About a Mover," "The Rains Came," and "Mendecino," all of them produced by Huey P. Meaux. A Dallas Mexicano named Sam Samudio did a similar image change, donning a turban and calling his band Sam the Sham and the Pharoahs. Cranking out nonsense lyrics pegged to a driving organ beat with a faint resemblance to the polka, Samudio scored with the international hit "Wooly Bully" in 1964. Then there was Question Mark and the Mysterians, a Michigan band of Latinos with South Texas roots, who recorded the mystical, somewhat cryptic "96 Tears" in 1966, pegging their sound to an organ that bore distant kinship to the accordion.

Perhaps the most inhibiting factor to the development of a regional sound was radio, the most important form of mass communication in Texas Spanish-speaking communities. Spanish radio, as it existed in the Rio Grande Valley, Corpus Christi, and San Antonio, adhered to a policy that shut out both local announcers and local musicians. The Anglo radio station owners typically hired their programmers and announcers from Mexico, because Mexicans spoke Spanish properly, unlike border and South Texas Mexicanos. The Mexico First policy extended to the musical selections they played, emphasizing the same recording artists who were popular in Mexico at the time. Local performers were at best relegated to special programs that aired for a few hours every week.

The iron grip of "the mustache guys," as they were known, broke in the late fifties, when they began to be challenged by a new breed of broadcaster. Leading the charge were San Antonio radio mavericks like Henry "Pepsi" Peña and Little Junior Jesse on KUKA, and Scratch Phillips on KCOR, who were showcasing rock and roll and rhythm and blues; and Manuel Dávila, Sr., also of KUKA, who aired conjuntos, trios, and *orquestas*, the records that were getting played at sock hops and on jukeboxes. In Alice, a jock at KOPY named Miguel Ríos featured the latest releases by Tony de la Rosa, Isidro López, and Juan Colorado. At KINE in Kingsville, Mike Chávez did a program bilingually, mixing in three Top 40 songs with current *la onda chicana* (the Chicano wave) hits every hour. In Corpus, Domingo Peña, Freddie Martínez, and Johnny Canales put out the word on dances during their programs. These were exceptions. Otherwise, the Tejanos were shut out.

Maverick announcers like these saw an unfilled niche, one where they could sell advertising time on stations for sock hops, dances, personal appearances and records, just like the gringo Top 40 stations were doing. In 1966, San Antonio's KEDA-AM began spinning the best of South Texas—Sunny Ozuna and the Sunliners, Little Joe and the Latinaires, and Flaco Jimenez, followed incongruously by Little Richard or B. B. King. "At the time, the black guys weren't getting played on mainstream Anglo radio," explained broadcaster Manuel Dávila, Jr. "You might have heard it on Scratch Phillips' program on KCOR at night or Joe Anthony's *Harlem Serenade*. We were playing it because we liked it, because that's what our peer group liked."

The results were immediate. KEDA received as many as eight hundred cards and letters daily from listeners making requests or sending out dedications. Anglo jocks on the Top 40 stations, KONO and KTSA, even bought time to advertise, although they were competitors. "They would buy stuff for their dances on our station because our station pulled," Manuel Dávila, Jr., said.

Out of the mix, Radio Jalapeño was born. "We were trying to come up with a logo," Manuel said. "We weren't Mexican. I was trying to avoid the tag as a sleepy guy under a cactus. I don't want to have a serape and I don't want to use a sombrero. We're not that. We can't be 'Muricans because to the gringo, we're just Meskins. What the hell are we?"

Disc jockeys, studio engineers, and raw talent was a volatile combination. San Antonio became the hub of regional Mexican music, a sound that the Dinos, the Four Seasons of the Seashore, had absolutely nothing to do with. They were busy listening to rock and roll on the Top 40 radio station.

It was a heady time to be young and alive in the C. C. City, harmonizing in the street with friends, rocking and rolling your life away. The Harbor Bridge had just been completed, making it easier to cruise North Beach or over to Port A or just go back and forth over the four-hundred-foot span above the ship channel, honking your horn and yelling at the top. All of Corpus (pop. 167,690) seemed to be growing and prospering, presenting to the world the splendidly contradictory image of industrial hub and beach resort. The Chamber of Commerce couldn't make up its mind which one it was supposed to be, so Corpus was variously described as "The Young Giant of the Texas Industrial Empire," "The Door to Wonderland," and the "The Tourist Capital of the Southwest."

Abraham's conduit to this brave new world was the radio, specifically the two AM radio stations in Corpus that played Top 40, KRYS and KEYS, and KTSA, which could be picked up from San Antonio. Like most disc jockeys, KEYS personalities such as Charlie Brite made extra cash hosting sock hops staged at schools throughout the city. Two of Brite's favorite after-school hops were at Ella Barnes Junior High and Cunningham Junior High on the west side, where he warmed up before his evening shift on KEYS. By doing so, Brite learned what records the Mexican-American kids wanted to hear, and how they wanted to hear them. "I'd always do two slows and one fast, two slows and one fast, and one of the slows would be something *really* slow, like 'Talk to Me,'" explained Brite. Most of the records that the junior high kids requested were sung in English by Mexican-American teens from San Antonio—songs that weren't on the KEYS playlist. But Brite would play their records at the hops and observe the kids going crazy. His efforts to add the artists were consistently rebuffed by the KEYS program director, who said, "There is no way we are gonna play Spanish music, just no way."

"But it's English," Brite protested. "They sing it in English!"

Undeterred, Brite began sneaking the records on the air

late at night, after he knew the program director had gone to bed. The phones, the ultimate arbiter of taste in radio, would light up. When Brite was promoted to program director himself, he started adding the music that lit up the phone lines to the playlist and aggressively promoted live dances at the city coliseum starring the bigger regional acts such as Sunny and the Sunliners and Little Joe and the Latinaires. "Hispanic kids showed up because they liked English music, though they followed mostly bands who were part of their culture," Brite observed. "Anglo kids liked the music, too. You would see it at rock-and-roll shows all the time."

This phenomenon ran counter to the way Brite was raised in nearby Beeville. "The Spanish and the Anglo didn't mix much in the fifties when I was growing up. You didn't date a Hispanic girl or your father and mother would kill you. In turn, her father and mother would kill *her* if she would date an Anglo guy. It wasn't prejudice one way; it was prejudice both ways."

Brite got a fair amount of heat for crossing the cultural line in the name of rock-and-roll radio. "Anglo listeners would call and say, 'If you're gonna play Mexican music, I ain't gonna listen,'" he said. But Pandora's box had been opened. Corpus was crawling with Mexican-American bands doing rock in English. One exceptionally popular group, George Jay and the Rockin' Ravens, led by a fellow named George Balli, recorded an instrumental called "La Pachuca," an answer to the Sunglows' "La Cacahuate," that went straight to number one on the KEYS Top 40 survey. Their success was no doubt helped along by their manager, Jungle Jim West, who happened to be another KEYS D.J.

Brite, along with a music promoter named Carl Becker and an investor named Morgan Spear, had opened an eight-track recording studio on Chapparal Street downtown, where one day, three young Mexican guys walked in and introduced themselves as the Dinos. They wanted to make a record.

"They did these four-part harmonies in three parts that

I couldn't believe,'' Brite said. ''Seff Perales, the lead singer, had such feeling in his voice. He had just a little bit of an accent, but he had real emotion in his voice, too.'' The other two, Bobby Lira and Abe Quintanilla, were impressive as well.

Brite huddled with West and decided to roll the dice. The Dinos went into the studio, stood around a microphone, and harmonized to a song titled ''So Hard to Tell,'' which Brite and West paid to have pressed into a 45 rpm single, releasing it on the J. W. Fox label owned by Johnny Herrera. Signing on as the band's managers, Brite and West hyped the song on KEYS, making sure it received exposure during both their shifts, and booked the band for personal appearances at sock hops and dances in Corpus, Kingsville, Woodsboro, and anywhere else in the coastal bend where they could attract a crowd of teens. The record hit the KEYS charts and made the Dinos local heroes in Corpus Christi in 1959. For the followup, West and Brite recruited a group from El Campo called the Counts who featured a horn section and took the Dinos to Doyle Jones's recording studio in Houston. The second Dinos single, ''Give Me One Chance,'' was composed by east coast doo-wop idol Teddy Randazzo, who'd written songs for Little Anthony and the Imperials, among others. The Dinos heard the song in a movie and sat in the theater while the film played and replayed several times, just so they could get the words right. Their perseverance paid off. The record went through the roof, getting extensive airplay not only in Corpus but on KILT, the dominant Top 40 station in Houston. ''We sold, ourselves, just by playing the song on the air and at concerts and record hops, about 150,000 copies [a figure Brite may have inflated over the years],'' Brite remembered. ''I mean, it was unbelievable. Jim would sell them out of the back of his car.''

The business Dino, Abe Quintanilla, was pleased with the response but wanted to know why little of the dough was finding its way into his pocket. ''When they came in, they wanted to do everything free, you know, anything to get on the air," Brite said. "But after 'Give Me One Chance,' they were getting so many bookings, Abe and I did have a few words. He didn't like playing for free after a while."

The Dinos began fielding offers to perform. Visions of stardom danced in their heads. In all, they would record some ten 45 rpm singles sung in English, and in live shows covered the music of the Beatles, Ray Stevens, Johnny Tillotson, Tommy Roe, Sam and Dave, and the Five Americans, among others. Unfortunately, the ugly issue of race came up frequently enough to remind them that all teenagers were not created equal. A club owner in North Beach, just across the harbor channel from downtown Corpus, was shocked to discover the band he'd booked was made up of Mexican kids. He paid them not to play. On one out-of-town booking north of Houston, the Dinos had to ride in the back of a bus to the concert and were denied motel rooms reserved for other members of the package show they appeared on. The other singles that followed—one original called "Twistin' Irene" and two covers, "Ride Your Pony" and "Lover's Holiday"—sold poorly. But the real impediment to advancing their career was a letter from Uncle Sam.

In October 1961, Bobby Lira received his draft notice. He was to report for a physical in San Antonio. Abraham and Seff agreed to go with Bobby, with the understanding that if all three passed muster, they would apply for induction into the special entertainment division in the Army. Lira failed the test, so the three returned home to Corpus. The following month, Abraham received his induction notice, and he was drafted into the Army.

Actually, the service was a ticket to see the world, even if it meant being away from the other Dinos for two years. He spent most of his hitch stationed in Fort Lewis, Washington. While doing his time, he met a young woman named Marcella Samora. Like Abraham, she was Mexican-American (and part Cherokee Indian), with Texas roots, her father hailing from Amarillo and her mother coming from southern Colorado before both had followed the crops to eastern Washington State, where they'd settled. Abraham courted Marcella and they married on June 8, 1963. On December 13, shortly after Abraham had been discharged from active duty, Marcella gave birth to their first child, a boy named Abraham Quintanilla III. For a month, Abraham struggled to make ends meet by working as a fry cook. Then he and his wife and son headed home to Corpus Christi, living at 3518 Leopard while Abe briefly worked as a deliveryman while resuming his music career.

The Dinos were waiting for Abraham, but shortly after his return, he learned that the rules of the music game had changed. The guys were still harmonizing, but they were being pressured to go with the times. One of the first engagements the band had after Abe ended his hitch in the service was a dance in Sinton, a farming town north of Corpus. The crowd that had turned out to see the Dinos was mostly Mexican farm workers who did not share the band's enthusiasm for American pop and rock music, as the mixed audience they usually drew did. They wanted to hear the songs of their homeland, not "In the Still of the Night" or the Dinos' hit "Give Me One Chance."

"Play Spanish music," a voice yelled.

"What are you, a bunch of queers?" another person shouted at them.

"Who do you think you are, gringos or something?"

The Dinos were all Mexican-Americans. The music they sang was in English. Neither was acceptable to the crowd that had paid their money at the door. "We didn't know any Mexican music and were just singing doowop," Abe later recalled. "Pretty soon, the whole dance was in an uprising over it. They closed the dance and refunded money."

That was putting it mildly. The crowd ran the band off the stage and out of the building. Sheriff's deputies had to be called in to escort the Dinos out of town. It was a sobering lesson.

The second revelation came on the *Domingo Peña Show*, the music program that aired Sunday mornings on channel 3 in Corpus. Peña was an engaging local television star made for the little black-and-white box, the first local Mexicano on the tube. He was flamboyant, outrageous, and entertaining, known for driving a Cadillac and wearing two-tone black-and-white patent-leather Beatle boots. His extroverted tendencies, perhaps a compensation for his affliction with polio as a child, were on full display every week preceding the regular broadcasts of bullfights and boxing from Mexico. Every episode of the *Domingo Peña Show* started with the battle cry "*Amacízate, abuelita!*," which roughly translated is "Hold on tight, little granny!," before Peña presented a cavalcade of musical acts from Corpus Christi and South Texas performing in front of a live audience at the station's studios. Because it was the only program like it in the region, both Mexican-American and Anglo-American entertainers vied to play on the show, all urged on by Peña shouting his catch phrase, "Put it on! Put it on!," his heavily accented English coming across to some ears as "*Poo dit ohn! Poo dit ohn!*"

The charismatic Peña had a lock on the Corpus *onda.* Besides television, he worked a daily shift on KCCT-AM, playing records by acts from South Texas, and promoted *bailes* at Memorial Coliseum on Shoreline Drive downtown and, later, at the Stardust Ballroom on South Padre Island Drive. His influence was so widespread that if the only date he could secure for a New Year's Eve *baile* at the coliseum was on December 27, the whole city would celebrate New Year's Eve four days early.

Most of the bands on Peña's show sang in Spanish, even if they were playing rock, doo-wop, or R & B, because, at least in South Texas, that's where the money was. No matter how well Seferino, Bobby, and Abraham blended their voices, the color of their skin seemed to be a limiting factor. Musically, they were as good as anyone. But the cultural differences, not to mention the racist tendencies of the people running the show in show business, inevitably stood in their way.

The Dinos finally changed their minds at the behest of

Johnny Herrera, the proprietor of a little hole-in-the-wall record shop at 1026 Port Street called House of Music. The whitewashed cinderblock building wasn't much to look at from the street, but inside was a beehive of creativity, reflecting the myriad interests of the shop's owner. Of all the people who made Corpus the cradle of Tejano music, as it would one day be known, few could claim to have played as seminal a role as Herrera.

Johnny Herrera was born in the Rio Grande Valley and raised in Corpus. He was well educated, having graduated from North Texas State Teachers' College in Denton and earned degrees in journalism and English, a rarity for any Mexican-American in his day. Like Abe, though, Herrera had a passion for music. He wrote songs not because he thought he'd get rich, but because it was his preferred form of expressing himself. He was good at his craft, too. His composition "Un Mal Amor" was recorded in 1946 by Duo Tejano and the pioneer South Texas big band leader Beto Villa. Another Herrera original, "De Rodillas Vendrás," was covered by Carmen, one half of the popular duo Carmen y Laura, backed by legendary accordionist Narciso Martínez, aka El Huracán del Valle and Isidro "El Indio" López, later recognized as the father of Tejano music. He also recorded Lydia Mendoza, considered the greatest Mexican-American female voice of modern times.

In 1949 Herrera broke more ground as a performer by recording the country music standard "Jealous Heart" in English and Spanish for the Melco label. Two years later, he recorded the same song as "Corazón Celoso" for Decca Records, effectively preceding Johnny Rodríguez's chart-topping bilingual version—erroneously credited as the first Tex-Mex country music crossover hit—by twenty-four years. Herrera cut a cool image on stage with his orchestra, earning the nickname of El Suspiro de las Damas, or The Sigh. His music reconciled the two sounds that dominated Spanish music—the basic accordion-guitar conjunto sound that was derided as "cantina trash" music, and the more sophisticated *orquesta* sound that emphasized brass instruments and written arrangements.

One song he wrote and performed, "Por Ningún Motivo," was extensively covered in Mexico, which gave Herrera firsthand insight into the difference between Texas-Mexicans and Mexican-Mexicans, in the form of a promotional trip south of the border.

He was no stranger to racism in Texas, where he'd been called "pepper belly" and worse. On the other side of the Rio Grande, Herrera discovered prejudice of an entirely different kind. Mexicans, he learned, were as bad as Anglos.

At the offices of RCA Records in Mexico City, an executive asked him, "What are you?"

"Mexicano," Herrera replied.

"What part of Mexico are you from?"

Herrera replied he was from Texas.

"No, no, no, then you're a *norteamericano*."

Herrera satisfied his inquisitor by telling him then in that case, he was a Tejano, a Mexicano from Texas.

The experience made Herrera prouder than ever of his regional heritage, so proud that on the records he subsequently released, he variously described the musical style of each composition as *bolero tejano, ranchera tejana*, or blues Tejano. He made Tejano music, not Mexican music.

Herrera performed mainly to promote the songs he'd written. He preferred to stay in the background, especially after surviving a serious car wreck with his musicians in Roswell, New Mexico. So he taught high school in the small town of Ben Bolt, opened a lounge in Corpus, and finally opened the House of Music record shop across the street from the lounge, where he sold the latest 45s as well as recording and releasing singles on his Gaviota label.

One of the first youngsters Herrera encountered was a wiry, muscle-bound young man named Bobby Lira, who delivered beer to the lounge that Herrera co-owned across the street from House of Music. Lira was a singer, he told Herrera, and he sang with this harmony group Herrera should check out someday. They called themselves the Dinos.

Through Lira, Herrera became acquainted with the other Dinos, the dazzling lead vocalist Seferino Perales, and the third voice, a young man with Mario Lanza cheekbones, pouty lips, and dark, smoldering eyes, Abe Quintanilla.

Abe wasn't much of a singer, but Herrera realized he had a head on his shoulders, since he was the one who conducted band business. Herrera had always said that he'd wanted others to do his songs and the Dinos seemed perfect for the task at hand, even if they needed some training. They became part of a loose group of musically talented *batos de Corpito*, whose numbers included Oscar Martínez, Johnny Avela, and Freddie Martínez, who dropped by every afternoon to drink Cokes, listen to records, compare songwriting skills, and, as Freddie Martínez put it, "talk about the bad times." The outspoken Herrera conducted the gatherings, adding lines to songs they'd written, challenging them to improve their lyrics, always inspiring them to come up with something better. In the process, he raised an entire generation of successful musicians. By hanging out at House of Music and learning the ways of Johnny Herrera by osmosis, they were mentored in the dual mysteries of art and commerce, getting the lowdown on the business of music from one who had learned the hard way.

"When I got married, I'd get up in the morning and get dressed and leave and my wife couldn't figure out where I was going—I wasn't going to work," Freddie Martínez recalled. "I would go and hang out at the record store and talk about who was doing good—Little Joe, Isidro, and Sunny—and how we were all struggling. We all wanted to get something going, and finally the Dinos got a little something going—nothing big but they got something going. They were doing good. And then I got my thing going."

For their part, the young men enjoyed goading Herrera. Freddie would offer an idea to Herrera and have him put it together as a song. Oscar Martínez told him, "Whenever you get mad, I learn a lot from you." Johnny was more like them than their parents. He also gave them a home away from home, offering a spare bedroom when romance called for it, even loaning his car to Abraham when he needed it.

Herrera had a message for the Dinos, one that he learned back when girls still called him The Sigh. Singing in English may come naturally to the boys, but if they wanted to survive through music, the Dinos should sing in Spanish.

"You've got to get into the Mexican market," Johnny Herrera kept telling Abe. "You're never going to compete with the Four Aces. Look at Sunny." He was right.

In 1964, the year Abe Quintanilla, Jr., came home from the service, the Texas Mexican-American musical movement toward assimilation into the pop mainstream ground to a halt. Sunny Ozuna, the one who had started it all, left Huey P. Meaux and, under the guidance of Manny Guerra, started singing in Spanish to his fans. "Talk to Me" had landed Sunny an appearance on Dick Clark's *American Bandstand* show, a breakthrough that remains a source of pride to Texas Mexican-Americans. But after enjoying a nice run of popularity as a national recording artist, Sunny intentionally altered his sound to appeal to the audience that came to his shows and bought his records. "Cariño Mío" wouldn't get him back on *Bandstand*, but it would keep the crowds who paid the cover charge moving around the floor, which is what it was all about. René and René followed suit.

The music that Mexican-American bands were playing had been commonly referred to as Tex-Mex, or simply as Spanish music. Now there was a new handle to go along with the new attitude—Chicano music, inspired by the Chicano political movement sweeping the Southwest. A Chicano was neither Mexican nor American but both, and Chicanos were imbued with a pride of culture and a pride of place that distinguished them from other Latin-Americans. The concept of Brown Power filtered into the local dance-hall circuit and on to jukeboxes and radio stations. It wasn't a consciousness so much as a sound, dubbed *la onda chicana*, or the Chicano wave, by Johnny Gonzales, the Dallas promoter. Not only did *la onda* give the music an identity, it prompted the kids who'd been assimilating to discover the heritage of their parents. Bands stopped emulating their white counterparts and started looking inward. The polka became trendy again. Spanish lyrics prevailed. The words meant something more than just love. "Las Nubes," sung by Little Joe y la Familia, became the anthem of the United Farm Workers union.

The Dinos were caught in the middle of the transition. Like most of their counterparts, they had been weekend warriors who used entertainment and the opportunity to prance around a stage as a means to pick up girls, amuse themselves, and make some pocket change. Ultimately, they realized that in order to survive they had to give the people what they wanted. And what their crowd wanted was to dance.

It all came down to language and money, Johnny Herrera told the Dinos. "I can't afford to do the English stuff. You can't compete with the major labels."

As a public service, he offered his own composition "Con Esta Copa" as the gateway to their new career, recording the Dinos' initial foray into *la onda* in a studio on Up River Road and issuing it in 1964 on Herrera's own Epitome label. ("Distributors had the hardest time with that label," Herrera later said. "They all pronounced it 'Ep-i-tohm.' ")

"Con Esta Copa" was a hit, getting play on jukeboxes and on Spanish-language radio programs in Texas, Arizona, California, and Chicago. "You heard it everywhere you went," Johnny Herrera said.

"From that time on, we did Chicano music," Abe Quintanilla remembered.

The Dinos became Los Dinos. They still dressed sharp, in matching collarless jackets with an embroidered *D* above the heart and white slacks. The only difference was that they were playing to an audience who wanted to hear the pop, rock, and soul hits in Spanish. They hooked into the *onda chicana* scene.

Unable to finance the cost of an entire album, Herrera encouraged the band to sign with Arnaldo Ramírez at Falcon Records, who released their Spanish-language hits in album form under the title *Con Esta Copa*, in 1964. All nine songs were Herrera originals, and the composer's picture was featured as prominently as the Dinos' on the back cover of the album jacket. Herrera didn't mind being a celebrity songwriter, though he knew it irritated some members of the band, specifically Abraham.

"Wherever they went, the girls wanted Johnny Herrera," Herrera said. "They were asking for me and I was not there. On television, Domingo would announce my name first."

The deal with Falcon gave Los Dinos wider exposure than ever, since Ramírez had more extensive distribution than any other Texas recording venture. Los Dinos answered the call by adding a horn section—two trumpets and an alto and tenor sax—and hitting the road, with Abe booking the eleven-piece ensemble across the Southwest. After releasing three albums for Falcon, Los Dinos jumped to Bernal Records, the other big record label in the Rio Grande Valley, which was run by Paulino Bernal, the leader of the hugely popular Conjunto Bernal of McAllen. The first release for that label was *La Tracalera*, named after Johnny Herrera's Spanish-language Texas song about a trucker searching for a love in all the big cities of Texas.

Back on the home front, Marcella gave birth to their second child on June 29, 1967. They named their daughter Suzette Michelle.

The 1968 Bernal release *Los Dinos a Go Go* displayed the band's dual appeal at its best. They were strong on soul and rhythm and blues, but their music was specifically for the *batos y rucas* who were Texas-bred with Mexican roots, as was the case with their cover of the Young Rascals' "Groovin'," which had been reworked into "Lluvia," though the melody remained the same.

Going Chicano meant more money in the pockets of Los Dinos, but it would forever inhibit their ability to aim for the Top 40 charts. Instead, they concentrated on road work, going south to the Rio Grande Valley, where they introduced *la onda*'s brass-section style to La Villita in San Benito, and the Squeeze Inn in Brownsville; and out west to Rio Grande City, Laredo, El Paso, and Calderon's Ballroom in Phoenix, the last stop before heading to the West Coast and all the way to the Yakima Valley of Washington State.

No matter where the band went, there were always reminders of intolerance, the prejudice that whites and browns were separate and not equal. Sometimes it was merely in the look on someone's face. Sometimes it was more obvious, like the signs posted in cafés, at swimming pools and skating rinks, outside rest rooms and water fountains, all over South and West Texas: NO MEXICANS ALLOWED. NO DOGS OR MESKINS.

No matter how talented they were and how sweet their four-part harmonies sounded, the race and culture they sang to would forever limit their appeal. Perception was three-fourths of the problem. Mexicanos in Texas came from peon stock, and Anglos constantly reminded them of it. As one Texas-Mexican put it, "Cubans came to the United States in 1960, started out washing dishes in a restaurant, and today own that restaurant. We came over during the 1910 revolution, started out as dishwashers, and three generations later, we're still dishwashers."

Abe was the business guy, but his reputation was that of a fighter who engaged in backstage fisticuffs with Seff, usually over something trivial like what song they would open with. Between the mounting bills and the responsibility of having a family, it became more and more difficult to stay on the road. Abraham was gone so long on one trip that little A.B. didn't recognize his daddy when he came home. By 1969, the crowds were thinning out, the gate receipts were declining, the whole music scene was changing. Abraham threw in the towel.

Los Dinos would continue without Abe, cutting more

sides for Bernal Records and continuing to cover Johnny Herrera's compositions. In 1974, Los Dinos sang their last harmony and hung up their rock-and-roll shoes, leaving behind a body of work that spanned twenty 45s and six LPs.

It would be another six years before Johnny Herrera would actually receive a handsome royalty check for writing a song: "Si Quieres Verme Llorar," which was covered by Lisa López, "was so big it was even covered in Mexico by the Magic Organ of Juan Torres," Herrera said. "That song was like cancer, it spread around everywhere, right around Christmas," selling particularly well in Puerto Rico.

Following Hurricane Celia, which had effectively blown away his shop in 1970, Herrera moved the store to its present address on Andrew Street, a half block that is sandwiched between Port and the Crosstown Expressway, where he continued holding court, selling records, and offering observations on the curious business of music.

Abraham had devoted almost fifteen years to music. By virtue of his position as the band's business representative, he had helped connect the network of dance-hall owners, jukebox operators, and record-label entrepreneurs who made it all happen. Now he was leaving it behind. As painful as it was to admit, it was time to settle down and make something of himself. Leaving *la onda* was like leaving his baby. He was walking away from his chance to shine, to step onstage, to see people actually take their hard-earned cash out of their wallets and pay to hear him sing.

A different kind of reality awaited him up the coast.

2
L. J. Girl

ABRAHAM QUINTANILLA'S TICKET OUT OF the music business was the world's largest petrochemical refinery. He arrived with his family in Lake Jackson and announced to his mother that the prodigal son was finally quitting show business and the attendant lifestyle that she disapproved of so strongly. Abe wasn't exactly a stranger to the vicinity. Abraham, Sr., worked as an auto-body repairman on Plantation Drive, next to the old Kentucky Fried Chicken; Abe's little brother Eddie was in nearby Bay City; and his sister Gloria and her husband, Henry Ramírez, were down in Freeport, where Henry's dad and mom as well as Abe's youngest brother Isaac lived and where his sister Yolanda would eventually work as a nurse in the emergency room at the Freeport hospital.

The change of career and scenery required him to lose more than his pride. Unlike Corpus Christi, whose population was mostly Mexican-American in 1970, there wasn't much of *la onda* to speak of in Lake Jackson. There were hardly any Mexican-Americans in Lake Jackson at all, much less any Mexican-American music. To make it in Lake Jackson, you had to fit in. Abraham didn't mind that part. Compromises were made tolerable by the hourly wage at Dow. The big challenge for him was to get over music.

Taking up his brother-in-law Henry's suggestion, Abraham applied for work at the Dow plant, although he was discouraged because he lacked a high school degree. Despite that, he was hired as a shipping clerk and tow motor operator in October 1969, and moved the family into a humble wood-frame rental house at 109 Ivy Court in Lake Jackson. The four-room structure was a production model like all the other houses on the street, some of the first housing constructed in Lake Jackson back in the forties. Still, the cul-de-sac location beneath the tall pines and shady hardwoods draped with Spanish moss gave the place sort of a fairy-tale feel. The neat little lawns, the driveways with vans and pickups and the occasional boat or RV parked in the yard, suggested material wealth was in reach of the residents.

Less than a year after settling down, Marcella became pregnant. She gave birth to her second daughter at Freeport Community Hospital, on Easter Sunday, April 16, 1971. The child's arrival was preceded by some strange events. Before she discovered her pregnancy, Marcella was told by a doctor that what ailed her was a tumor which needed removal. When she sought a second opinion, the other doctor told her she was expecting. Both she and Abraham, now a man of thirty-two, were convinced their third child was going to be a boy; so convinced, that they'd picked a name for their second son: Marc Antony. When the little girl arrived instead, they were at a loss for a name. Another mother sharing the room with Marcella offered a suggestion: Selena. That was her choice for her baby girl, which turned out to be a boy. Marcella and Abraham agreed it had a nice ring to it, especially when pronounced Seh-lee-na, Anglo style, rather than Seh-leh-na, as in the Spanish. What a pretty name: Selena.

The Quintanillas' giggling baby girl was a peanut, weighing a mere five pounds and ten and one-half ounces. Small as she may have been, it was evident to all who saw her that she was a bundle of energy.

After their second daughter's birth, the Quintanillas moved again, first to Bay City, about forty miles southwest of Lake Jackson, then to Angleton, less than ten miles north of Lake Jackson, where the family lived at 813 Chenango.

María Calderón Quintanilla passed away at the community hospital in Lake Jackson on January 18, 1972, three months before Selena's first birthday. Mary was fifty-two. She was survived by her husband and her children: Abraham, Jr., Isaac, Eddie, Hector, Yolanda, Gloria Ramírez, and Cynthia Fanelle.

Three years after the little girl's birth, the family moved back to Lake Jackson, where they settled in a larger wood-frame house under a huge oak at 146 Trumpet Vine, not far from Ivy Court. Here the exteriors were a little more decorative, the yards a little bigger, and life a little more pleasant. The homes were still built on blocks, in anticipation of the inevitable heavy rains and floods, with bar ditches in place of curbing and sewers for drainage. All things considered, the level of comfort had definitely improved.

The little girl was something special. "They dressed her like a princess—so frilly. She would sit on the edge of a desk and anybody who saw her was captivated," said Harold Lindloff, an officer at the First State Bank, who vividly recalled the three-year-old who tagged along with her parents. "Everyone had a feeling that she was destined to be more than the average child. She was so beautiful. She was vibrant. The way I remember her, because of her teaching she respected her elders but she always had a twinkle in her eye, you could always cut up with her. She had that aura, something magical."

Lindloff's contact with the family was usually with Marcella, who did the banking, although both Abrahams also dropped in. "Abraham, Senior, was all business. He was the strong figure. Abraham, Junior, always had a twinkle, he was very likable. You'd get so mad at the way they handled their business but you still could not help but like them."

L.J.—Lake Jackson—and Dow were inseparable. The land had once been part of the Abner Jackson plantation, which had been abandoned after the hurricane of 1900 that destroyed the nearby seaport city of Galveston. For most of the first half of the twentieth century, the land lay fallow, ceded to the surrounding coastal jungle, save for some cow pastures and a few rice and cotton fields. Then, in 1940, about the same time air-conditioning was beginning to make this part of Texas habitable, the Dow Chemical Company made a conscious effort to build a vast petrochemical refining complex at the mouth of the Brazos River, carving a town around the plant from the dense vegetation. Twenty-nine years later, when Abraham Quintanilla arrived, a trailblazing spirit still prevailed in the community. There were poisonous snakes to kill, poison ivy to eradicate, and, always, mosquitoes and humidity to endure.

But as hostile as the environment was to humans, the conditions made for a beautiful lushness of the land once the wilderness had been tamed. The live oaks were particularly majestic in Lake Jackson. The magnolias, azaleas, dogwood, japonica, sago palms, smooth carpets of immaculate green grass, and English ivy surrounding all the lovely new middle-class houses lent an air of the Old South to the town. But unlike the Confederate states, or the eastern extreme of Texas for that matter, Lake Jackson carried little baggage from the days of slavery. Segregation ordinances were nonexistent, despite the fact that the community was overwhelmingly white. Fewer than forty families out of the three thousand living within the town limits in 1970 had Hispanic surnames. Most Mexicans and blacks lived in Freeport and Clute, where older, cheaper housing was plentiful, as were the jobs connected to the fishing industry and Dow's older plants, where magnesium cells and chlorine were manufactured. By contrast, most homes in Lake Jackson were less than thirty years old and were subject to stringent building codes that, among other things, outlawed trailer houses within the town limits.

The benevolent hand of Dow blessed the community with a sense of culture and refinement not found in other Brazosport communities. Its citizens were chemists, engineers, doctors, lawyers, and other white-collar workers, a highly educated workforce. In the place of bars and lounges, of which there were none, the citizens of Lake Jackson were wealthy and culturally sophisticated enough to support a symphony orchestra, beginning in the sixties. At the same time, they were grounded enough in family values to foster a wide array of houses of worship. Episcopalians, Presbyterians, Methodists, Baptists, Church of Christians, Lutherans, Catholics, and Baptists were so well represented that school activities were rarely scheduled after six P.M. Wednesdays, in deference to midweek church services. Similarly, no one made a big deal out of the significant number of children, including the Quintanillas', who weren't allowed to square dance in physical-education classes or attend parties because of their religious beliefs.

Lake Jackson accepted the Quintanillas, who often went door to door to spread the word of Jehovah, on those terms. As long as they conformed to the standards defined by Dow, the church, and the community they were welcomed. The town seemed insulated from the problems pervading neighboring towns like Freeport and Clute—much less Houston, fifty miles away—mosquitoes, ticks, fleas, flies, snakes, stickers, and thorns notwithstanding. The Quintanillas had bought in, making payments on a nice house, Abe doing all right on the salary paid him for loading railroad boxcars that brought plastic to the world.

Abraham's passion was still music. Whenever work got the best of him, he'd seek refuge in playing his guitar and looking back wistfully on the time when he had a dream to follow. One day, Selena walked in and sang along while he strummed his instrument. She'd seen her daddy playing guitar, seen how he'd encouraged her brother to play the borrowed Sears bass guitar he'd been given and urged her sister to practice on the set of drums he'd bought. She could contribute by singing, she showed him.

Her eagerness to please did not go unnoticed. Abraham could tell she had the same appreciation for music that he had. Her brother and sister could play, as long as he made them practice. But his littlest one had the gift.

"I saw all the qualities in her at a very early age," Abraham later said. "She could dance and had charisma as a little girl, she had stage presence. I knew she would go places."

The Quintanillas eventually found heaven on earth, or something close to it, at 104 Caladium. It was a larger, neater frame house with a pitched roof and painted shutters. A palm grew in the front yard, along with several pink-blossomed mimosas and a thicket of dense vegetation crowding against the garage. To the neighbors of the Quintanillas, Selena was a gregarious, athletic girl who was something of a tomboy. Their impressions of her were formed watching her play kickball, roller-skate on the pavement, chase fireflies on summer evenings to a droning symphony of cicadas and locusts, and hang out with the other kids on the Caladium Court cul-de-sac around the corner.

The green tangle of steamy, sticky vegetation was a life force constantly threatening to overtake Snake Jackson, as the locals sometimes referred to town. It left an indelible imprint on Abraham and Marcella's littlest child. "I remember how green it was," she would say many years and many miles later. "I loved Lake Jackson because of the green grass, the trees. I remember eating at the Sonic and the Dairy Bar. I remember how it would flood where I lived, and my friends and I would play in the water. I was a little tomboy when I was growing up. I used to like to play football with the guys and, you know, normal things like hide-and-seek, and get ahold of my brother's bike and try to teach myself to ride it. I hurt myself a couple of times. That's normal.

"What else did we used to do? Oh, now that I think back on it, this was really stupid. We used to get my mom's sheets, you know, the fitted sheets, and we used to go outside and hide from the cars on the front lawn.

We would make bubbles and hide under there. And if we got seen we would go stand on the corner and make these ugly faces. I know it's stupid. And then, what else did we do? Oh, we had these monkey bars in the back of our house and we used to get my mother's sheets and tie them to the bars and make little cocoons and just hang in there all day.''

Meredith Lynn Cappel was Selena's partner in mischief on the block, on the playground, and in class at O.M. Roberts Elementary School, a modern institutional building that opened in 1960 in one of Lake Jackson's more affluent neighborhoods. ''Me and Selena and another girl, Becky Button, we used to act like we were so bad and athletic,'' Cappel said. ''We used to rule the field during P.E. Selena could run faster than anybody. We wanted to show everybody we were stronger. We did not like the prissy little girls.''

At school, Meredith Lynn and Selena liked to get in the back of the inevitable single-file lines students assembled in to go anywhere as a group. ''We used to see what we could get away with,'' Meredith said. Selena had a favorite skirt that would swirl out like a parachute whenever she twirled around. Once, while standing at the rear of a line, Meredith Lynn dared Selena to flip her skirt up and show her panties. But just as she did so, their teacher, Mrs. Pérez, looked directly at them. ''We were just frozen in time,'' said Meredith Lynn. ''She held us out in the hall and gave us a lecture. It was awful. That stuck with me forever.''

Still, both girls were considered good girls because they knew when to behave. ''Both of our parents were strict in a good way—it was 'Yes, ma'am,' 'No, ma'am,' and you didn't talk backtalk,'' Meredith Lynn said. ''She was never, ever disrespectful of Mrs. Pérez. We had the fear of God put in us by our parents. We knew if we did something wrong we'd get whippings and everything else. I'm glad my parents were like that now, looking back. You just did not question what you were told. I remember if it was getting close to four o'clock, [Selena] would just drop everything, no questions asked. 'Gotta go.' I remember her dad was really strict."

These were the days of sweet innocence. It was easy to fit in and please her teachers, like Mrs. McGlashen in first grade. "I remember going to school predominantly with Americanos," Selena recalled years later. She neither spoke Spanish nor was encouraged to learn it, because Mexican culture was practically nonexistent. Lake Jackson was the center of the white-bread world, "a real small hick town," as Selena put it.

Selena might have been a rough-and-tumble kid, but she also loved playing with dolls. Marcella once gave her daughters identical dolls. Selena's was easy to identify because, as Suzette recalled, "Selena fried its hair by curling it so much. She made it this purple outfit out of shiny material."

In the kids' universe, parents were merely bit actors. "We were forbidden to go into her house," said Meredith Lynn. "Her parents were like mine—really strict. And they were never around. Her parents worked and mine worked. I guess we were latch-key kids, but back then it was okay. But we were never allowed to go into each other's houses."

Both Matt and David Read, neighbors of Selena's, were in awe at how tightly knit the Quintanilla family was. "They stuck with each other, looked out for each other. I never recall seeing those kids fight. It was so unlike regular brothers and sisters," said David. Matt's mom, Carmen, told the Brazosport *Facts* some years later, "There wasn't a lot of free time for those kids. They may have worked harder and shouldered more responsibilities than their peers, but that did not inhibit Selena's bubbly personality. She would just laugh. Never would she cry, never was she rude or ugly. She just had such a good outlook on life. She was such a happy child."

A next-door neighbor, Mrs. Sam Johnson, recalls the Quintanilla family's music. "Their garage was on the other side of the house from our house, so we were never disturbed by the music. They put carpet up all around the garage, sound-proofed it as best as they could. They never played late, never gave anybody any problems. They were very good neighbors but we never really got to know them that well because our kids were different ages. We could hear the music, but it was never loud enough to bother us."

Ah, yes, the music. Music was more than a pastime around the Quintanilla household; it was mandatory. Suzy, A.B., and Selena would often be called in from playing outside to come to the garage to practice. Abraham gave them no other choice. Even his brothers urged him to lighten up and let the kids be kids and play, but Abraham was not swayed. "They think this is fun," he told them. Besides, there was a goal, as Carmen Read found out. She had attended a PTA meeting at Roberts Elementary where the featured entertainment was young Selena, in one of her first public performances. "She loved to sing as a child," Read said. "She didn't speak Spanish as a child, but she could sing it perfectly. Selena had a beautiful voice, even as a little girl."

Selena's motivation was typical sibling rivalry. If Dad was going to spend all that time and effort showing A.B. how to play bass, then she would vie for his attention by singing. "I guess I got a little jealous, so I went out and got this musical book that my dad had with old songs and I started making my own melody and singing in front of them, hoping he would notice me," Selena told writer Joseph Harmes in 1992. "And my dad started teaching me. And I guess he noticed that I picked up right away and my timing was there. You know, I knew when to come in and when to go out and all that.

"We had our little family band right there. My cousin ended up moving down from Washington because my mother is from Washington. We have relatives over there. And he played the drums. My sister came [back] playing drums when my cousin moved back to Washington. She fought it. She thought it was so unfeminine to play the drums. But we had our little band."

Selena liked the attention and found that singing helped

her overcome the terrible feeling of shyness that enveloped her whenever she was around people. "Our relatives would come over and Dad would always try and make us play for them. And, you know, when you are kids—my God, I was only six years old—and it's like 'No!' You know, you start throwing these little tantrums. Eventually we broke out of it."

A.B. had an obvious gift for music as well as art, and was destined to teach. His ninth- and tenth-grade teacher at Brazoswood High School, Rod Cannon, remembered "Abe Lincoln" as a talented, if somewhat introverted, guitarist in the jazz ensemble. Sister Suzy had a quick mind, a sharp wit, and the physical wherewithal to play drums, although she didn't think it was the kind of instrument a girl should play. But Selena was different. She just knew. Her cues, her sense of timing, her expressiveness while performing—it was like she'd been born into show business.

"When I realized that Selena could sing, I saw the continuation of my dreams," Abraham later said.

In truth, Selena was no child prodigy. She had to be trained for a show-business career. Whatever talent she was blessed with, her father nurtured and cultivated through hard work and hours of practice, something the other kids on the block did not quite understand. "I was always scared of her dad," said Shaunda Clark. "I had to be out of the house by the time he came home." Meredith Lynn Cappel formed a similar impression. "I remember sneaking into her house one time—we were getting sweets or something," she said. "There was music equipment all over the house. I remember standing in her den and you could see the drums in one room and a guitar in another room. Selena said, 'Oh yeah, my sister plays the drums, my brother plays guitar.' We used to love to ask her to sing songs. It gave you chill bumps how powerful her voice was, and this was in third and fourth grade. She'd do it during recess and when we walked home from school. Any Top 40 song she could sing. She didn't just sing it, she really got into it."

In choir, students had to greet the music teacher, Mrs. Peacock, by singing "Good morning" to her. Merely singing was not sufficient for Abraham's girl, however. "Selena would just belt it out," said Meredith Lynn. "Selena knew so much about music and it would make the teacher mad. If she was wrong about something, Selena would correct her. It was funny. I remember being kind of jealous about that, how good she was."

Mrs. Peacock didn't remember things quite that way. "She was a natural. I didn't teach her a single thing. Her dad was real controlling. He wouldn't let her sing Christmas carols because of being Jehovah's Witnesses. She couldn't even have 'Happy Birthday' sung to her. One day she came in and said, 'It's my birthday but you can't sing "Happy Birthday" to me.' We sang it to her anyway."

As proof that she was destined to make music, one day in 1978 Selena brought Meredith Lynn and Shaunda a 45 with an orange label. Both girls were impressed by the way she autographed the record in bold, dramatic handwriting.

Abraham taught his kids to enjoy all kinds of music. To better appreciate harmonizing, he turned them on to the Imperials gospel group. The music of his fifties youth became their music. He coached them to sing phonetically in Spanish. The kids had their music, too. Lying on the sofa in the sound-proofed practice room Abraham had built for them, Selena learned music and came to be partial toward the black female vocal group Taste of Honey, disco diva Donna Summer, and Australian pop-rockers Air Supply.

To Abraham, it was all part of the Tex-Mex experience of his youth. "It is influenced from so many different directions, so many types of music, that we accept any kind of music as long as it is good." To Selena and her brother and sister, almost everything sounded good.

At school, little Selena had no trouble blending in. "She was a quiet, good worker. She wasn't a troublemaker, not out to get attention. She was a sweet little girl, an average student, not outstanding but not below average," said her second-grade teacher, Pat Diehl. "All the kids liked her. There were never any problems. She was a happy little girl, an average happy little second-grader. She dressed like the other kids, not flashy, not dirty. She had no language-skill problems. She was an average reader in an average group." Selena's first-grade teacher, Mrs. Nina McGlashen, concurred, describing her as "a perky, enthusiastic, happy little girl. She was well liked and had a bubbly personality." She also demonstrated an entrepreneurial streak at a young age, buying candy and reselling it at school, which impressed her father. "She did other little things like that, that showed she knew how to handle money."

The smiling *chiquita* with the thick mane of flowing black hair that she often braided and tied in a knot, was the sole brown-skinned person in her third-grade classroom, other than her teacher, Mrs. Annie Pérez. "I didn't remember at first that I had Selena as a student," Pérez admitted some fifteen years later. "She was an ideal student. You usually remember the outstanding ones—the really good ones or the bad ones. She did everything she was supposed to do. She was an average student scholastically, did her work, was obedient. She had a glowing personality, but was quiet at the same time. On the playground the kids would call out 'Selena!' She was friendly with the other students."

There were occasional clashes between teachers and Selena's parents. Her musical aspirations, or those of her father, were affecting her schoolwork.

"I was making real good grades but I had a couple of teachers that were being real . . . they felt like my father was doing child labor," Selena said to Joseph Harmes in an interview. "Of course, we got all that straightened out. But eventually they started thinking she is not doing anything, she's not missing school, 'cause we would only do it on the weekends."

What did stick out in the minds of some teachers and friends as much as the music was her religious upbringing.

"She was a Jehovah's Witness," recalled Meredith Lynn Cappel. "In our school that meant any time there was a party, she had to go to the library or she went home. She missed out on all the fun and I hated that. I had a birthday party and she couldn't come."

Selena would tell her friend it was no big deal. "I'm sure she was disappointed, sitting in the library while we were having our party, but she never pouted about it," Meredith Lynn said. "As soon as we were back in class everything was fine again."

The tenets of the Watchtower Society, founded in 1884 by Charles Taze Russell, were indeed strict and specific. Jehovah's Witnesses believed that they were the one true Christian faith described by the apostle Paul; when God returned to destroy the whole wicked system of things on Earth, the true believers, the 144,000 Christians described in Revelation as "brides of Christ," would be resurrected and take their place alongside Christ in the theocracy of Heaven. Blasphemous religious teaching, oppression by big business, and the tyranny of human governments were all products of Satan. Witnesses refrained from saluting flags, accepting blood transfusions, and they claimed military-service exemptions. Abraham and Marcella's brood were not members of Jehovah's Witnesses, per se—otherwise Abraham would not have served in the military—but they counted themselves followers of the faith.

It was the *abuelos*, Abraham, Sr., and Mary, who were the true believers. Abrán neither drank nor fooled around. Every day he left his job doing auto-body repair and painting to go home and tend to his wife, whose health began to fail in 1971. He wasn't hesitant to urge friends and co-workers to come around to the ways of the Lord. He became so frustrated trying to convert one acquaintance, Sam Flores, that he called him *cabeza de repollo*—he had a cabbage for a head.

Being subjected to the rules and constricts of the faith did not impede Selena from being one of the most popular kids in school, mainly because of her friendliness. "I don't think she ever had any enemies," said Meredith

Lynn. "She was always giggly and funny. She was so self-conscious about her body—she used to hate her bottom! But she wasn't fat. She just had a big bottom. The only thing she was shy about was thinking her bottom was too big."

In her class picture, taken April 11, 1980, about the same time Abraham and Jim Serda were planning their restaurant venture, a toothy, wild-maned Selena stands in the front row, radiating a smile bigger than life, outshining her fellow students. She knew a thing or two about projecting. She'd already performed professionally, her father saw to that. The kids had won two hundred dollars in a talent contest at the Wharton County fair. They'd gigged at the Starlite Ballroom in Houston, a music club and restaurant in an old grocery store which was owned by Emmanuel and Cruz Velásquez and featured Mexican-American bands. Abraham had gotten his children bookings opening for a new Houston band called La Mafia, and for Grupo Tejas, a spinoff from the popular Latin Breed. She had already recorded at Sugar Hill studios. The band played weddings, birthdays, parties, wherever Abe could get them an engagement. When the occasion called for it, such as the wedding anniversary of Santos Serda, Sr., Abraham would sing with her. "I was scared for her, proud, and happy when I saw that people were liking her," Marcella said. "It wasn't easy at all—it was very hard for everyone, but I think it drew us together."

During the day, Abraham Quintanilla, Jr., toiled in metal warehousing, in building B-201 on the Dow Chemical campus. One co-worker who used to chat with him during breaks, Louie Matula, said it was easy to see where Abe's priorities were. Driving a forklift and loading boxcars wasn't his thing. "He really loved to play music. His first love was [his kids'] band. They played around at different places in the area. He was a pretty good worker but was more interested in his music than his work. They would play until late and then he would come into work. Abe was an opinionated, outspoken guy who knew what he wanted. Working at Dow was just a way to get enough money to further his musical career.

"He couldn't wait to blow it all off."

Papa Gayo's restaurant opened at 121 Circle Way late in the summer of 1980. A photograph of the ribbon-cutting ran in the local newspaper, the Brazosport *Facts*, depicting the owners, Abraham Quintanilla, Jr., and Santos "Jim" Serda, Jr., and a little girl between them who was misidentified as Selena Serda. Marcella and Jim Serda's wife, Carol, ran the kitchen. A.B., Suzy, and Selena bussed tables and helped out. The waitresses were Jehovah's Witnesses recruited from church. In the evenings the men came in to help out. But less than a month after the place opened, Abraham joined them full-time, quitting Dow to take over operation of the restaurant while Jim Serda held on to his day job. Abraham left much of the food part of the operation to the wives. He had grander plans. One had to look no further than the advertisements that ran in the newspaper announcing live entertainment Thursday through Saturday featuring Selena and Company ("The only place in the Brazosport area where a family can eat a good meal and enjoy live entertainment") to see where he was focusing his efforts. Abraham was back in show business.

"I was going through a mental battle," he later said. "I missed the music and wanted to get back into it." While working his day job at Dow he helped Jim Serda rewire, plumb, and generally transform the rectangular brick building that was the former home of Agnew Beauty College into a restaurant. The location was near the heart of the Lake Jackson business district, though the confusing road gridwork made it difficult to reach from the main highway.

Such minor details did not deter Abraham, who beckoned readers of the Brazosport *Facts* to try the best flautas in the Brazosport area and hear Selena, "the sensational nine-year-old singer."

Putting the children to work as entertainers was not part of the original plan for Papa Gayo's. "At least on my part it wasn't," said Selena, whose memories of the restaurant were of eating lots of flan and chile con queso. He was looking for all kinds of entertainers. On December 13, the restaurant hosted a special $7.95 dinner night featuring Bobby Reed's tribute to Elvis, his son Taylor's magic show, and a style show featuring fifteen girls who'd taken a nine-week self-improvement course called Attitudes started by two local women. The girls modeled fashions from the Corner and the La Velle shops, with their hair done by Maximillian's.

Abraham also solicited acts through the newspaper for the restaurant. One of the persons answering his ad was Rena Dearman, who showed up at the Quintanillas' house on Caladium with her friend Kevin Barnett, with whom she was performing country music under the name Blue Midnight. Abraham liked what he heard.

"You're hired," he told them, not as a featured act at the restaurant but as members of the band the Quintanilla kids were playing in, Southern Pearl. Rena, eleven years older than Selena, signed on to play keyboards and sing back-up vocals. Barnett played guitar but soon left and was replaced by a handsome fellow named Rodney Pyeatt, though Abraham played guitar, too.

One night, Primo Ledesma, a disc jockey who hosted a weekly Spanish-language radio show in Freeport, drifted into Papa Gayo's for a listen. "I went to the restaurant and heard Selena singing," he recalled. "I thought, 'Man, they're good.' Her father came over to me—I had known him since way back when he was with the Dinos."

"She's going places," Ledesma predicted to him. "She's got it all—the voice, moves, the smile."

Abraham feigned disinterest, shaking his head.

"I won't take her childhood away from her. I'm not going to push her," he told Ledesma. Undeterred, Ledesma asked if he could tape Selena. He had brought his tape recorder along with him. He always carried it around, in case he came across a story or interview.

Abraham nodded his approval.

Selena sang while the tape rolled.

The following day, during Ledesma's show broadcast over KBRZ in Freeport, he announced, "We've got a new talent on the radio today" and played the tape he had made the night before.

The call buttons on the telephone lit up immediately. Who was that little girl with the voice that wouldn't quit? Child singers had always been popular in the Latin music world, but this girl was something else. She sounded like a new sensation.

Ledesma called the girl's father from the studio. "What was your daughter's name? C-E-L—"

"No, no." Abraham Quintanilla corrected Ledesma. "S-E-L-E-N-A. Selena."

On his next visit to Papa Gayo's, Ledesma learned that the little girl's star was already rising. Someone offered her two thousand dollars to sing at some opening in Houston, Abraham said. He wasn't going to do it, though, mentioning his desire to protect her childhood. But when Abraham ran into Ledesma again, he told him they did go, and that her career was taking off.

Unfortunately, Abe's culinary path to riches and success was not meant to be. In fact, his timing couldn't have been worse. He was inexperienced as a restaurateur, with a tendency to seat as many patrons as he could fit in, plying them with tostada chips and free soft drinks while they waited for as much as an hour for their orders to arrive. The problem was aggravated by the fact the kitchen help spoke Spanish and the waitresses spoke English. The location, though downtown, was not easy to reach. At a time when margaritas were being touted as the perfect accompaniment to Mexican food, it was against the law in Lake Jackson to sell liquor by the drink. Papa Gayo's, though, did happen to serve beer and wine. Despite a decent lunch crowd, Lake Jackson just might not have been ready for home-style Mexican cooking that was far more authentic than at franchises like Monterrey House and El Torito. Finances became so tight that Abraham ceased taking out advertisements in the Brazosport

Facts by January. By the first of March 1981, Papa Gayo's doors were shut. It was replaced a month later by a new restaurant, the Coral Reef, which specialized in seafood.

Even through the eyes of a carefree, happy-go-lucky child, things looked pretty bad. "We had to file for bankruptcy," Selena later said. "We lost our home [though the mortgage was ultimately paid off when they sold the house to Teodoro Longoria]. We lost our restaurant. We were [almost] literally out on the street."

In November 1981, the family moved in with one of Abe's brothers in a trailer park in El Campo, about seventy-five miles west of Lake Jackson, where Selena attended fifth grade. Abraham worked for his brother's trucking business, delivering gravel.

Through all the trials and tribulations, Abraham's faith in music never wavered. He worked day gigs because he had to. He pushed music because he wanted to. He hustled gigs for the band at weddings, country clubs, wherever he could find them. After the restaurant shut down, the former Southern Pearl and Selena and Company became Los Dinos, even though the personnel remained the same, with Rena Dearman on keyboards and Rodney Pyeatt on guitar. The band still played country and some pop and rock, but now they also mixed in songs that Rena and Rodney knew as Spanish music; Abraham referred to it as *musica tejana*.

The *musica tejana* sound was a quirky style that sounded even quirkier if one didn't understand the Spanish lyrics; but it was easy to dance to, which was the basis of its appeal in the first place. Rena and Rodney weren't Tejano by birth, or even assimilation, but they knew a good music gig when they saw it. Abraham was really determined, so it was easy to make a commitment to stay with the band, especially now that the little girl who sang at Papa Gayo's was blooming into a charismatic young teenager. They were so convinced they made a commitment to themselves, and married.

The next year, the Quintanillas moved back to Lake

Jackson, where Selena attended sixth grade. Their residence this time around was number 211 of a faceless sixties-vintage two-story brick apartment complex at 401 Garland, a few blocks from their old homestead on Caladium but several notches down the economic scale. It was a tough adjustment, but at least there was one side benefit. Abraham had entered Selena in a weekly talent show called Starmania, which was held in the ballroom of the Villa Hotel in nearby Angleton every Saturday night. The talent search was promoted by a local entertainer named Bobby Reed, who'd performed his Elvis tribute at Papa Gayo's. When Reed started hosting the Starmania contests, Selena won the qualifying rounds for seven consecutive weeks by singing "Feelings." Just as millions had migrated to New York or Los Angeles to get to Broadway or Hollywood, Abraham wanted to be where the action was.

Surprisingly, the gypsy-like wanderings hadn't affected Selena's schoolwork. She was a bright student and made up the work she missed due to the moves and the absences caused by playing music. She placed second in the fifth-grade spelling bee in El Compo. Nonetheless, some teachers voiced concerns about her attendance, fearing that Selena's father was sacrificing her education at the expense of the singing career he envisioned for her.

Primo Ledesma saw the world Abraham had built for his family in Lake Jackson collapse around him for the last time. "[Abraham] had to start driving a dump truck. They moved to the apartments on Garland. He didn't want anybody to know he was driving a dump truck. He wore sunglasses and a hat and kept the windows mostly rolled up [a considerable sacrifice of comfort, given the Gulf Coast heat and humidity]. It was a big old ugly thing. Then one day he parked the truck in the Kettle parking lot across the street, by where the Dumpster's at now, and they just took off. He didn't want anybody to know. That truck stayed there six or seven weeks before it was towed off. I saw it early on and knew whose it was, but I didn't say anything."

Abe packed up the van and took the family back to Corpus. That's the way it would be. They had to give up a boat, motor, and trailer—spoils of the good life in L.J.— but took the amplifiers, speakers, and instruments with them. Music was the way out. He believed in music, a faith he understood like nothing else. His kids had talent, especially Selena. Abraham knew how to keep a band going; he'd proved that the first time around with his Dinos. He'd prove it again with these Dinos.

If these were desperate times, Selena didn't show it. While Abraham scouted things out in Corpus, she stayed with relatives at the Magnolia Apartments in Angleton. A neighbor, Yolanda Flores, said that Dina, as her aunt and uncle called her, would sit with Flores on a bench outside every evening and entertain herself by singing. Occasionally, she held Flores's six-month-old daughter and sang while dancing with her in her arms.

"Despite all the family's problems, she wasn't sad or depressed," Flores said. "She was very wrapped up in her music." Selena told Flores she was going to be a star, but that when she was, she wouldn't forget Mrs. Flores's baby girl.

Selena saw the move back to Corpus as something that was necessary for the whole family to do. "I guess we can honestly say that that was when we started our musical career. It was like we had no other alternative to make money. This was the best way."

3
Chicano Hollywood

W HEN ABRAHAM QUINTANILLA, JR., FINALLY moved
his brood back to Corpus Christi, he was following
family again as much as he was chasing money. Abraham,
Sr., who had bailed him out of more than one shaky investment in the past, had already settled with his second
wife in a tiny four-room white frame house at 1611 Floral,
one block from the Koch refinery in a poor, mostly black
and Mexican residential neighborhood scrunched between
the interstate and the ship channel. Brothers Hector,
Eddie, and Isaac were in Corpus, too.

The hardships Abe had encountered after he'd left Dow
gnawed at the depths of his soul. Making it in show business was his only escape. Marcella and the kids were doing their part, swearing fealty to him, trusting that he
could make the band concept work, just like the family's
kids on the *Brady Bunch* on television. But it was a grueling, thankless task, trying to promote an act while holding
on to day jobs that were temporary at best. That kind of
work led nowhere. With music, there was at least hope.

Taking the name of Abraham's old band might help the
kids get bookings. "I encouraged the name Los Dinos
because the name had been used by a very popular group

of the fifties and sixties," Abe told a reporter a few years later. "Reviving it would automatically provide greater publicity and promotion for Selena," he reasoned. What he couldn't do on his own, his children would do for him.

Once again, it all boiled down to language. The plan was to drop the country music bit and stick with playing *musica tejana*, the style he had converted to with the original Los Dinos. In order to achieve the kind of success she was capable of, he would continually teach his little girl how to sing in Spanish, which made Corpus an even more agreeable place to be, since it was where *la onda* was happening.

Since the seventies, the Mexican influence had been asserting itself again in Corpus through sheer numbers. There were more Latins than Anglos living in the city, and they were finally grabbing for their piece of the pie. With the average Mexicano about ten years younger than the average Anglo, the old *patrón* system of white bosses lording over brown peons was coming to an end. The political balance of power shifted in 1976, when Carlos Truan beat Mike McKinnon for the office of state senator representing Corpus Christi.

Finally, the economic buying power of Mexican-Americans was being noticed. In 1983, three local firms were among the top four hundred Hispanic businesses in the United States. For the first time, there was a full-time Spanish-language television station in the city, KORO. Corpus's major grocery chain began using bilingual signage in many stores and increased stock in ingredients used in Mexican foods.

Still, there were many battles to fight. The city was behind only Odessa, Texas, as having the most sharply defined separation between Latin-Americans and Anglo-Americans, according to a study conducted at the University of California. Half of the eligible Mexican-American population in Corpus had not registered to vote. The drop-out rate from public school was eighty percent for Mexican-Americans living in Corpus Christi; their median education was four and a half years, compared to a twelve-year average for Anglos.

These problems were not Abraham's. He was more than happy to be back on his old stomping grounds. People in the barrio already knew about Los Dinos, *his* Los Dinos. No matter how small the pond, it was nice to be a big fish again. Abraham knew most of the important players and operators on the scene. Back in Lake Jackson, he was just another faceless blue-collar worker at Dow. In Corpus, he could hustle a session at Hacienda out of Roland García or hit on his old acquaintance Freddie Martínez for a break on studio time.

When it came to celebrities, Corpus Christi could claim Farrah Fawcett, whose toothy smile and fly-away blond hair had made her a worldwide sex symbol; Sam Neely, a bland folk singer in the John Denver mold; country-folk singer Don Williams of the Pozo Seco Singers, who actually came from nearby Portland; actor Dabney Coleman; musician Tony Joe White, who performed locally with the Kon Tiki Trio before he hit it big as a Louisiana swamp-styled singer with "Poke Salad Annie"; and Lou Diamond Phillips, who portrayed Hispanic music legend Ritchie Valens in the movie based on his life.

Corpito's Mexican-American celebrities, virtually unknown outside of Texas, carried a much higher profile among the local *gente*. Steve Jordan, the Jimi Hendrix of the conjunto accordion, whose experimentations laid a considerable amount of groundwork for modern Tejano music, liked to refer to Corpus Christi as the Chicano Hollywood. You had to drive no farther than Ocean Drive, where Freddy Fender parked his fifties- and sixties-vintage hot rods on his front lawn, to realize that. Living legends such as bandleader Isidro López, singer Chelo Silva, and accordionist Tony de la Rosa drove the city's boulevards and shopped its malls. Two natives, Freddie Martínez and Roland García, ran record labels that actually made money.

Spanish radio provided a consistent forum for leaders and the public at large. More people in the city listened to Spanish radio than to English. KUNO station manager

Luis Alonzo Muñoz credited the Chicano movement with building pride in the culture. "The gringo had been saying, 'You're an American, don't speak Spanish, and blah, blah, blah.' And all of a sudden they answered, 'So what?' They started being proud they were Mexican-Americans. And from that day on it has never stopped. They want to learn Spanish."

Mexican-Americans also wanted their own music, something that KUNO, with a playlist that emphasized Mexican International songs, did not always give them. Back in 1974, while Abraham was doing time at Dow, the Dávila family from San Antonio bought KCCT-AM and began programming the station like their station in San Antonio, KEDA-AM. Mexican mariachi and Spanish-international music records were shoved aside in favor of Texas artists, most of them singing Texas style *la onda chicana* or *la onda tejana*. The format, identified as Radio Jalapeño, immediately found an audience in Corpus that hadn't been previously exploited. Proof was the crowd of ten thousand that flocked to an outdoor concert that KCCT organized at Cole Park.

Selena's career endured several false starts on the heels of Papa Gayo's demise. Abraham arranged for Selena to record "Tomorrow's Rains Fall Today," an English-language version of "Si Quieres Verme Llorar," at Hacienda Studios in Corpus, but it was never pressed. He tried down the street at Freddie Records, the studio and record label run by his old *compadre* from his House of Music days, Freddie Martínez.

"One day Abraham brought Selena in here and said, 'I'd like you to hear my daughter.' I listened to her and immediately said, 'This little girl is very good,' and we did the very first album she recorded," Martínez said. "She did one album here and then she did the second one. We never put the second one out and we sold the master to Abraham. I don't know what he did with it."

The sessions at Hacienda had gone nowhere. The Freddie sessions, produced and engineered by Rick Longoria, then a salesman for the record company, fared a little better. Two singles were actually released on Freddie in 1983, "No Puedo Estar sin Tí" backed with "Se Acabó el Amor," and "Ya Se Va" backed with "Tres Veces No," but they garnered little airplay and generated virtually no sales. Those songs and four other tracks, including a remake of the original Dinos' "Give Me One Chance," became a cassette album titled *Selena y los Dinos* that was later reissued as *Mis Primeras Canciones*. Twelve other songs Longoria recorded, including "Si Quieres Verme Llorar," "Sweet Dreams," "You Needed Me," and a Spanish version of "A Hundred Pounds of Clay," have not been released.

Whatever the potential of Selena y los Dinos, Freddie Records was only going to go so far in betting on the band. They already had La Sombra, Ramón Ayala, and Laura Canales to push. Selena may have been young, sheltered, and impressionable, but she knew the score. "We did singles," she recalled. "I don't think they wanted to waste that much money on us. I guess because I was so young, they'd say we'll give her another six years before she started making it. Dad would get so upset. But needless to say, they were right."

Freddie Martínez did more than just give Selena's nascent recording career a small push. Many credited him as the one who started the whole *onda*. During the sixties, back when Sunny Ozuna, Rudy and the Reno Bops, the Royal Jesters, the Dinos, and all the young South Texas-Mexican bands were singing in English and riffing off American pop, rock, and soul sounds, Freddie Martínez was sticking to Spanish, playing the polkas, *rancheras*, and *cumbias* that were the essence of the music he'd grown up with in Texas, including the regional sound of the Mexican north popularized by Ramón Ayala, Trío los Panchos, Los Alegres de Terán, and Lucha Villa, and the boleros that brought tears to the eyes of listeners no matter what side of the border they came from. Martínez's idea of keeping up with the times was incorporating the latest Latin dance trends, like the mambo or the cha-cha, with whatever the other Mexican-American *orquesta* acts, like Sunny, Little Joe, and Augustine Ramírez, were doing.

For ten years, Martínez toiled in the dance halls around Corpus Christi, Alice, Kingsville, and Robstown, broadening his circuit to Houston, Brownsville, and West Texas, doing what he did best, which was keeping the dance floor filled. He'd recorded for Falcon, Zarape, La Polka, and Ideal, but never enjoyed much success. But on his fourth album, recorded and released in 1972, Martínez's perseverance paid off.

A disc jockey from Laredo discovered the B side of a single that Martínez had released from the album and couldn't stop spinning it. The song was a tearjerker of a ballad, "Te Traigo Estas Flores," written by Joe Mejía, and it instantly generated a barrage of listener requests. Jukebox play was phenomenal. Copies of the record couldn't be pressed fast enough. In spite of a loosely run distribution system, the album that the song appeared on broke the one-hundred-thousand sales barrier, the first Tejano record to do so. The song had such universal appeal, it even sold in Mexico, overcoming the long-standing Mexican prejudice that Texans making Mexican music were nothing but unrefined hicks from the sticks. Martínez was greeted with open arms when he toured Monterrey, Torreon, Tijuana, and all across Mexico, where he was accorded the formal title of el Embajador de la Onda Chicana and the slightly less eloquent moniker El Pocho del la Voz Maravillosa. He even performed at Madison Square Garden in New York.

Freddie Martínez proved there was money to be made in the field of *musica tejana*. Good money. He made enough money to buy Studio B, where he recorded, and started up his own label, Freddie. The entire Spanish-language music scene across Texas was going through a radical transformation. The mom-and-pop operations, the garage bands, and the independent entrepreneurs were doing so well with their respective ventures that outsiders were taking note.

Onstage, there was an entirely new cast of personalities. In the late seventies, *la onda* had gone through a dry spell, with only a handful of bands, like Little Joe; Latin Breed; Laura Canales, *la reina de la onda chicana*, as she was billed; Austin's Augustin Ramírez; and the Tortilla Factory from San Angelo, having much to say musically or drawing crowds to dances. But by the early eighties, a new wave was sweeping the scene. La Mafia started to hit out of Houston, Mazz broke out like gangbusters from the Rio Grande Valley, and Ram Herrera from south San Antonio was breaking hearts after breaking away from accordionist David Lee Garza. La Sombra was stirring up so much fan interest in Texas from their home base of Aurora, Illinois, with a catchy little tune, "Mi Güerita Coca-Cola," that they moved to Corpus to be closer to the action.

The music, which had always stressed variety, was becoming even more inclusive. All the bands did polkas, but *cumbias, huapangos*, and merengues were also being worked in, along with the English-language pop, rock, and rhythm and blues songs heard on the radio and jukebox. MTV, and the musical and fashion styles that went with it, was making just as strong an impression on Tejano youth as it was on youth elsewhere around the globe. The scene in Corpus was growing to the point that the 1982 eighth annual Mike Chávez Awards presentation (the local Tejano award) drew more than three thousand to the coliseum to see Mazz perform and walk away with most of the awards. Meanwhile, up in San Antonio, Chávez had competition in the form of the new Tejano Music Awards, which had begun in 1979. Dance halls and clubs were giving *la onda* acts more play dates. Cover charges escalated above ten dollars. The audience was dressing up, showing its affluence. So were the entertainers. Little Joe, who'd been wearing a fringe vest and headband, was now decked out in a tuxedo.

At the same time, the popularity of conjuntos remained strong and ran the gamut from modernists such as David Lee Garza and Snowball and Company featuring Laura Canales to the conservators of the old style such as Cuatitos Cantu, Flaco Jimenez, Rubén Naranjo, Tony de la Rosa, and Mingo Saldivar. The fan base was replenished by converts newly arrived from Mexico and from conjunto's country-and-western type appeal among the more assimilated members of the audience. Although it could be confused with music being made in Mexico, conjunto used a heavier, punchier drum sound than the thinner snare-drum sound and accordion-saxophone harmonies preferred by the *norteños* of northern Mexico.

Another phenomenon occurring in the Rio Grande Valley would have a significant impact on *la onda*. Two radio stations were reinventing the way music and information were being transmitted to Mexican-Americans. One station, KITM-FM, was a small 3,000-watt station broadcasting out of Mission that had spotty reception across the Valley. But its eclectic format, which mixed Tejano music with Spanish-international hits and English-language country and pop hits, was considered revolutionary, for no reason other than it mirrored the diverse tastes of the Tejano listener. Similarly, the station's bilingual announcing style reflected the way modern Tejanos talked. While the format was short-lived, the English-Spanish manner of speaking was soon embraced by other stations across the American Southwest. One of the first was another Valley station, KIWW-FM, the first 100,000-watt-station FM signal to broadcast a full-time format featuring *musica tejana*. The wattage and the audio quality of the FM signal meant that the latest Tejano singles would sound as good as the singles on the *gabacho* stations. And like KITM's, KIWW's announcers weren't Mexican nationals stressing proper diction and pronunciation but Texas-Mexicans, who not only spoke Spanish with a local dialect but breezed effortlessly between Spanish and English, just as Mexicanos in South Texas did in everyday conversation.

By talking like their audience and playing the music their audience preferred instead of the hits popular in Mexico, KIWW went on to thrash soundly KGBT, the Spanish-language giant in the Rio Grande Valley, in audience ratings, and to influence other stations throughout the region to follow their lead. With radio talking the talk of South Texas and playing the songs heard in the clubs and dance halls, Tejano music suddenly became a very hip commodity.

The Quintanilla kids were not so easy to convince. They liked what they heard on the Top 40 radio station, not Spanish music. And they wanted to play the music they liked. But Abraham would not let up. You may not like this music, he told them, but this is the kind of music you can make money with. He knew. He'd been there.

On many a night, he patiently sat with Selena, helping her memorize the phrases. She would learn how to sing in Spanish, even though she could hardly speak it.

Corpus felt like home to young Selena, since most of her aunts and uncles and cousins and her *papi* were nearby, as always. But it was a definite change of scenery. Lake Jackson was all humidity and vegetation. Corpus was just as flat but nowhere near as jungle-like. Perched on the northeastern edge of South Texas's harsh brush country, it was unusually barren for the coast. The saving graces were the palms planted downtown and along Shoreline and Ocean drives, where *los ricos* lived, and the gusty breeze constantly blowing off the water. It was even windier than Chicago, the Windy City, a teacher had once told Selena.

For the first few months of their return, the Quintanillas stayed at Uncle Eddie's. Then, in early 1984, Abraham was able to swing a deal to start making payments on a new brick tract home in the Molina subdivision, a few blocks down the street from where his brother Hector lived. Molina was a mostly Mexican-American working-class neighborhood, with a smattering of blacks and whites, on the southwestern edge of Corpus. Less than a mile from South Padre Island Drive, the city's newest freeway, and within view of cultivated farmland, Molina had been developed after World War II and earned a reputation as a good place to raise a family.

Most homes were small but well maintained, with neat

yards, some surrounded by chain-link fences. Older cars and pickup trucks were parked on the streets and in driveways. The Quintanillas' house, at 709 Bloomington, was in the newer part of Mo Town, as some locals liked to call it, near West Oso High School, where the brick homes, sidewalks and curbing, and somewhat larger yards suggested that its occupants were already enjoying their prosperity.

Abraham pursued his prosperity two ways. His listed occupation was working at Corpus Christi Motors on Leopard Street, helping his younger brother Isaac run his truck-leasing business. His real job was managing and directing Los Dinos. Even when he was renting out heavy trucks, his mind was on the kids, the need for them to practice and the urgency to get them out in front of the public. On weekends, he'd load them into the van, hook up the little trailer he'd built to carry their equipment, and hit the road, playing any kind of gig he could book. Abraham was behind the wheel, Marcie rode shotgun, and everyone else piled in back. "We lived together and slept together—it was a real close-knit thing," recalled Rena Dearman, who played keyboards in the first reincarnation of Los Dinos. "It was a sacrifice, but we loved it. We knew there was a reason for it."

Los Dinos paid their dues, working weddings and anniversaries and more than their fair share of benefits and fund-raisers, anywhere Abraham thought he could get exposure. When the occasion called for it, Abraham would join the band, singing duets with Selena or helping out on guitar. He called on everyone he knew to give him a break. Gregorio "Goyo" Villarreal, the owner of the all-purpose dance hall, truck stop, and restaurant in Mission called Greg's, remembered Abraham bringing Selena to his place in 1981. "He pleaded for an opportunity the first few times. He really needed the work."

The promoters weren't exactly chomping at the bit. The juvenile angle was worth a few tickets perhaps, but the concept of a female fronting a band didn't play in *la onda*. The crowds on the circuit came to see men, not women.

Machos made the world go round, not chanteuses.

"They were a band, they could play, they weren't totally garage, but they weren't great," remembered Rubén Cubillos, who'd first met Abraham and his children at the Starlite Ballroom in Houston. "They were kids making noise, they'd be out of tune. But they had that drive, and they were out there."

So was Abraham. "He was the ultimate stage father," said Mike Chávez. "He had so many doors shut in his face, but he wouldn't take no for an answer. This guy went against all odds. How many times was he told she had no talent, that they were just another band? He handled her career, he kept her clean, even if he came off as rough, difficult to work with, and would fly off the handle at the drop of a hat."

Just keeping the band together was a feat. Rena and Rodney weren't getting along, and they finally left the band in 1983 on their way to a divorce. They were replaced by two Brazosport-area musicians: Mike Dean, who took over keyboards, and Del Balint, a rocking guitarist.

Dean was a musical prodigy from Angleton who'd dropped out of the Berklee School of Music to play keyboards and later went on to engineer hits for rap stars the Geto Boys. It was this version of Los Dinos that recorded Johnny Herrera's "La Tracalera" at Manny Guerra's, beginning a long association with the producer. Dean and Balint stayed with the band almost two years before Abraham replaced them, in 1985, with two Corpus Christi teenagers, Ricky Vela, who played keyboards, and guitarist Roger García.

Merely getting to gigs and back was a task unto itself. "All I remember is every time they turned, I rolled off the seat," Selena said a few years after that. "We lost a lot. We really did. We would get home and we would have just enough money for our expenses and we would end up with nothing. But we all wanted to make it, so we did everything we could." Abraham instilled that desire in all his children. He wouldn't let them forget that they were entertainers and it was their job to entertain, as Selena related. "There were a lot of disappointing times. But even when we got ten or twenty people to show up, we always believed that Hey, these people paid to get in, we should go do a good show."

The money was in live performances. Making records was a nice vanity, but even the big acts like Little Joe were lucky to sell fifty thousand units, a level where a musician could actually live off retail sales. Still, recording was considered the nobler venture. In the tradition of the original Dinos, A.B. was credited for composing "Call Me," though it borrowed shamelessly from "Slipping and Sliding" and "Land of 1,000 Dances." Selena still had a way to go perfecting her Spanish, mangling the phrase *voy a gozar* to *yo va a gozar* on "Parece que Va a Llover" and singing *mejorte alo*, not *mejorte hallo* on "Tres Veces No."

Shortly after the Freddie sessions, Abraham found better reception to Selena y los Dinos in San Antonio, where he signed with Bob Gréver of Cara Records, the hot label in *la onda*. Two singles were recorded and released that year on Cara, "Encontré el Amor" backed with "Soy Feliz," and "Se Me Hace" backed with "Estoy Contigo," followed by six more sides over the next eighteen months that were then compiled as the album cassette *The New Girl in Town*, released in 1985.

Ten years earlier, while Freddie Martínez was chasing pots of gold in dance halls and ballrooms in the United States and Mexico courtesy of "Te Traigo Estas Flores," Bob Gréver, then a music executive in Mexico City, packed his bags to set up shop in San Antonio. He came from a family of prominent *chilangos*. His grandmother Maria established the family's music legacy by writing the classic love song "Júrame," which was still being performed decades later on both sides of the border. Soon after he hit town, Gréver formed the Cara label, largely to push his grandmother's catalogue of songs through his Golden Sands publishing wing. Gréver astutely formed alliances with composer Luis Silva, signing him to a contract with Golden Sands, and producer Manny Guerra, who ran Amen, the hottest studio in San Antonio. Utilizing Silva's and Guerra's considerable talents, Gréver created a veritable hit factory. Its cornerstone was the Latin Breed, whose members included survivors from the San Antonio doo-wop harmonists the Royal Jesters. He added other bands, arrangers, producers, and composers one by one until his operation became a virtual Tex-Mex Motown, whose artists were reinventing the music they'd grown up with. By the time Abraham brought his kids to Gréver's attention, Cara's roster included the two new heavyweights of *la onda*: Grupo Mazz and La Mafia.

Gréver's greatest contribution to the career development of Los Dinos was hooking them up with Manny Guerra, from whom young Abraham III, A.B. learned much about studio electronics, and getting the band radio exposure. His promotional team was effective in generating airplay, particularly in San Antonio. And whatever the San Antonio stations were playing, the radio guys in the rest of the state were sure to pounce on.

The fifth Selena y los Dinos single for Cara, "Oh, Mamá," was a particularly interesting teen confection, with a hook based on Selena's adolescent squealing whenever she sang the title lyrics. Although it sold well under fifteen thousand copies, the extensive airplay of the song helped Los Dinos develop as a live act. The most important showcase for both the single and the band was an appearance on the *Johnny Canales Show*.

While Abraham had been away in Lake Jackson, Domingo Peña, the host of the only weekly music show on Corpus Christi television and a man who'd given the original Los Dinos a big boost, had been usurped by his protégé Johnny Canales, who started broadcasting his own TV music show from Corpus Christi in 1979. Like Domingo, Canales was nothing more than a master of ceremonies, albeit an engaging one whose charisma was as elusive and inexplicable as Ed Sullivan's. The *Johnny Canales Show* had a huge audience in Corpus and elsewhere in South Texas, with new stations being added nationwide every week.

For their first television appearance, Los Dinos were dressed for action in matching space suits and combat boots, which the kids had painted to resemble walking collages shortly before they went before the cameras to lip-synch. Selena was only thirteen, but she already demonstrated a knack for knowing her way around a stage. With her short hair combed back and wearing guitar-shaped earrings and a necklace, she radiated confidence while chatting up Canales. He teased her in Spanish for not speaking the mother tongue and drawling those few words she tried to pronounce, such as *pintaron*, which came out "peen-tahr-rahn." For the record, she performed a serviceable if not altogether convincing lip-synch to the single "Oh, Mamá," literally squirming as she squeaked out the title words of the harmless *juvenil* ditty.

In an article in the San Antonio *Express-News* on November 8, 1985, Ramon Hernandez wrote about an upcoming appearance by Selena y los Dinos in Rosedale Park as part of a caravan of Tejano stars. "The best description of her voice and the band's sound is to listen to Lulu's 'To Sir with Love,' which [Selena] sings in Spanish as 'Un Primer Amor,' " Hernandez wrote, also comparing her to Brenda Lee. Selena was quoted as saying the band's goal was to "Chicano-ize with a popular fusion of Mexican, rock, and pop."

She had sufficient name value to have three of the songs she'd recorded at Freddie Records three years earlier show up on a compilation called *Texas Class* that Freddie put out, featuring Patsy Torres, Laura Canales, Zandra, and "Selina," as her name was incorrectly spelled on the cassette jacket. The newspaper articles, TV appearances, and cassettes with her name on them might have looked impressive to others, but in reality, the saga of Selena y los Dinos was trying to stretch two-hundred-dollar guarantees for a night's worth of entertainment into a working wage for an entire family. If there was a bad gig, Abraham paid

Ricky and Roger first, since they weren't family, then spread what was left among the clan. Sometimes their pay was nothing more than Whataburgers, the family's favorite fast food. "If we got five or ten dollars, my God. We were like, You're kidding me. We were all happy," Selena said. "This was great. We could go to Weiner's and go shopping."

From the children's point of view, playing and traveling was mostly fun. They all loved music, both listening to it and making it. There were always pranks and jokes to keep them amused during the long miles of boredom. Baby sister was the biggest cutup of all. She loved making the others laugh, pulling tricks like putting toothpaste in Oreos or breaking the silence by imitating an opera singer hitting a high note.

But Easy Street was not part of their neighborhood. "A lot of times, we all felt it," Selena related. "Because, like I said, we are a real tight family. When one person is hurting, everyone is hurting, and that's how we work. And it was really frustrating. At times it was like, Let's give up. Let's everyone get jobs and stop working and get money and just give it up. But, I don't know, something always just held us to the music."

Abraham made the most of the gig money. He built band tours around lodging opportunities, Selena remembered. "See, the funny thing about Dad is, we would go see our relatives in Washington and Dad would somehow get bookings over there and we would play. So we made enough money to come back and, you know, survive," she said. "Dad has always been like that. If he can get the band to play, he's like, Go for it."

At all costs. For a while, Selena tried to keep up with her studies at West Oso Junior High School, four blocks from home in the older part of the Molina subdivision. To get to the school, a long one-story red-brick building shaded by mesquite and Chinese tallow trees, she would walk past a couple of blocks of homes that were smaller and less attractive than hers, another low red-brick building that housed John Skinner Elementary, where she would have gone had she grown up in Molina instead of Lake Jackson, and the imposing iron gates at the entrance of Our Lady of Pilar, a Catholic church across the street from the Molina Veteran's Park. The house of her uncle Hector, a maintenance man, was a half a block farther down Bloomington, across the street.

Selena was an exceptionally bright student, well liked by her classmates. The band, however, came first, as her father saw it, causing her to miss classes frequently on Fridays and Mondays. The family was still scraping by, but they were going places and it was Selena who was taking them there. She was a singer, first and foremost. The family members had staked their futures on it.

That was the way it was more often than not, in Molina and in almost every other Texas barrio. Except in rare cases, academics always deferred to economics. It had been so ever since children left school during harvest season to help their families pick crops and the attitude still prevailed. Selena did music, and music was family, and she had to put family before books.

It had been a bone of contention between Selena's teachers and her father since Lake Jackson. Marilyn Greer, Selena's seventh-grade reading teacher at West Oso Junior High in Molina, had several run-ins with Abraham. Greer acknowledged that Selena's grades were excellent and that she was diligent about making up the work she missed when she went out of town to perform on weekends. It was the long-term effect she was worried about.

"Selena was probably a valedictorian-quality student," Greer later said. "She was not only beautiful, she was very, very intelligent, and she conducted herself like a lady, which coming from the barrio was not an easy thing to do. You're talking someone who was bright, a minority, and female. This child could have gotten a four-year scholarship with any major university in the country." Greer expressed those concerns to Abraham, but he wouldn't listen. His Selena was a singing star, he told her, a child prodigy destined for a career on the stage. The school principal, a fan of the original Dinos, backed up Quintanilla. If the *patrón* of the house said it was thus, then that's how it would be, especially since she was making money.

The response frustrated Greer no end. Quintanilla was acting like an old world Hispanic, posturing like a macho man who'd been insulted. "They even threatened me with child labor," he would later tell *People* magazine. "I said, 'Child labor! That's not what this is about! My kids have talent!'" That priority made it inconsequential that Selena had the chance to have her future education paid for. Look at Jodie Foster, Greer tried to reason with him: she went to Yale and still had a successful film career. Abraham didn't know Jodie Foster from Houdini. He believed in music, period. Considering where most other kids in the barrio were heading, with too many girls getting married at sixteen and too many boys quitting school to work for an hourly wage on a dead-end career track, Abraham believed he was doing the right thing.

But he set Greer off when he mentioned he didn't like the people Selena was associating with at West Oso, either.

"Oh, sure," Greer shot back sarcastically. "She keeps better company in nightclubs at two A.M."

If he had to, Abraham told Greer, he would take her out of school and educate her himself. It was his prerogative. What did she need to learn, anyhow? As if to prove his point, he arranged for Selena y los Dinos to play in the gym at the junior high, carting in sound equipment and running the mixing board himself. That would show the teachers what Selena was doing on weekends.

Greer remained unimpressed.

The following year, Abraham pulled Selena out of the eighth grade at West Oso Junior High for good. She would just have to apply herself harder by taking correspondence courses from the American School in Chicago, the same institution that educated the singing Osmond family.

The memory of the run-in stayed with Greer for years

to come. She'd seen her share of Little League fathers, cheerleader moms, and other parents pushing their children, but Abraham took the cake. "He always came across as a second-rate musician whose career was such a failure all he could do was live through his kids."

Throughout the tug-of-war over Selena's education, the absence of the mother was conspicuous. "She was never involved," recalled Marilyn Greer. Marcella remained in the background during these clashes, as she did in most instances. Abraham left no doubt who wore the pants in the family. But Marcie's presence was crucial. She kept the family tight. In that respect, she embodied the *madrecita*, whose role in the traditional family unit was to offer comfort to her children while standing behind her husband. "In traditional Mexican homes, every child was taught the mother is a sainted person, loving and forgiving in all ways," said Texas A & I sociology professor Stanley Bittinger. "Traditionally in Mexico, most families are patriarchal; the dad makes the decisions. But in traditional Mexico the father has historically always been very aloof, too, whereas Mom is loving and forgiving. Children felt warm ties to the mother."

It was no small wonder, then, that Selena's role model was her mother. She was proud that she had her mom's personality. Selena described Marcella by saying, "She is loving, sentimental, honest, uncomplicated. My mom is everything that is good. I want to be like her."

Still bombing around in the van working the clubs and the dance halls, Los Dinos changed label affiliation in 1986, leaving Cara for GP, Manny Guerra's label. It was an easy change, since the band had already been using Manny as their producer and doing their recordings at his studio. Gréver may have been the smartest businessman on the scene, but when it came to pure artistry, Guerra was the heaviest cat in all of Tejano. His career began as the drummer for Isidro "El Indio" López's big band, regarded as the first true Tejano ensemble. After dropping out of Burbank High School in San Antonio, he joined Sunny and the Sunglows, Sunny Ozuna's first group, recording a single for Joe Anthony's Harlem Records, "From Now On," and "The Lasso," which Guerra wrote. He hit the top of the pop charts with Sunny's "Talk to Me," the record that changed the course of *la onda*, before breaking away with the rest of the Sunglows and scoring another success with "La Cacahuate," a polka instrumental that hit the pop charts again and sold five hundred thousand copies. After years of working on the circuit, Guerra turned up the level of sophistication in the studio. Amen was one of the best studios in Texas, and he had all the necessary gear and personnel to augment what many considered to be the best ear in the business. Out of that soup, Guerra created an *orquesta tejana* sound that paid tribute to bluesman Bobby "Blue" Bland; the pop brass of Chicago and Blood, Sweat, and Tears; Kool and the Gang; and the Commodores, as well as El Indio, Beto Villa, Sunny, Little Joe, and the rest.

This would make for a nicer arrangement than the one with Bob Gréver. Manny would make the records. Abraham hustled the gigs.

For a Mexicana girl, her fifteenth birthday marked her *quinceañera*, the lavish sweet-fifteen party that celebrated her passage into womanhood while reaffirming her faith, a coming-out party that introduced a young lady to society, to the church, and to the community. The celebration often included a mass, a reception, a dinner, and a dance, with the expense rising into the thousands of dollars. The gifts typically given to the honored girl included a medallion, which symbolized the religious expression of faith and placed the young woman under the protection of the saint whose image was on the medal; a small gold ring, which symbolized the tie between the woman, the community, and God; a crown, or tiara, which represented the victory the young woman had won by living a Christian life in the modern world; and flowers, which represented new life and the girl's new commitment and responsibility to the community. A girl typically had fifteen attendants, or *damas*, and their escorts; and several *padrinos de bau-*

tismo, friends or family members serving as the baptismal parents, who helped pay for the event. Although the affair resembled a wedding, the actual function was more like the ultimate birthday party. The roots of the custom extended back to rites of passage observed by the ancient Maya and Toltec cultures of Mexico.

Unfortunately, Selena Quintanilla didn't have time to have her own *quinceañera*. She was too busy leading her family band, promoting her music, trying to build a career.

For her fifteenth, she scored her first magazine cover, her picture appearing twice on the front of the *Tejano Entertainer*, one depicting her in a coquettish pose, smiling offstage like a *ruca*, her hair still short but teased up; the other capturing her singing onstage, holding a microphone and looking very suave with mirror sunglasses, her father standing behind her. The headline accompanying the images read: "Selena y los Dinos Make Sudden Impact on Tejano Music Industry." The story inside, by Leandro Rivera, described the fifteen-year-old Selena as "making an impressive contribution to the Hispanic music industry as the youngest female vocalist in the Tejano onda music circuit today.

"Under the management and guidance of her father, Abraham, Selena has arrived out of practically nowhere with a hardy grasp on the top-ten listings of frequently aired recordings throughout the vast network of Spanish-programming radio stations." The band, Rivera wrote, "obviously recognize the lack of competition in the circuit and are presently taking advantage of the temporary 'sick-leave' absence of the great Laura Canales, the renowned *reina de la onda*."

It was no secret in Tejano circles that Laura Canales liked to party and could keep up with the big boys when it came to having a good time. Whatever personal problems she may have had, they were troublesome enough to keep her offstage, creating a void on the scene for a female performer which someone like Selena might fill. Abraham was consumed with Canales, worried that she might mount a comeback and destroy whatever momentum Selena had established.

Ramon Hernandez, who'd been doing record promotion for Bob Gréver and Manny Guerra, put his publicity skills to work to help Selena, writing the very first bio and fact sheet:

> Selena (Quintanilla) is a 5-feet 4-inch powerhouse of energy. Born in Freeport on April 16, 1971, she now makes her home in Corpus Christi. This Aries lady is in such demand for personal appearances, she does not have the time to attend regular school. Therefore, she is obtaining her education through correspondence courses. They say behind every successful man, there's a woman. In this case, behind a very successful young lady, there's a smart man—her father, Abraham Quintanilla, a former singer with the original Dinos from 1957 to 1972.
>
> Selena, her brother, Abe Jr. (bass), and sister, Suzette (drums), are a second generation of Dinos. Its other two members are Ricky Vela on keyboards and Roger García on guitar.
>
> The GP recording artist became interested in music at the age of six. She made her first public appearance at her father's Mexican restaurant in Lake Jackson at eight and recorded her first record at nine.

PROFESSIONAL MUSICAL CAREER HISTORY

1980–81 Southern Pearl
1981– Selena y los Dinos

DISCOGRAPHY

Singles
1983 "Encontré e Amor"/"Soy Feliz"
1983 "Se Me Hace"/"Estoy Contigo"
1984 "Escríbeme"/"Anque No Salga el Sol" (written by Johnny Herrera)

1984 "La Tracalera" (written by Johnny Herrera)
1984 "Ya Se Va"/"Tres Veces No"
1985 "Oh Mamá"/"Un Primer Amor"
1986 "Dame un Beso"/"Con Esta Copa"

Cassettes
1985 *Selena y los Dinos*—Freddie 1294
1985 *The New Girl in Town*—Cara

LP Albums
1986 *Alpha*—GP LP-1002

Awards
1983 TASA Zenzontli Award: New Female Vocalist
1984 Tejano Music Awards: Nominated Female Vocalist of the Year
TASA: Texas Association of Spanish Announcers in Texas
1985 Tejano Music Awards: Nominated Female Entertainer and Vocalist of the Year
1986 KFLZ Que Feliz Award: Female Vocalist of the Year

Television Appearances
Domingo Show   Johnny Canales Show   Estrella de Tejas
Mundo Musical   Noche de Estrellas   Cita con Carlos

Out-of-State Performances
California, New Mexico, Florida, Illinois, Oregon, and Washington

GP Guerra Productions: Manny R. Guerra

Hernandez also designed a promo card showing a picture of Selena surrounded by snapshots of her as a baby, a toddler, a little girl, a juvenile singer, and with her brother, sister, and dad playing behind her. On the card,

Selena listed her favorite food as pizza, *Moonlighting* as her favorite television program, and "Curiosity" as her favorite song. Her Personal Philosophy: "Be at your best at all times."

In the span of a year, Selena y los Dinos released three consecutive singles that generated considerable radio airplay—"Dame un Beso" (Give Me a Kiss), a spicy *ranchera* written by A.B. and Ricky Vela, with a cover of Abraham's Dinos' first Spanish crossover hit, "Con Esta Copa," on the flip side; a recycled oldie-but-goodie slow dance triplet in English called "A Million to One"; and a salsified remake of "La Bamba." All three A sides demonstrated a new maturity in her voice, as well as a maturity in her band's ensemble sound due to her brother's emergence as an arranger, producer, and composer. Manny Guerra had seen it all and done it all; A.B. simply soaked it all up like a sponge.

"Dame un Beso" was the first hit. "Within the past *tres meses*, Selena has taken a step forward on other female singers," Abraham told one reporter. "Her most recent recording, 'Dame un Beso,' has earned her the number-three hit position on the top-ten listing in Dallas, number-one in El Paso and Lubbock, and has also earned an Album of the Month honor in New Mexico." The father-manager went on to establish his knack for hyperbole. "Selena has a natural gifted ability to sing. At the age of six, Selena's voice sounded like that of a twenty-five-year-old grown woman."

"Dame un Beso" was followed up immediately by "A Million to One," released in June 1986. A swaying, sentimental bellyrubber, it had been popularized by the black vocalist Jimmy Charles. Selena y los Dinos were pretty faithful to the original version, with Selena singing in English and dragging out her phrasing on the word *one* like a natural-born hillbilly girl. Like Los Dinos of yore, all the kids had a talent for that soulful doo-wop that had a special place in the hearts of most Tejanos. It also was right in line with the Tejano attitude of reaching out to other sounds and reinventing them in the right context for the local fans. Polkas and *cumbias* filled the dance floor and paid the bills for bands and record companies, but the performers' creative instincts were more closely attuned to contemporary sounds, specifically English-language pop, jazz, rhythm and blues, and country. "They were Tejano plus Top 40," said Ramon Hernandez. "They were doing a lot of Rocio Durcal tunes they turned into polkas. That was one of the singers that Selena looked up to. Tejano music just took a Mexican tune and Americanized it."

"A Million to One" did especially well in San Antonio. "S.A.'s always been an oldies-but-goodies town," explained Ricky Dávila, who held down the morning shift at KEDA-AM, which gave heavy emphasis to the song. "A Million to One" fit right in. "Whenever she sang in English, she sounded black," Dávila said. "She could sing the Commodores like Lionel Ritchie sang." The single suffered from the usual limited distribution, but nonetheless shot straight to the top of the charts at KEDA. It was the first number-one record for Selena y los Dinos in the number-one market for her music.

The two singles were the impetus for a slew of awards that came their way in 1987, notably the Tejano Music Awards' recognition of Selena as Female Entertainer of the Year, an award that shocked the house at the San Antonio Convention Center Arena with the news that a fifteen-year-old kid had dethroned Laura Canales. (Selena's reaction, as reported on the front page of the San Antonio *Express-News*: "God, that's neat. At least I know I'm accomplishing something.") Selena was the only female to be nominated for any category outside Female Vocalist of the Year at the Mike Chávez Awards in Corpus Christi, and was recognized in the Simon the Diamond's People's Choice Awards competition as Female Artist of the Year. "Dame un Beso" also earned the Tejano Music Awards' nominations for both Song of the Year and Single of the Year; an Album of the Year nomination went to the cassette *Alpha*, as well as a Most Promising Band nomination and a Female Entertainer of the Year nomination for Selena.

Los Dinos were staking out turf as a performing act. One of their strongest fan bases was developing in El Paso, in far West Texas, on the fringe of the Tejano scene where international acts from Mexico traditionally attracted a larger audience. The single "Dame un Beso" was getting plenty of spins on KBNA, the bilingual station with the highest ratings in the city, as well as on KAMA and KALY in El Paso, and XZOL and Radio Cañón in Ciudad Juárez, Chihuahua, Mexico, on the other side of the river separating the United States from Mexico. No fewer than three local bands—Kalhua, Sierra, and Río Grande—were already covering Los Dinos material.

The interest created quite a buzz for the band's appearance at a package show in El Paso that featured several Mexican-international stars. Selena marched through her set like a trouper, then upstaged one of the show's biggest acts, the great diva Lucha Villa, whom Los Angeles writer Greg Barrios described as sounding like "Marlene Dietrich with a cold." Selena was called back to duet with Villa and brought the house down by imitating Villa; or so Barrios thought, until he learned after the show that Selena had a bad case of *roncha*, hamburger throat. The next morning, Barrios interviewed the up-and-coming star and discovered that more than anything she wanted a black Mercedes-Benz. She may have been only fifteen, but she was already a material girl.

The title of the new cassette album issued in April 1987, *And the Winner Is . . .*, referred to all the citations and plaques Selena was taking home and hanging on the wall along the staircase. She wasn't just a winner, but a winner who knew how to win with grace and humility. "I look at each show as an opportunity to reach out, prove ourselves, and give the people a good time," Selena said. "I guess we're really addicted to the public."

A third single following in the footsteps of "Dame un Beso" and "A Million to One" was issued that summer. Taking note of the success of the Miami Sound Machine, a Cuban-American band that put a pop spin on a traditional Latin dance called the conga and broke into the mainstream with their lead singer, Gloria Estefan, Los Dinos tackled the traditional sailor's song from Veracruz, Mexico, called "La Bamba," updating it with a semi-salsified interpretation that hit the *Billboard* Latin chart on August 8, 1987, and eventually reached number twenty, Los Dinos' very first national exposure. Abraham noted the song had been a million-seller for Ritchie Valens in 1957 and Trini López in 1963. "Both are Mexican-Americans and maybe some of that magic will rub off." He couldn't help but add, "As it stands now, radio stations in Corpus are playing her records on the average of one each thirty minutes." Unfortunately, "La Bamba" by Selena y los Dinos entered the charts just before the same song was covered by the east Los Angeles Tex-Mex band Los Lobos. And Los Lobos' version was on the soundtrack of the recently released film "La Bamba." Abe couldn't compete with Hollywood. Los Lobos' version shot up the charts, while Los Dinos' version fell off. "Because we were an unknown group, they knocked us away," Abraham said.

It could hardly be considered a setback. When Selena y los Dinos made their second appearance on the *Johnny Canales Show* on April 26, they performed in front of an audience of thousands gathered in the *plaza principal* in the center of Matamoros, the Mexican border city across the Rio Grande from Brownsville. At sweet sixteen, Selena was filling out. She had graduated from the space-suit stage uniform to a silver, sparkling *matadora* outfit with a short vest and slacks that complemented a physique considerably curvier since her last appearance on the show two years earlier. With her hair a little longer and a little wilder, hoop earrings, and long, painted fingernails, there was a tinge of sexuality projected from the stage. Her moves were still minimal and basic—stepping in time to the music with A.B. and occasionally sashaying her hips—but the confidence was there. The whole act had upgraded. Ricky was playing a Korg synthesizer, and Suzette had graduated to Roland syndrums that softened her image. A.B. looked like he finally knew what he was doing onstage.

If there was any impediment to their progress, it was language. Selena's banter with Canales was still child-like and centered once again on her inability to converse in Spanish. Canales related his attempts to cajole her into speaking more Spanish, teasing her about her request that "When we do an interview, let's do it in English." After performing her version of "La Bamba" in the plaza, Selena finished in English, cryptically speaking into the microphone, "Am I bothering you?"

Selena y los Dinos were now bonafide Tejano circuit riders, meaning they worked the Texas market, playing the same town every month or two with occasional forays to the Southwest, the West Coast, the upper Midwest, and other regions where there were enough Mexican-Americans with Texas roots to come out and dance to Tejano. The band's optimism about their future noticeably increased after a show in San Antonio that was attended by a young woman named Bonnie García, who saw Selena and fell in love. Selena was young, attractive, and knew how to shine, exactly the kind of image García was looking for to help sell Coca-Cola to Hispanics, which was her mission at the Atlanta-based soft-drink bottler.

The first concrete sign that money was becoming as much a factor as music in *la onda* appeared in 1985. Hacienda, the label Roland García ran next to his real estate company in Corpus, signed a distribution agreement with RCA International. Though Selena y los Dinos had no success with the recording they made there, Hacienda now boasted a roster of popular contemporary acts such as Johnny Hernández (Little Joe's brother), Rubén Ramos, of Mexican Revolution fame, singer Gary Hobbs, and accordion virtuoso Steve Jordan. RCA's interest in distributing the lineup marked the first time in recent history that a major music label put money down on *musica tejana*. (RCA's Bluebird label had been recording Texas-Mexican accordionist Narciso Martínez and singer Lydia Mendoza since the thirties, while Capitol first enjoyed success in the forties with Freddy Salinas of San Antonio, a crooner from the Sinatra school.) That same year Little Joe Hernández achieved another milestone when his thirty-sixth album, *Little Joe's 25th Anniversary*, was released on CBS International, which later became Sony. In effect, it made Little Joe the first Tejano act signed directly to a major since the rock-and-roll era of the early sixties. Little Joe stayed with the company until 1992, when he won the Grammy award for Best Mexican-American Album for *16th de Septiembre*, then released his next album, *Timeless*, on his own Tejano Discos label.

Shortly thereafter, Bob Gréver solidified his own distribution agreement with CBS, releasing Mazz's greatest hits package to take advantage of CBS's superior distribution system. By then, Gréver had all the young guns signed—La Mafia, Selena, Joe Posada, and Mazz. None of the deals were of much benefit to the artists, the labels, or the distributors. "They came in and sort of flirted with it," said Freddie Martínez, Jr., who took over day-to-day operations of his father's label. "I don't think they had the people in place that really understood this market. I think they just sort of saw the buzz happening at the time and felt that maybe they could come in here and cash in on what the independents were already doing. I think they were just expecting too much too soon. It wasn't worth the time, money, and effort that they were putting into it." But they certainly set the stage for the land rush that would follow. Tejano wasn't just a popular ethnic regional music anymore. It was an economic sleeping giant, waiting for the right people to discover it.

In many ways, the state of the art was a continuation of the energy sparked by *la onda* movement of the seventies. The creative edge was being defined by Grupo Mazz out of Brownsville, specifically by singer Joe López and his sidekick-arranger Jimmy González, who modernized the sound through the use of synthesizers while simultaneously taking it back to its foundation by adding accordion to the big band's ensemble. But Mazz were victims of their own success. "They were like little kids

in a candy store," said Mike Chávez, who served a stint
as the band's road manager. "In three years they went
from being broke to having as much money as they could
ever want, so much they didn't know what to do with it.
They were spoiled. They didn't want to break ground anywhere." Ramiro Burr, the music writer for the San Antonio *Express-News*, concurred: "They're great musicians
but they're so disorganized. They're like Guns 'N Roses—
they're controversial, they don't show up for gigs, they
have no assets."

Mazz's lack of ambition was compensated by La Mafia's desire to do things bigger and better. The Houston
band brought Tejano into the contemporary context of an
arena concert rather than a mere dance-hall *baile*. Led by
charismatic singer Oscar González and his brother Leonard, the band augmented their sonic attack with a light
spectacle that dazzled the eye as much as the music
pleased the ear.

Mazz and La Mafia's flashy dress, elaborate stage gear,
and monster P.A. systems updated the sound of Tejano to
something new and completely different. This wasn't their
abuelos' music anymore. Los Dinos got a first-hand taste
of how the sound was changed, thanks to Abraham's pes-
tering his way into bookings to open for both Mazz and
La Mafia. If nothing else, there was an up-close glimpse
of how the successful bands worked and played. The first
time they opened for Mazz, Abraham thought he'd
showed up at the wrong show, there was so much high-
tech equipment and stage gear. He realized the business
had changed quite a bit since the days of the original
Dinos. It wasn't just Little Joe standing up there singing
a *ranchera*. This was spandex, long hair, glitter, flash pots,
MTV. The line between fantasy and reality had blurred.
On one occasion, Oscar of La Mafia, who had given Selena a gold necklace with a fourteen-karat gold microphone charm, was shocked while singing into a
microphone in the middle of a show. Though he had to
be taken to a hospital to be treated for burns, the crowd
cheered and applauded, thinking it was part of the show.

For the Dinos, just being in Houston, La Mafia's home base, was an education. Compared to Corpus or San Antonio, it was more of an international town. Every strip-mall nightclub told a different story, with Puerto Ricans grooving on salsa, Central and South American enclaves hooked on *tropical*, the Guatemalans and Hondurans into marimba, and new arrivals from *la frontera* sticking with the *cumbias* of local hero Fito Olivares, whose numbing monobeat punctuated with fat baritone sax riffs was so popular he'd often play two dances in one night.

After seeing what full-blown stage-production gear could do for a band like La Mafia, Los Dinos wanted the same, even if they couldn't afford it. So in lieu of a professional light show, Abe and the kids improvised two lighting racks by placing a regular bulb fixture inside a big coffee can then spray-painting the whole thing black. "Then we would buy the plastic colored film and make a little frame, so it would show red. To make the light show, it was all regular on-off switches," said Rubén García, a neighbor from Molina who occasionally did roadie work for the band.

García started hanging out with the Quintanillas in 1984, his last year of high school. "I met Suzette first, then I met A.B., then I met her father, and then I met Selena," García said. "She was always an isolated child. She never got much slack to come outside.

"When the band would play here in town, we would go and see them and talk. I would try to get more of my friends to go see them with me. I would walk the streets and go by their house and talk to them. They didn't have nobody working in the band. It was just the mother, the father, and the band. They had a van and a little trailer. Everybody had to load the equipment. So they invited me to help them unload and set up. That was in 1988."

In March, the band's price for a show inched up again after Selena walked off with Female Vocalist of the Year honors at the Tejano Music Awards for the second year in a row. Abraham's efforts were finally beginning to pay off. Part of his job was cultivating decent working relationships with the promoters who controlled each market. If Selena could draw a crowd big enough for the promoters to make money at the door and for the band to stay on the road, or if they could sell some extra tickets as an opening act, they could do business together.

By now, Los Dinos were working a string of clubs and dance halls extending from South Texas west to Arizona and New Mexico. It was still a threadbare existence. For his labors, García was paid enough to cover his motel room and one meal a day, out of gig money that averaged between three hundred and six hundred dollars per performance.

Nonetheless, Abraham was adamant about making the band stick to the basic tenets of show business. For example, before a midwinter gig in a dilapidated old warehouse in the dusty West Texas town of Big Spring, Selena had taken sick. Her nose was running, she had a temperature, and her throat felt raw. But she went onstage like a trouper.

"When her dad said, 'Get up,' that meant get up," García said. "It was to a point where it was like he would say, 'Ya'll aren't getting out of the van looking like that, are you?' He was all on top of them. He was really strict with all of them. But after a while Suzette and A.B. got more release. They were more released than Selena was." When the money got good enough, Suzette and A.B. got their own motel rooms. Selena always roomed with Abraham.

At another gig in Carrizo Springs in southwest Texas in December 1988, only five paying customers showed up. "Abe made us give them their money back," García said. Before Los Dinos took the stage, the father prepped his musicians in no uncertain terms. "Those five people out there, you're going to play the full four hours for them."

Abraham was just as relentless dealing with other groups. Mazz frequently had Los Dinos open for them, which Los Dinos did mainly for the exposure, since the opening slot paid only a few hundred dollars. "There were times when I didn't pay them at all," said Mike Chávez, who was working as Mazz's road manager. "The only time I remember I had a hassle with Abraham was when we were playing San Marcos on a football-Friday night and we took them with us. It was a bad night. We brought in twelve hundred at the door and I got a call from Joe's brother. He said, 'I've got a problem. Abraham wants to beat the shit out of me.' We did twelve hundred at the door and had six hundred in expenses, and Abraham wanted the six hundred we'd guaranteed him. He gets on the phone and demands his six hundred dollars. I told him if I paid him six hundred I'd never book him again as an opening act. In the end, I told Lorenzo, Joe's brother, to split the six hundred with him.

"That's what I hate about Tejano music," Chávez said. "Everybody's a prima donna. I've had La Mafia threaten to cancel because they didn't get two-thirds of the stage. There's always arguments about who can or can't use the lights, whether the opening band can use the drum riser. Mexican bands come to play. They want to know when they should start, when they should stop, and that's it."

It was hard and it was easy. At least they had each other. When no one else was left to lean on, family was there. Abraham's education of his children in the ways of the music business was ongoing, even if it was at the expense of their formal education. When he went to check out other bands, the kids came along. On several occasions, he brought them to the coliseum in Corpus to hear Laura Canales, *la reina*, and talk with her backstage. The title was one that only Canales deserved. "She paved the way for everyone who has come after her, including myself," Selena would say some years later. "She had really opened up a lot of doors. I think she was the first lady to draw in crowds and bring in people. I really respect her because of that."

Canales grew up in Kingsville and started singing in the early seventies at the age of sixteen, after a neighbor, Oscar Solís, who was working with a valley combo known as Los Unicos, encouraged her to come along to gigs with him and sing. After Los Unicos broke up, Canales became part of a splinter group, Snowball and Company, then fronted a band who performed as Felicidad featuring some of the same members.

Canales dropped out of school to pursue a music career that paid her very little. Her father encouraged her to sing, while her mother, a college administrative clerk, encouraged her to get an education. But her father died shortly after Canales started singing professionally, which forced her to make her own way. The lessons she learned came through first-hand experience.

"My dad was my only supporter. He used to go with me, pick up a six-pack, and have fun, dance with all the girls. But he died in seventy-seven. After that, I'd come home crying and Mom would say, 'Quit! Get out!' I never had anyone to talk to. In this music business you don't belong to yourself, you have no private life; you belong to the public," she said. "They put you on this pedestal and you can't do anything wrong."

Laura's preeminence as the female voice of *la onda* gave Selena a blueprint to follow. But Canales's stormy personal life, including her failed marriage to fellow musician Balde Muñoz and her wild ways offstage, was a textbook example of what not to do if one wanted to get ahead in the business. "She was a very hardworking entertainer," said Vilma Maldonado, the Tejano music critic for the McAllen *Monitor*. "She strayed awhile to different things, to do different things in life. She married and then divorced—these were things that promoters or managers would throw in her face. They would take advantage of all that and they knew what buttons to push."

The lessons Laura learned were hard. Rosita Ornelas, the dean of Tejano music disc jockeys, whose afternoon show on KWED-AM in Seguin was a South Texas broadcasting institution, didn't mince words about how important it was for an artist to stroke radio. "She used to jump on my case because I wouldn't go to the radio station and say hello before the dance," Canales said. "She'd tell me,

'You musicians are so stupid. You should always take advantage of the radio station. Even if you're tired, you're sleepy, go wash your face and brush your teeth and go to the radio station.' "

Her wild reputation notwithstanding, Canales was considered part of the old school of Tejano, where money was made on the road and a hit record meant selling ten thousand units. Selena represented the new generation. As Selena's star rose and hers waned, Canales finally settled the issue by putting entertainment on the back burner and enrolling at Texas A & M at Kingsville to pursue her college degree in speech therapy. "I'm going to teach my people to say 'chicken' instead of 'shicken.' " In breaking the barrier, she'd made it easier for Selena and her peers to be accepted.

"Even though on the surface it doesn't look like there's prejudice, there is," said Vilma Maldonado. "There's some old-fashioned sonofabitches out there who can't stand the fact that women are in the limelight. They will make you miserable. The men somehow feel that the women still have to pay their dues, no matter what, to be in a man's business."

There was one advantage Selena had over her, Canales recognized. Once, at a show at the coliseum in Corpus, Laura imparted a bit of advice backstage to Selena, telling her, "Good luck in your future, be careful, don't let anybody take advantage of you."

"Are you kidding? With *my* dad?" Selena replied.

It made Canales wistful, as she later related. "Shit, I wished I'd of had someone like that, a rock. Somebody that you can trust beyond reason. You can turn around and go to sleep and know that they're going to be watching you, making sure nothing happened to you."

Four years after she left Los Dinos, Rena Dearman caught up with the band at Bobby Jo's Club in Angleton, near Lake Jackson. A.B. had called her up and suggested the old bandmates get together. A.B. and Suzy were pretty much the same as ever, Dearman remembered. But little

Selena wasn't so little anymore. "I saw Selena for the first time since she had grown into a teenager and it was amazing." She had a streetwise, almost tough look, accentuated by her sensibly short haircut, her *cacheton* chubby cheeks, and her offstage preference for wearing black.

For most of Selena's career, music had been like child's play. "It was kind of a hobby . . . I didn't see the business side of it. We used to play for relatives just for the fun of it. With your relatives, you know who they are and you feel confident around them. You know that they're going to automatically be proud of you because you're related." Now she understood the urgency to succeed commercially that her father felt. His coaching was paying off. "When you go out on the road and make a profession out of it, it's new to you every time and you . . . wonder if they are going to accept you or not. I can say I started taking it seriously at the age of eleven."

Selena had an amazingly solid grasp on the price she'd paid. "I miss going to school and having friends; that's normal for anyone my age," she admitted. "I had a very boring childhood because I never had the opportunity to associate with anybody my own age due to my career. I miss being around kids my own age.

"I've never been to a football game or had a date in my entire life," she confided to Ramon Hernandez. "As for dancing, I only dance with people I know. I don't dance with strangers unless they ask my dad for permission. I also enjoy seeing other people dance. Then I go backstage and practice the steps I saw." Having a relationship was out of the question. "Sure, fans and admirers write me proposals on notes, but they're in a flirting or joking way. You know how the story goes."

The story was that it all came down to business. That's how Abraham saw it, and he was running the show. That didn't mean she'd given up on furthering her education. "I might take a couple of college correspondence courses," she said, though that wasn't the only outside project she envisioned. "I've been designing clothes for quite a while now, so this year I might be opening up a boutique here. [But] really and truly I try not to think that far ahead. I like to take things one day at a time. I've noticed that in this business, you don't count your chickens before they hatch. There can be a lot of disappointments if you do that.''

Nor did it mean she was denied companionship. She told friends about a medical student she was seeing on the sly. On occasional weekdays, she flew up to Dallas to hang out with Alfred Hinojosa, an older man who was co-owner of La Bamba nightclub, but only if Suzette went along as chaperone.

The bottom line was that show business was her life. Her friends were her family, band members, roadies, and whoever she ran into on the road. Reality was dingy dressing rooms in cavernous dance halls, endless sound checks, midnight performances, the smell of smoke in her clothes, and long road trips. Travel was anything but a broadening experience. ''I enjoy sightseeing, but I've never been to the Galleria in Houston because we don't know our way around,'' she said in 1989. ''We are constantly on the road, but the only opportunity we really get to know a city is when fans invite us and give us the grand tour. Otherwise, it's roadside restaurants, hotel rooms, and dance halls.'' If there were lessons to learn, they would be Spanish lessons or voice lessons. Selena was going to be a Tejano star. She needed to live up to her billing.

Selena Quintanilla had greeted the new year of 1988 with a new hairstyle, tinted contacts, and a determined attitude. She would survive. Los Dinos had moved up from a van and trailer to a bus they called Big Bertha. From the outside, it sent the message that Los Dinos had arrived, they were a real band. Inside, it was a different story. The vehicle lacked heating and air-conditioning. Since there were no bunks, everyone slept either on the floor in sleeping bags or atop the equipment. Abraham was the driver as well as the roadie, soundman, booking agent, promoter, and crew chief. A.B.'s new wife, Vangie, and Abraham's spouse, Marcella, did the lights. Lodging was usually Motel 6. Meals were taken at Denny's, Jim's, Whataburger, and the Waffle House.

Ramon Hernandez, whose regular job was promoting artists on Manny Guerra's GP and RP labels, also wrote a column in the San Antonio *Express-News* about the Tejano scene. He'd grown up around Mexican-American music and was on a first-name basis with all the big-name stars. But this band was different. He liked the modern, cutting edge approach to Tejano they were taking; he got along with band members and family; and he loved the star performer.

Hernandez had first heard of Selena in 1984, when she was thirteen. "I was working with Bob Grèver as a publicist and writing for the *Express-News*, and Grèver gave me several 45s of Selena. At the time, she already had a cassette out, but they needed some new publicity pictures for her. So I went to Corpus, called her dad, and they came over to my mother's house. That was the first time I met her, that was in 1985. I thought she was good. It was there, like a diamond in the rough. If you listen to her first cassette on Freddie Records, which came before Cara, she was quite good for a little girl.

"We became instant friends, Abraham and myself. Selena already had that showmanship in her. She was not nervous, she wasn't shy or anything. She was very outgoing and very willing to please. Whatever I told her to do—pose like this—she would do it. She had no makeup, her hair was short and curly and windblown. But when she flashed that smile, she just melted your heart."

The black-and-white photos depict the fourteen-year-old Selena wearing music-clef earrings, a gold chain necklace, and two rings—one with an egg-shape stone on the ring finger of her right hand, the other a smaller ring on the middle finger of her left hand. Her long, painted fingernails were fake. In some shots she smiled that radiant smile; in others she was close-mouthed and pensive. Several poses were done with her father, whom she embraced while standing behind him, looking over his left shoulder.

In only one shot does Abraham in his tinted glasses appear to be smiling.

"I think he's trying to project a certain image," Hernandez said of Abraham. "I have a lot of friends who refuse to smile, although we joke and kid around. For the whole world, they want to project a certain image. That's the way Abraham was. A lot of people considered him as cold, or mean, just because he looked serious. He spoke to you in a real gruff voice. But underneath it all there's a heart of gold. Just like the time, he and I and his father and his brothers were at the body shop that Eddie owned. All his brothers and his father kept calling him Junior. He turns to me and says, 'You better not write that they call me Junior.' He was that way because he had to deal with all those club owners, I think. He'd have to be firm to collect the money after all the gigs."

Hernandez was sympathetic to Abraham's mission. "I think he saw that he could realize his dreams through his daughter. It was evident. The original Los Dinos disbanded at the height of their career. They all got married, they all went into different professions. Everything he wanted that he could not attain as a teenager, as a performer—this was his chance."

His immediate goals were the same as any band's: expand your horizons and get out of Texas, as long as you cover your costs. There would come a time when Abraham would compare the experience to going on vacation every week. In truth, it was a grueling existence, especially for Abraham, the bus driver, road manager, business manager, sound mixer, and everything else. "I don't know how he made it," marveled Hernandez. "At three in the morning, you're collecting money from the club owner, you have to wait until the equipment is loaded, then you have to be up and get everything ready in the morning while everyone is still sleeping." If there were ever any discrepancies in gate receipts or trouble with the club owner, Abraham had to take care of it without burdening the rest of the family with his troubles. "What went on between him and the club owner went on behind closed doors," Hernandez said. "He never talked about any disagreements or run-ins. He kept the information to himself. That was one way to keep the pressures off the kids. I never saw them pressured. It was always a happy-go-lucky group. They would talk about songs or stage presentation among themselves, but it was always constructive. They were trying to improve. They weren't negative about it. There was never infighting or disagreements. I don't recall him raising his voice when I was in their presence.

"There was humor. I remember going to sleep on the bus and Abraham called out, 'Good night, John-Boy. Good night, Selena-Girl.' "

Hanging out with the band, Ramon Hernandez got to see a side of Selena few others had known. She could cook, he learned, but on the road, she craved Jack-in-the-Box tacos. She had a boyfriend no one knew about. Her real calling was fashion. She liked to sketch clothing designs and began sewing her own stage outfits during downtime on the road. If it wasn't for music, she told him, she would be headed for Seventh Avenue in New York. Hernandez recognized how serious she was when she took him upstairs to her room at 709 Bloomington. Hernandez was in awe.

"There was this dressing mirror and bright lights, and there were all these Styrofoam heads with hairpieces on them, lined up like it was Dolly Parton's bedroom." Hundreds of shoes filled her closet. "I couldn't believe it. I think when she saw how I reacted, she was embarrassed." But it fit in with her image as the consummate entertainer that Hernandez knew her to be. "During photo sessions, she couldn't keep still. She was like Jonathan Winters on Johnny Carson, always bouncing around. She was always full of life, full of joy." When all she could see were lights and smiling faces, she felt so free, so untouchable. It was what the hard work and sacrifice were all about.

In 1988, Ramon Hernandez followed Selena y los Dinos on a typical run that began with an afternoon gig in San Antonio, then a gig in Dallas that night, then a gig the next night in Waco. "They did a *tardeada* [an afternoon performance] in San Antonio," Hernandez said. "And they were sick and tired. They had gone to bed late the previous morning. They had to pack up their gear and get on the road to Dallas. In Dallas, they had to set up at the Gómez Palladium, get to the Motel 6 in Garland, try to shower and change before it was time to go to work. At one, they were done, so they went out and had a late breakfast at Denny's, got a few hours' sleep, then onto the bus and the next gig in Waco."

The bus offered brief moments of respite and contemplation, as well as a classroom for Selena's correspondence classes. It was their home, albeit a derelict one. The ancient diesel engine put out a lot of smoke and ran rough. Once, a security guard told Abraham he'd have to shut it off because of the noxious fumes.

Abe refused. "If I cut it off, it may never start up again," he said.

Laredo disc jockey Luis "The Bird" Rodríguez first encountered Selena and the band when they were broken down on the side of the road. "I was driving my truck from a ranch when I saw an old brown bus parked on the side of the highway. I stopped to offer help. There was a man jacking up the side of the bus. He said that the tire was flat." Rodríguez took the man, Abraham Quintanilla, down the road to have a friend fix the tire. When he returned to the bus, he asked the kids, "Who are ya'll?" Abraham replied, "We're Los Dinos."

After gigs, Rubén García would escort Suzette and Selena to the bus and lock them inside before returning to the club to break down the equipment. Sometimes, Abraham would let him drive. Selena would get up in the middle of the night and sit alongside him, making small talk and keeping him company.

"How's the bus running? You doing all right? Need anything?"

Once, late at night, García overheard her talking to A.B. "He asked her what she wanted from her life," recalled García.

"I really want to have children," Selena said.

• • •

Abraham kept the band on a short leash. "The Quintanilla kids didn't grow up on the street like I did. They were straight," said roadie García. "I gave them advice of what not to do that I did. A.B. was always making music at home. When he wasn't working, he would sit at home all day with his instruments. When we would get to a gig early, they would rehearse. On the road, in the bus, in the motel, that's where the music was being born. They would take portable keyboards and the tape machines. A.B. saved money and bought a two-track recorder. He'd put the pieces together, they would work on one song, and when it was ready, they would go into the studio, spend eight or nine hours a night. Selena wouldn't come in until last. They would go in, make the music for the song, record the demo, take it home, and then she would go into the studio and sing it."

The kids would play in the kitchen, play in the garage, play wherever it was convenient to make music. Neighbors frequently gathered in front of the house on Bloomington to hear them rehearse. But that creative freedom did not translate socially. Selena was shielded from the outside world by Abraham. "Her dad wouldn't trust her with nobody," Rubén García said. "I was over the house a lot and one time A.B. said I was just trying to get close to them to get to her. But I didn't. She became just a real good friend. Eventually, A.B. and the family realized I wasn't after her."

Abraham's fears had some basis. Following one performance in Muleshoe in West Texas, a Mexicano holding a knife confronted Rubén García shortly after he'd put Selena and Suzette on the bus.

"Open the bus," he said. "I want to see Selena. I want to talk to her and be with her."

García used his fists to deny him access.

Two albums were released by Selena y los Dinos in 1988, both for Manny Guerra's RP label. The first, *Preciosa*, and the second, *Dulce Amor*, brought her career into sharp focus. A *Billboard* poll indicated that Selena was the most requested artist on ten out of fifteen radio stations programming Tejano music. Selena had made her peace with Tejano long ago. Although the band played a blend that mixed rhythm and blues, dance, and pop with strains of salsa and *cumbia*, she was Tejano first and foremost.

"When Dad introduced it to us, we were like, 'No! You can't make us play it,' " she admitted to Vincent Rodríguez, Jr. "There were times we would come in to practice and we would start crying, 'We don't want to learn this music.' But we learned and now that's all we listen to on the radio and we like to play it."

The awards and citations were nice, but the gigs paid the overhead. Nano Ramírez, who booked the Villarreal convention center in McAllen, kept getting phone calls from Abraham, who was nothing if not persistent. "You need to take Selena out there," he would tell Ramírez.

Ramírez was unmoved. He wasn't getting any requests for Selena. "Nobody wants to go dance to female artists," he told Abraham.

"But she's got the Tejano Music Award," he protested.

"There's no demand out here," Ramírez replied.

"Well, goddamn, I'll never go play with you," Abraham barked before slamming down the telephone receiver.

Three months later, he'd be back on the phone with the same pitch.

There was no better place to watch Selena's personal metamorphosis and the changing of the guard of the whole *onda* than the 1989 Tejano Music Awards at the San Antonio Convention Center. Rudy Treviño's brainchild brought more credibility to the music scene than any single event. It was already an industry function without rival, having effectively aced all the competing awards shows. But it was becoming a fan event, too, much like Nashville's Fan Fair. You could vacation in San Antonio, hear a lot of good music, and meet the performers. The podium at the ninth annual Tejano Music Awards ceremonies in San Antonio, manned by singer Vicki Carr and comedian-actor Cheech Marin, was becoming a familiar place to stand for the Quintanillas. Selena made several trips there to pick up awards for Female Entertainer of the Year and Female Vocalist of the Year.

The event was marked by an unprecedented display of backstage schmoozing and sucking-up to Abraham by reps from all the new major labels who were setting up shop in San Antonio. It so happened that the night's big winner was without record label, having fulfilled contractual obligations to Manny Guerra.

The successful suitor was José Behar, who nailed down the contract on behalf of Capitol-EMI Latin where he was a vice president. Afterward, Behar was ecstatic, telling the *Caller-Times*, "We see so much potential . . . she's going to get the support she deserves as an artist. We feel that Selena is not only a great Tex-Mex artist but she can be a major star in Mexico and the South American market. If we can accomplish that goal, we're excited about [the possibility] of her crossing into the Anglo market." For her part, Selena chalked it up to good timing. "I feel very fortunate," she said. "I just happened to be at the right place at the right time."

When Selena turned eighteen that year she became not only a woman, but also a full-blown commodity, signing with Capitol as well as finally inking a deal with Coca-Cola. A year earlier, while fooling around with his camera, Ramon Hernandez had produced a bottle of Coca-Cola and asked Selena to pose with it. She would be the perfect spokesperson for Coke, he thought. No person better represented the new blood than Selena. She was primed with good looks, talent, show business smarts, and saw nothing but blue sky ahead. She had a voice that could growl ferociously, do a bedroom croon, or sound sweet, fragile, and totally wild all at once. Her range went from deep and sultry to high soprano, hitting the upper register like an ululating Indi-pop starlet. She had a natural *chichi rara* style that complemented her classic Aztec facial features, accented, in the great Latina tradition, by excessively heavy dark eyeliner. Her body was filling out with curves that added another potent weapon to her performing arsenal, a simmering, sensuous sexuality. Her flower was in full bloom.

By the summer of 1989, Selena y los Dinos were working on their first album for Capitol, entitled *Selena*, at Manny Guerra's in San Antonio and Sunrise Studios in Houston, coming up with a blend of "Tex-Mex and Latin pop," as Selena described it. In addition to the hit single "Contigo Quiero Estar," the recording, produced by A.B., included "My Love," a paean to the pop singer Madonna, and "Sukiyaki," a cover of the sixties hit by Japanese crooner Kyu Sakamoto, with Spanish lyrics. The rest of the album stuck with the usual polkas and boleros. Capitol-EMI's record promotion staff worked the radio stations as no independent producer had before, getting more chart action for Selena than she'd ever enjoyed. Meanwhile, the label spun off the single "Contigo Quiero Estar" (I Want to Be With You), which peaked at number eight on *Billboard*'s Mexican Regional chart, Los Dinos' highest chart position yet. The airplay fueled more road work, and they traveled through such traditional Tejano strongholds as Arizona, New Mexico, Indiana, Illinois, and Washington State while making inroads to Florida and other non-Tejano Latin markets. Part of the summer was spent touring with Ram Herrera, the Latin Breed, Jean LeGrand, and David Marez as part of the ninth annual Tejano Music Awards' Caravan of Stars, which stopped in Corpus on August 5 to play Memorial Coliseum.

The big difference now was how the music was being sold. Content was important, but now, so was image. For the album cover, Selena underwent a makeover. "I had seen the stuff she was doing with Manny, and to me it did not appeal because she was a beautiful young girl who looked older, maybe to compete with Laura [Canales]," said creative director Rubén Cubillos. "My reaction was, 'You're beautiful the way you are. Let's keep you as natural as possible. You're young, you're fresh, you're contemporary, let's show that.'

"She picked out this outfit and her mom looked at her

and said, 'Your daddy ain't gonna like that, he's gonna fight that, he's gonna have a cow.' And I said, 'No, the important thing is if you feel comfortable.' She was just mesmerized with everything—the jewelry, the hair.''

Cubillos brought in a makeup artist and a full crew and went on location to a limestone fill out by Bitters and McCullough roads on the northeastern edge of San Antonio. "I kept talking to her, bringing her confidence up. She kept looking at her dad, and I said, 'Don't look at your dad, this is about you, I want you to feel that you're beautiful, I want you to feel like you own this whole thing right here.'

"Abraham would come in and out and we'd discuss. He came in and had a conversation with me, saying, 'Selena doesn't like this makeup.' To this day, the company still swears that this is the worst album cover they've ever gotten. Because they didn't understand it. What I liked about it was the warmth of her skin. She's got that look. I wanted to take off all this makeup stuff. She's not a model. She's not anything but a nice, fresh young woman with talent.''

The cover shot unveiled a Selena at her most sultry and beguiling: dressed in a halter, with a bare midriff, flowing sheer skirt, long dangling earrings, elaborate gold necklace, and short hair with bangs. Standing tall but expressionless, as if her mind were wandering, she looked for all the world like a Mayan princess. But the makeup, the hair, the professional talent, and the production did not impress the band or their manager. "Abraham didn't like it," said Ramon Hernandez. "Her nose looked too flat."

Rubén Cubillos did not consider Abraham's involvement as meddling. "He's not a control freak, he's a father. We want the best for our kids and we never want anybody to take advantage of our kids, never. You're looking at a man who's investing his emotions, his money, his time, his passion, his whole love, man. He wants to make it work and he doesn't want to spin his wheels. He had no time to be hanging around wanting to be somebody. He was on a mission. He knew he was going to be successful.''

Ten years earlier, while Abraham was dreaming of his restaurant, Tejano was a distinctive regional pop style noted for Latin rhythms and set to Texas dance-hall time, with sentimental Mexican lyrics, a bilingual soul cry that didn't require translation, and the polka at the heart of it all. Creativity was the driving force. Now Tejano meant a glitzy sound with a splashy look and the promising prospect of riches only hinted at. It was way beyond uptown. It was big business. And Abraham was going to get his share. He knew his way around the Texas scene, he was ready to take the show big-time, and he had the act, including two new boys—Pete Astudillo, a Laredo singer hired to harmonize and duet with Selena and write proper Spanish lyrics for A.B.'s compositions, and Joe Ortega, added as a second keyboardist to play alongside Ricky Vela. Abraham was always pushing while Selena was busy trying to master Nintendo, planning shopping attacks on Dillard's and K-Mart, drawing her designs, and gluing the shiny baubles on metal or leather or stage fabric. They were out on the road as much as they could afford, four nights, five nights a week. The traveling Quintanillas were pulling some decent change, with increasingly frequent five-thousand-dollar guarantees and advertising tie-ins. Album sales were up. Selena had broken another barrier: she was the first female Tejano artist to sell fifty thousand copies of an album. There would be plenty of time to conquer the gringo audience in her homeland. First came the rest of the Latin world, where the initial wave of Selenamania was breaking out.

The changes reverberated through Corpus. ''Something has burst,'' observed Dr. Clotilde García, the city's first female Mexican-American leader. ''Years ago, our children had no ambition, no role models. Today, they want it all, and they're getting there.'' The majority of the coastal bend's national and state legislative delegation was Hispanic. Three of the nine city council representatives were Mexican-American, as were three of the seven school-board members. Corpus was ninth in the nation in the number of Hispanic-owned businesses. Mexican-American women were no longer segregated on separate floors at Eckhardt Hall dormitory at Texas A & I, in nearby Kingsville.

Selena was being positioned to cross over into the Spanish-international market, something no Tejano act had ever done. She was already learning the market, how it was different from Texas, what she had to watch for. She had shared a December 4 bill in Brownsville with Alejandra Guzmán, the daughter of famed Mexican artist Enrique Guzmán, and Dueto Dominó, both of whom were acts hitting in the international scene. Backstage, Selena and Alejandra Guzmán spoke a long while about acting and dancing lessons. Guzmán had practiced both before she launched her singing career. Selena would do the same, whatever it took. Dance. Act. Learn Spanish. Hold the Coke. Smile into the camera. Meet the radio guys. Turn on the crowd. Belt it out. All for one and one for all.

4
Star Time

ON JANUARY 10, 1990, CAPITOL-EMI Latin bought Cara Records from Bob Gréver, conveying with the sale the most desirable roster of artists, composers, producers, and arrangers on the Tejano scene and making Gréver a wealthy man. The recordings of Mazz, La Mafia, and Emilio were now available through CEMA (Capitol, EMI, Manhattan, Angel) Distributors. La Mafia, though, were left in a most uncomfortable position, since they were in the process of cutting a new deal with Sony despite the fact that they still owed two albums to Gréver. For their part of the bargain, EMI brought the necessary financial clout essential to selling Tejano not only to young Mexican-Americans but to young Latinos everywhere. The tools that Capitol, Sony, and the other majors brought with them were the same ones used in the general-market music business—videos, press kits, promo photos, radio tours, production gear, contract riders. For the first time on the Tejano scene, there was money.

The old guard—Gréver, Manny Guerra, Joey López, Freddie Martínez, Roland García—was notoriously tight with budgets and even tighter with advances and expenses. Capitol-EMI and Sony talked five-figure advances, recording and video budgets, and marketing campaigns without flinching.

José Behar, the guiding force of Capitol's Latin division, was a player. A lean, handsome *cubano* with a thick shock of dark curly hair, he was already on a roll when he walked into Hollywood's Capitol Tower, a skyscraper resembling a stack of phonograph records, in 1989. He'd started a few blocks away at La Brea and Sunset at Herb Alpert's new Latin division for his A & M Records label in the mideighties. He was a shaker behind the "Cantaré, Cantará" Latin superstar charity recording project that emulated "We Are the World," a critical success but a flop as a benefit, since it failed to funnel much funding to the poor. Later, Behar ascended to the helm of CBS's Latin division before moving to Capitol, where he rose to president. The experience gave Behar a solid grasp on the big picture and inspired a game plan. Acts singing in Spanish could be as big as acts singing in English, he believed. But first, the Spanish acts had to be groomed and marketed like the English acts were. "We don't live by concert attendance, we live by record sales," he told writer Greg Barrios. "We're trying to break [acts] nationally and get them out of the regional area because we feel they have potential to cross over to the national scene."

Sales in Texas were already attractive enough to stir up major-label interest, Behar noted when he saw the figures generated by Cara artists distributed by CBS, or Discos Sony, and by Little Joe, when he was with Sony. After signing Selena, and then Roberto Pulido in 1989, Behar inked Mazz the next year to a long-term contract, stealing them from under Sony's nose (Behar allegedly let Mazz's contract with Sony/CBS expire while he was at that company, then scooped them up when he went over to Capitol), and immediately moved one hundred thousand units of their live album in the first week of release. Mazz was the heart and soul of Tejano, defining and redefining the sound without straying from López crooning on top of a modernized polka melody or a slow *cumbia*.

Meanwhile, La Mafia, in a move to expand their audience base, started doing concerts in Mexico and throughout Latin America, striving to crack a market no Tejano band, not even Mazz, had cracked before. "Oscar had told me that they had been going down there for three or four years and spending money out of their own pockets just to promote the band and open up other markets," said Freddie Martínez, Jr. "They had a lot of faith in the Mexican market and they wanted to expand their business." At the same time, Emilio Navaira was setting himself up as Tejano's most promising crossover artist by moving into mainstream country music. The path had been prepared by Ram Herrera and David Márez, two singers who, like Navaira, did time with David Lee Garza's group, though Herrera and Márez were considered too old and too stylistically entrenched to make it in Nashville.

Then there was Selena. She was young enough, brash enough, and versatile enough to prove several marketing theories Behar had. To break a Latin act as a mainstream pop act, there were two routes: singing in English, or singing in Spanish, breaking foreign markets, then coming back to America from abroad. Behar recognized the latter route was the smarter way to go; since Selena was such a chameleon vocally, she could sing anything. With a little marketing, advertising, and promotion, he could take her to the next level, singing to other Latin audiences. If she could survive there, then she was headed for the Gloria Estefan, Julio Iglesias stratosphere.

Mumbles of displeasure from the mom-and-pop independents greeted the majors' move into San Antonio. Their reward for serving as the backbone of the regional music business was that they were co-opted and swept out of the way. What did these Hollywood turkeys have in mind for the future of *la onda*, anyway? But the acts weren't complaining, not with the advances they were being offered. "When there's blood in the water, the sharks are there," as Manuel Dávila explained. "It comes down to units. It helped us a lot. All of a sudden, we had distribution. We had been recognized as valuable enough to make a buck off of. But it hurt, too. They signed everyone up. They were just gonna keep throwing stuff against the wall until it stuck.''

Even before the labels arrived, corporate bets had already been placed. One catalyst was Lionel Sosa, a slender, soft-spoken gentleman who ran Sosa, Bromley, Aguilar, and Associates, a San Antonio firm that happened to be the largest Hispanic advertising agency in the country. No small part of Sosa's talent was his ability to persuade major national advertisers that some of their money should be spent on selling directly to Americans who spoke Spanish, something Sosa knew how to do quite well. One major client was Coca-Cola USA, who bought in early, in the late eighties. Their representative was Bonnie García, an energetic, independent woman who grew up in San Antonio, went to school at Burbank High School, and then worked her way to her present position in Atlanta, where she handled the twenty-million-dollar Hispanic advertising budget.

García called on Sosa one morning in 1987 with a message. ''She had someone who she wanted to make sure we signed,'' Sosa said. The night before, she had gone with her mom and family to some little dive in San Antonio where she'd seen the future of Coca-Cola. Her name was Selena.

''Get a contract together, we're signing her up,'' García instructed.

It actually made sense to have the sixteen-year-old girl be a spokesperson for Coke. Music had always been a strong vehicle to sell products. Put the right music with the right lyrics, and people respond. García brought some of Selena's recordings and sample audio commercials singing the ''Sabor para Siempre,'' a Taste for All Time, tag line to Sosa. ''I couldn't believe the clarity of her voice,'' he said. He was also struck by the contrast of how she sounded singing for Coke and how she sounded singing in front of her band. ''How come it sounds so different on the jingle, with our musicians and mixing, and how come her voice seems to be drowned out on the other music?''

García was committed to making Selena part of the Coca-Cola team. "She would always be excited about her," Sosa said. "And she actually became her very close friend and her biggest supporter. Wherever Selena was playing, if Bonnie was somewhere close by, she'd be there. It was like this client that was paying her all this money . . . was kind of an awestruck fan as well."

García's enthusiasm was infectious. Al Aguilar, president of the Sosa agency, had been a believer since 1985, when he shared the stage with the young teen as a co-presenter at the Tejano Music Awards. Chuck Morrison, a high-ranking marketing executive with Coca-Cola, bought in after seeing one performance. "She is the next Janet Jackson," he declared.

The sponsorship not only dropped some $145,000 a year in the Quintanillas' laps, split four ways, as all band income was; it also brought exposure to Selena like she had never had before. Television commercials were filmed in Mexico (she would do three for the company). Jingles were recorded. Posters and point-of-sale displays were created. Personal appearances and tour support were underwritten. The wholesome images of Selena and Coke were intertwined and aggressively marketed, not just in Texas for the edification of Tejanos but in all parts of the United States where Hispanics were targeted.

What she did in front of a camera or microphone was only part of the package. "This kid had this innate ability to remember everybody's name, be totally gracious, know who everybody was," Sosa marveled. "I've spent all my life trying to figure out politics and who's who and who has the power, and she instinctively knew it. Maybe she didn't know it, but she was just wonderful to everybody, whether it was the assistant at a shoot or the president of Coca-Cola. She knew who everybody was, went out and hugged them, and made it seem like it was a privilege for her to be doing what she was doing. You always got that feeling, like [she thought] I'm so lucky to be here.

"Our agency was trying to sell the concept that some Hispanics are totally Spanish-dominant, some Hispanics are totally English-dominant and don't know a damn word of Spanish, but most Hispanics are bilingual, bicultural, a blend," explained Sosa. "You've got a bunch of kids that are from the U.S., educated in the U.S., nobody taught us to read Spanish, to write Spanish. We speak and understand it because Mom and Dad do. So as we grow up, we wind up with this thing of being able to sing it but not to speak it comfortably."

The very nature of Tejano perfectly complemented the soft drink. The old Tejano fan listened to nothing but Tejano as a means to hold on to his roots. The new fan was a more modern animal who wanted to hear covers of the latest pop tunes as well as the reformulated versions of *rancheras*, polkas, *cumbias*. The new fan attended rock shows, listened to jazz, enjoyed country music, heavy metal, or grunge, but wanted their *cultura*, too. It was part of living in Texas, where anyone who liked music, regardless of their ethnic heritage, was exposed to a cornucopia of sounds. It was also part of growing up Tejano. Conversing in English and listening to songs sung in Spanish came naturally in that part of the world. Selena did Whitney Houston tunes, just as Emilio covered John Michael Montgomery and other Nashville hat acts, and La Mafia paid tribute to the Beatles. They were all merely giving the audience what they wanted.

The new decade began with a makeover, longer hair, and the first Coca-Cola endorsement. Selena's drawing power was evidenced by her immediate inclusion on two various-artists albums, one a greatest-hits package on Capitol-EMI, culled mostly from earlier RP recordings, entitled *Personal Best*; and another greatest-hits package consisting of masters owned by Bob Gréver of Cara that he had sold to CBS. The old guard was getting left behind. Manny Guerra's services as engineer and producer were less in demand. "He was sitting on the volcano and he was part of the explosion. He got blown away," Manuel

Dávila said. Johnny Herrera placed fewer and fewer songs on Los Dinos' albums. Polkas were out. *Cumbias* were coming on strong.

Selena was a millionaire at age nineteen, or so the hype would have the public believe. The truth was that most of the band's earnings were plowed back into equipment, instruments, and road gear. There was plenty of room for improvement, Selena believed. For all her life, she'd cruised along singing phonetically, but the demands of the fans, the radio, and the press necessitated a better command of *español*. "One thing is that if I ever have children later on, for sure I want my children to know Spanish," Selena would say two years later. "It only makes you a better person or even smarter to know two languages. If that barrier is not there you can cross both lines, talk to English and Spanish people. And it gets you a lot farther in business and personal [communication]."

It was precisely that attitude that made Selena such a valuable commodity to Coca-Cola, to the record company, to anyone interested in tapping into the burgeoning Hispanic market. She was *pura* Latina, from her *morena* features to her embrace of family values. But like the vast majority of kids of her generation who had assimilated into American culture, she grew up speaking English, and only when she reached adulthood did she begin to delve into her cultural heritage. She represented the new woman, one who could carve out a career in a male-dominated, machismo-driven industry and yet evoke a femininity that telegraphed the message that you could have your family values and still project sexuality.

"To an old man like me, she was like [a] daughter," Sosa said. "To a twelve-year-old, she was the sexiest thing that could be."

Her image was so clean that she was enlisted as a spokesperson by the Texas Prevention Partnership, sponsored by the Texas Commission on Alcohol and Drug Abuse, making public appearances on the state agency's behalf. Her message was a simple one: "With a positive attitude, you can be anything you want to be" is how she put it to a gathering of two hundred at Fulmore Junior High, in San Antonio.

Selena polled her audience to find out who wanted to go to college (over half raised their hands), previewed some commercials she'd shot, sang an a capella version of "Enamorada de Tí," and advised students to stick to school. "If you drop out, you could end up cooking fries at McDonald's for the rest of your life," she warned.

A group called Tierra Tejana took Tejano into the rap and hip-hop idioms with their hit "Las Hijas de Don Simón." Variety was still the essence of the Tejano sound. "Tejano's always been influenced by what's going on in American Top 40," said Ramon Hernandez. "From big band swing that influenced *orquestas*, the crooners who influenced Sunny and Little Joe, the same with the rock-and-roll, disco, Urban Cowboy sound. I don't know if it's assimilation or going with the flow. The polka never went out. It's still there, it's just different arrangements."

A typical piece would begin with an elaborate buildup heavy with fanfare before kicking into overdrive with that 2–4 glide and a backbeat that merely skipped across a melody instead of pounding it home. Highly influenced by the brass-rock sounds of bands such as the Chicago Transit Authority and Blood, Sweat, and Tears, rather than by the grittier rhythm and blues created in Memphis and Detroit, Tejano could be construed as sort of an MOR version of reggae reworked for Texas-Mexican coastal sensibilities.

Even so, Selena y los Dinos were not pure Tejano. She was a Tejana by birth, as were her brother, her sister, and her other bandmates. She had come up the ranks of Tejano music. But she'd gone beyond those confines to become an international music artist. It was part of José Behar's plan. Given the band's penchant for cumbias, merengues, and other Latino sounds, it made sense to push them toward international music as a means for preparing for the English crossover.

Capitol, so far, "has been a good romance," Abraham remarked.

On March 9, 1990, Selena once again walked off with Female Entertainer of the Year and Female Vocalist of the Year honors at the Tejano Music Awards. In May, a west-coast swing included a date at the Hyatt Regency in Oakland sponsored by Coke. But the new corporate clout backing the band didn't become clearly visible until *Ven Conmigo* (Come with Me) was issued in September. Instead of at Manny's, the band cut the ten tracks at Zaz Studios, on the far west side of San Antonio, where owner Joey López ran a one-stop Tex-Mex hit factory. Bands and conjuntos from both sides of the Rio Grande could walk into López's studio, take their tapes and artwork next door to the pressing plant, and walk out with ready-made product to hawk in a forty-eight-hour turnaround. While Selena y los Dinos weren't in that kind of rush, they entered the Commerce Street facility with more musical firepower than ever before. José Ojeda replaced Joe Ortega as the second keyboardist and Mike Orosco played guitar, replacing Roger García, although the six-stringed instrument was still mostly used for background in the band.

The musical versatility was broader-based and more adventurous than any mainstream Tejano act, La Mafia included, since Little Joe ruled the *salones de baile*. There were three old-school contributions from Johnny Herrera: "La Tracalera," the musical Texas travelogue that received an injection of modern polka elements into its *ranchera* framework; the sentimental "Después de Enero"; and "Aunque No Salga del Sol," one of the most poetic works ever written by a Texas composer. *Ven Conmigo* discarded the concept of a two-sided single sandwiched between a bunch of polkas and an oldie-but-goodie or two. World beat was the way to go now. The ballad "Yo Te Amo" was neither Texan nor Mexican but was rather the embodiment of Spanish international music in the guise of a slow *cumbia*. The same elusive qualities were evident in "Ya Me Voy," by international star Juan Gabriel, a native of Juárez, Chihuahua, just across the Rio Grande from El Paso.

The album's grabber was "Baila Esta Cumbia," a

straight-ahead rendering of a *cumbia* which bore many resemblances to the work of Fito Olivares, a Tejano by residence who was born in Camargo, in the upper part of the Rio Grande Valley. Olivares was a veteran of the popular border band Tam y Tex. He made his money specializing in beat-heavy cumbias, modern variations of the mambo themes articulated by his hero Perez Prado. By updating the sound into a pounding rhythm that was given more weight than the words or sentiments, Olivares had already hit in Mexico, the Caribbean, and Central and South America with his smash hit "Juana la Cubana." With the exception of Freddie Martínez's 1972 song "Te Traigo Estas Flores," Tejano music had not yet overcome international barriers.

The album signaled a change of direction for the band itself. A.B. had finally arrived as a producer, and he and Pete Astudillo were taking over as writers, credited with writing the majority of the songs on the album. Johnny Herrera had contributed his original compositions for the last time. Polkas were no longer an essential element of their recordings, as Los Dinos broadened their scope, a move that put additional importance on Selena's versatility. David Lee Garza was brought in for accordion fills to lend a Tejano flavor to the title cut.

"*Musica tejana* is just *musica tejana*," reasoned Selena. "The only thing you can really do with it is maybe add a new synthesizer sound or put some live strings in it and make it progressive in that way. But I don't think you can really mess with the beat."

The album shot to the top of *Billboard*'s regional Mexican chart, remaining on the chart for fifty-six weeks, an unprecedented feat for a Tejano act, with the energetic dance number "Baila Esta Cumbia" reaching number eight on the regional singles chart. The record ultimately went gold, which in Tejano terms translated into sales exceeding fifty thousand units, something that no group fronted by a female had ever accomplished. "And that's when the band was really freaking out," Selena said to Joseph Harmes. Abraham was proud of what his daughter had done on an artistic and commercial level as well as on a broader scale. He may have come off gruff, tough, and thoroughly macho when negotiating on behalf of his daughter, but behind the bluster, he sounded like a feminist at heart. "The biggest obstacle we have to overcome is due to the Latin culture," he was quoted as saying in the Corpus Christi *Caller-Times.* "The Latin is *el hombre.* He's number one and puts the woman behind. All the people and promoters involved in this business are males. And then her age was another factor against her. It's not like this in other markets, but in this market, they don't feel a woman can draw a crowd like a male entertainer can. That's the kind of mentality we've fought ever since we started. But the more doors they shut on us, the more determined we became. We've just started seeing a change."

One sure sign of a change was the high school degree she received from the American School of Chicago in December of 1990. She may have had all she wanted materially, but she could not quench her thirst for learning. She'd applied to take college courses by correspondence from a California school, and had been accepted.

Selena was getting so hot that Abraham was finally able to persuade Nano Ramírez to bring the band to McAllen. The Rio Grande Valley had been the last pocket of resistance in Tejano to Selena's music, and now they were coming around. Ramírez started bringing in Los Dinos at the Villarreal convention center west of town four times a year, drawing from 1,000 to 1,500 fans consistently, the same rotation he used for Emilio and La Mafia. The only act bigger was the Valley's own Mazz, who played the venue six times annually, consistently selling out the 2,000-person-capacity room.

Cameron Randle, the president of Arista Texas records and former director of a Nashville management firm, met Selena through Emilio Navaira, a new act he'd been turned on to while managing the Texas Tornados, a supergroup of fiftysomething Tex-Mex stars, including conjunto accordionist Flaco Jimenez, balladeer Freddy

Fender, San Antonio rocker Doug Sahm, and Sahm's sidekick, Augie Meyers. Randle showed up for a Texas Tornados gig at the Tower Theatre in Houston early one night to check out Navaira, and he was floored.

"What I saw was completely unprecedented. I saw an ocean of young Hispanics in their twenties and thirties, and all the guys were in George Strait standard-issue starched shirts, starched blue jeans, and cowboy hats. The girls were all wearing Rocky Mountain brand jeans. All I heard was the sound of screaming females. This wasn't the coalition of old hippies and music junkies who were turning out to see the Texas Tornados. This was a segment of music society I hadn't experienced before.

"After the show I went backstage and talked to Emilio and he said Selena was the other artist I should look into. I quickly learned the big guns on this scene were Emilio, Selena, Mazz, and La Mafia. My partner Stuart Dill and I eventually began managing Emilio in 1992, and we got a closer look at Selena because they were labelmates, duet partners, and both endorsed Coca-Cola. They were a team.

"She was the quintessential Latin vixen, the Latin version of 'I Dream of Jeannie.' Then to find there was an engaging personality behind that image—she was the total package."

In the middle of the summer of 1991, a dance with La Mafia, Emilio Navaira, and Selena drew nine thousand to the Summit, in Houston. A few days later Selena shared the bill with international acts Ramón Ayala, Pandora, and Fito Olivares, at the ninth annual Hispanic State Fair, in San Antonio. She made her third appearance on the *Johnny Canales Show*. The band, dressed in the black-and-white faux cowhide outfits and black vests designed by Selena, was hardly recognizable compared with the kids who'd sung along with their record and jived with Johnny four years before. Selena had fallen under the influence of Madonna, wearing a bustier, black tights with a big-buckled belt, and calf-high boots, and working the entire stage while she sang "Baila Esta Cumbia," her spicy dance number off *Ven Conmigo*. Behind her was the expanded version of Los Dinos, which now included the shy guy from San Antonio, Chris Perez, on guitar, who looked totally unsure of himself as he practiced his Temptations-style dance steps in time to the music. His choreography may have been tentative but the rock licks he played on his guitar were like spitfire, bringing a hard edge to the band that it had previously lacked. He was two years older than Selena but looked more like her younger brother. His playing, however, was mature beyond his years.

Between songs, Selena continued her ongoing dialogue with Canales about learning Spanish. She'd made progress, he said. When they first met, the only word she knew was *dinero*, money, as in "Papa, where's my *dinero?*"

Selena's social life revolved around the band. Her circle of friends consisted of people she worked with—family— and people she met while entertaining. No matter where they played, someone was waiting backstage to talk and take photos and provide nice company. But after the show, it was back to the motel room. Her contact with the outside world was carefully screened by Abraham.

Keeping her image up was a constant challenge. "Her figure was not by accident. She worked at it," said Ramon Hernandez. "On the road, it's not that you let yourself go; you have no choice. I've got pictures of her walking between the convenience store and the bus, carrying a pile of goodies—Twinkies, cakes, ice cream." But at home, downtime was spent working out and playing racquetball at the athletic club, as well as shopping and working on her designs.

On the road, everybody was Selena's best friend; at least, that's the way she made them feel. But she couldn't really count on any single person in the truest sense. Family remained the binder that held her life together, with her father keeping a tight rein on the whole affair. They all knew their roles and shared an element of trust that did not extend outside of their immediate circle. "We're a very unified family," Selena said. "Within the family we have aggressive and dominating personalities, but we believe the family is the most important thing of all. We're all stubborn.'' Within the unit, there was a distinct division of labor. ''Everybody knows their position in the band, nobody steps over their line as far as my dad's being the manager. We don't get into business or tell him what to do. My brother creates the music and we let him take care of that. My sister is in charge of the marketing. We don't step over that line. We all have our little jobs. We are just like a team.''

She was right on the mark. She had a father who was flexible enough to adjust to the growing demands of the marketplace, improving and upgrading the organization as the fan base expanded. She had a brother who wrote the songs that fit her like a glove. She had a sister who kept the beat and hustled the merchandise. She had a mother who gave the family unit a foundation that was built upon love and nurturing, qualities often lost in the soulless world of entertainment. Working together, they could fend off any adversity. Even bad talk.

''One thing that happened this year would be people talking bad about the group,'' Selena told one journalist. ''To me, when the public does that it's a letdown because you think so highly of the people that go to your dances and, I mean, these people are the ones that make you, you know what I mean? They are the ones who buy your records. But when you hear them talking bad about you, you get this kind of personal thing, like, 'Hey, what have I ever done to you?' ''

Abe backed up his daughter, telling the same reporter, ''I've always said, whether it is good or bad, someone will always talk about you.'' He knew some truths about show business, performers, and their public, and *la envidia*, the envy. But no matter what Selena's feelings toward her family were, no relative could satisfy the other yearnings that were stirring inside. Selena had made the transition from gawky teen to full-blown woman before everyone's eyes. Gone was the perky Brenda Lee cut, all function and little form. Instead, she let her raven hair grow thick and full, augmenting what nature denied with hairpieces. Her lips had filled out voluptuously; so had her breasts and hips. Her rear was "the kind you could place a beer glass on without spilling the foam," as one admiring disc jockey put it. She was the total Latina.

It showed in performance. Her personal bearing figured into the musical equation in a big way. The teen band that could have been confused for the Latin Partridge Family was fast evolving into a support vehicle for the singer, who was clearly the center of attention. Now, she possessed the power to turn men on. For the first time, Selena was being perceived as *una guapa*, a babe.

Whenever the house lights went up after the last encore, the illusion was shattered and Selena reverted to her traditional role as the kid in the family, just part of the team, doing her bit for the enterprise, and working the crowd, the promoter, and the radio guys, working everyone. One for all, and all for one. But deep inside, this commitment she had made way back in Lake Jackson along with Dad, Mom, A.B., and Suzette left her unfulfilled. There were yearnings welling up that her family couldn't meet. The Bible couldn't inform her about the stirrings inside. Her eyes turned elsewhere, looking, searching, needing somebody else.

Selena had worked with Chris Perez for two years. She'd met him in 1988 while he was still playing behind Shelly Lares, a pal of Selena's from San Antonio. He'd become a Dino just after the band had finished recording *Ven Conmigo*. She liked him a whole lot as a band member. His playing was impeccable, he showed up on time, and Dad liked him. He was also really fun to be with on his own. She loved the little wrinkled smile he had, his shy, demure manner, the way he carried himself on- and offstage, how he let his guitar do the talking, as he used to tell her. He was a good listener. And he was a good friend, like all the guys in the band, all of whom were considered family.

Now she found herself liking him in another way, too, in a way she'd never felt before in her life. It was strange for her, because she had always dedicated herself to her job. There wasn't any time for romance in this organization.

It started when a friend put a bee in her bonnet. "Do you have a crush on him?" her friend asked.

Selena looked at her funny. "Give me a break." She hadn't noticed Chris before, but the question made her start thinking. The longer she gazed at Chris, the more different he appeared to her. "We were friends," she said later. "I never thought I wanted to marry a musician." She started noticing him more and more. She couldn't take her eyes off him, and she didn't want to. "I don't even know how he felt about me."

There was one big problem. Chris never seemed to notice the way she looked at him, the way that all the play between them was becoming something more than professional camaraderie, at least in her eyes. Actually, there were *two* big problems: that and Dad. She went to A.B. for assistance.

One day, A.B. took Chris aside. "What do you think about Selena?" he asked.

"She's cool," Chris replied nonchalantly.

"No." A.B. asked again, "What do you think about Selena? Because she was asking about you."

Chris's face reddened visibly as he shyly smiled. He was a loner, a quiet one, who found release through his guitar. Selena interested in him? He felt more embarrassed than anything. No. Her? No way.

Love and time were two things that Abraham couldn't control. Selena had grown up before his eyes. You could see it in the proof sheets from the photo sessions for the new album *Entre a Mi Mundo*, shot by Al Rendon. The San Antonio photographer had worked with Mazz, Emilio, and all the big Tejano acts, and had been hired to shoot the cover in February. "I'd been doing some work with Capitol-EMI and she had an album due," he said. "Another photographer had shot some photos they didn't like and she needed a quick session."

Rendon rented a studio, hired a makeup artist, and had

everything set to go when the bus pulled up and Abraham introduced himself in a less than charming manner. His first words to Rendon were, "We don't want to use your makeup guy." Rendon's makeup artist, John MacBurney, privately complained that he couldn't deal with Abraham's interference.

But whatever their opinion may have been of the old man, they felt differently about Selena. "Now, she was real easy to work with," Rendon said.

Selena picked out an outfit that included a black top with a mesh, see-through midriff, a long-sleeved black jacket with black-and-white-striped long sleeves, a wide black leather belt, and tight black pants. The image suggested a mature young woman at the peak of ripeness, and as she posed, running her fingers through her hair, it was too much for Abraham to endure.

"Dad just got entranced," Rendon observed. "He was watching and said, 'This isn't my little girl, she's all grown up.' He got so choked up, he left the studio and stayed on the bus for the rest of the shoot." Her father started to realize she had grown up quite a bit.

"All the clothes she'd worn before, they weren't quite as provocative [as this]," Rendon said. "Then she went to town." Abraham may have found it difficult to accept, but Rendon's reaction suggested that Selena had a new type of fan: young males who saw the woman in the spotlight as a sexual animal. "After that I was hooked," he said. "I'd go to her performances." Backstage, he still saw the two contrasting images of Selena—with and without Abraham. "Alone, she was so animated, she'd hug you and just light up the room. Then her dad would come in the room and she'd clam up."

Selena's infatuation with Chris did not, would not subside. They saw each other every day on the road, but it wasn't the place to develop a relationship. They first admitted to each other the feelings that they each had at a Pizza Hut in the Rio Grande Valley, talking about it intimately in the parking lot. Chris, it turned out, was just as smitten as she was. "I never wanted to see anyone else,

I never went out with anyone else. It was just Selena and me." And Abe and the band.

To outsiders Chris seemed an unlikely choice. They were opposites, fire and ice. He was introverted and retiring; she was loud and boisterous. She could have had almost any Latino man in the world, and she picked her guitar player. But Chris wasn't a goody-goody by any stretch of the imagination. In December he'd been convicted of driving while intoxicated and evading arrest in San Antonio, which cost him $670 in fines and court costs, plus attorney's fees, lost work time, and having to explain himself to Selena.

They had to settle for stolen moments, on the road, back home, wherever and whenever they could. Abraham didn't mind Chris going places with Selena, as long as it appeared to him to be band-related business. Even he didn't suspect.

When he caught them embracing, Abraham didn't miss a beat. What did Chris think he was doing? Selena was no tramp. They were just kids. Sooner or later, Selena would realize it was just an infatuation. She'd see the light, if he had anything to do with it. For the first time since Papa Gayo's, though, he didn't have anything to do with it.

Try as he might, he couldn't smother the flames of passion. He'd given his daughter all he could, nurturing her, protecting her, managing her, guiding her career and her personal life. But this was one void he could not fill. As much as it troubled him, he couldn't control Selena's feelings for Chris.

When Abraham fired Chris, he hadn't anticipated Selena's reaction to Chris moving back to San Antonio and picking up a gig playing behind Patsy Torres. All it took was Selena's misery over the next four months for the angry father and protective manager to come around. His daughter would be accommodated, but on Abraham's terms. He asked Chris to come back but said he could be with Selena only if they married and only if they lived next door, in a house Abraham owned. A.B., his wife,

Vangie, and their two children already lived on the other side.

"I'm sure that any father who has a daughter has mixed emotions [about her marriage]," Abraham said. "All I could do was teach my kids as my parents taught us, that marriage is a sacred covenant."

On April 2, 1992, Selena told her parents she was going shopping and went with Chris to the Nueces County courthouse on Leopard Street. The twenty-one-year-old bride wore a Coca-Cola jacket, the twenty-two-year-old groom a white shirt. Both had on jeans. Judge Joaquín Villarreal III waived the normal seventy-two-hour waiting period, and Selena Quintanilla was married to Christopher Perez by Ben Garza, Jr., Justice of the Peace, in precinct 1 in Nueces County, who interrupted his lunch break to preside over the ceremony. Deputy Mary Truesdale processed and signed the license.

"Ever since I was a little girl, I'd dreamed of having a big, wonderful wedding, with a long white gown and a bouquet of flowers," Selena later told a friend, María Elida Saldívar. "But my love for Chris was so strong. I couldn't wait any longer for us to be husband and wife. I couldn't even wear my nicest dress because that would have made my father suspicious."

Judge Garza said, "I remember thinking, Where are their parents? They were so happy together, they deserved to have their family and friends around them."

A few weeks later, while on a music promotion trip to Las Vegas, Ramon Hernandez ran into his old friend Selena. It was the first time he'd had the opportunity to spend time with her since she'd become a Capitol-EMI Latin act. It was a heady trip for Selena, who was in Vegas to play a *Billboard* showcase at Caesar's Palace. Killing time in a casino, she won two thousand dollars at the slots and headed straight to a gift shop with her winnings to buy a leather jacket, which she later wore to the Premio Lo Nuestro awards show in Miami.

Selena introduced Hernandez to her husband, Chris Perez. Hernandez hadn't known that Selena had married, and he suggested that he take a wedding photograph of the couple. "I told Chris to pick up Selena for a photograph, and he tried to but she weighed too much. So she got on top of a sofa, he held out his arms and swung around, I took their picture before he dropped her."

Abe felt that publicizing the marriage would damage Selena's career, so he soft-pedaled the news, telling only those who asked. He told Selena it wasn't cool to talk about it in interviews. "He doesn't want to emphasize it," she told one reporter. Like it or not, career or no career, Abraham couldn't stop her, though he did convince her not to flirt with Chris onstage. This was a job, not some soap opera.

At the 1992 Tejano Music Awards at the San Antonio Convention Center Arena on March 6, Capitol-EMI Latin acts won all thirteen categories, led by Mazz's six awards (the line "and the winner is Joe López" turned into a running joke), three kudos for Emilio Navaira, and Selena's now perfunctory Female Vocalist and Female Entertainer citations. Selena demonstrated to her peers how to test the waters beyond Tejano by engaging in a well-received romantic duet onstage with Alvaro Torres, the first non-Tejano to perform at the annual event. Ever fashion-conscious, Selena straightened Torres's collar while singing to him. In a one-off, she had recorded "Buenos Amigos," a pretty if somewhat insipid ballad, with Torres, a Honduran pop singer who had a big following in Central America and Puerto Rico. Although Selena's name was inadvertently left off the album *Nada Se Compara Contigo* when it was released in February 1992, the single, which credited Selena, would prove some of José Behar's crossover theories. The duet was perhaps the most endearing and enduring vocal style in Spanish-language music, and it was expected that Torres would give Selena star power by association in areas of the Latin world where Tejano was not known. The plan worked, giving Selena her first number-one record on *Billboard*'s Latin singles chart, reaching the peak on June 6, the same month the band made their performance debut on the *Orale Primo* music program.

The album that followed, *Entre a Mi Mundo*, strengthened the Selena juggernaut. The album was recorded in San Antonio, returning the band to Manny Guerra's studio after they had sampled Joey López's facilities across town for *Ven Conmigo*. As in the past, Manny and his house engineer, Brian "Red" Moore, a former bass player with Patsy Torres, ran the board. A.B. called the shots as producer and arranger. For years he'd done his job, holding down the bottom of Los Dinos' sound with his bass, while learning everything he could about songs, songwriting, music, audio recording, electronics, instruments, and how they all interacted. He had prepared well, ably producing the *Selena* album and *Ven Conmigo*. Now he was experienced enough to make a statement. If the band had ever put together an optimum piece of modern music, it was "La Carcacha," a rocking pile driver of a *cumbia* highlighted by call-and-response chants, shouts, whistles, searing guitar fills from Chris Perez in his recording debut with the band, and Selena's mesmerizing snake-charmer vocals; she alternately trilled and growled about hanging out on the corner, waiting for her loved one to pull up in his jalopy. The tale of love in hard times was something the composer, A.B. Quintanilla III, knew well. There was also a properly overwrought *ranchera*, "Qué Creías," that Selena described as "one of those songs where a girl tells a guy off." This proved to be a big crowd pleaser in concert, since Selena recruited a young man from the audience to sing to, reminding the ladies how men take them for granted. Another *cumbia*, "Como la Flor," was equally catchy though done slow and easy. The title, Selena said, "comes from those flowers that they have at dances with the light inside. That was the idea behind that song." More than any other single song, it was regarded as the one that put Selena over with the Tejano audience, knocking La Mafia off the top of the regional charts in September. "Missing My Baby," written by A.B. and sung in English by Selena, was a state-of-the-art pop song that could have found a home on any radio station with a contemporary hits format, signaling to the record company that whenever they were ready to cross over, the Quintanillas were raring to go.

The album was significant for several other reasons. Like the previous release, *Ven Conmigo*, it sold the act as simply Selena. The words *Los Dinos* appeared only on the inside liner notes that listed the musicians. Furthermore, every song on the album was written in-house, with credits belonging either to A.B., Ricky Vela, or Pedro Astudillo, although "Qué Creías" had the markings of a traditional mariachi to the point that it bordered on outright theft. The last cut on the album, "Amame," was written by Astudillo and Selena Quintanilla, her first songwriting credit. The album also listed the name and phone number of Yolanda Saldivar, *presidente* of the Selena y los Dinos *club de admiradores*.

The formula was evidently working. The album entered the Latin top-fifty chart, where it would remain for the next sixty-two weeks. It reached number one on the Mexican Regional chart of *Billboard* and earned the accolade as the number-one Regional Mexican album of the year. More important, it earned platinum status for a Tejano record, signifying sales in excess of one hundred thousand units, and it eventually reached the three-hundred-thousand-sales plateau.

For years, the realm of Tejano had been riddled with name artists who were either temperamental, swollen-headed, or just plain unreliable. Selena had the snap to get it done and get it done right. During the Coca-Cola television spot she shot in Los Angeles, "There was Timmy T, who was super-hot on the radio; a very talented Puerto Rican act; another guy from New York; and Selena," recalled Rubén Cubillos, who was working on the commercial. "It was supposed to be the hottest Latin sounds from L.A. to New York. Each one was gonna sing a segment of the song. When it came time to record the tracks, Selena got in there and kicked ass. First two takes, and that's all we took. She shined. Sweet. She poured it on, did her cut, and she was gone. The others couldn't handle it that way.''

The Coke connection went both ways. Selena made Coke look good. Coke made Selena look good, exposing her to an audience way beyond Tejano. Typical was the event staged in Washington, D.C., as part of a celebration for the Hispanic caucus of the United States Congress. The soft-drink company arranged to hold a street dance in a parking lot in a largely Hispanic inner-city neighborhood. The event marked the first time Corpus Christi attorney Albert Huerta saw the girl from his hometown perform. Huerta, who accompanied his business partner, master of ceremonies Johnny Canales, and U.S. Representative Solomon Ortiz to the concert, came away impressed. "This girl is going places," he told Canales.

When Selena was booked to appear for the taping of a Canales show at the Bayfront Auditorium back in Corpus, Huerta knew how good the act was but was unprepared for the response. "Crowds were lined up for about a mile along the seawall by five o'clock in the afternoon." It was jam-packed as no Johnny show had ever been.

In October, the band headlined a Houston benefit for the Florida victims of Hurricane Andrew, one of the most destructive storms ever to hit the United States. The bill for the fund-raiser included Mazz, La Sombra, Fiebre, and David Lee Garza, and was strong enough to attract a crowd of twenty-one thousand. That same month, Los Dinos were the featured act at the Enchilada Festival in Las Cruces, New Mexico.

Selena-fever was also spreading south for the first time, thanks to the broad-based appeal of *Entre a Mi Mundo*. Mexico was especially receptive to "Qué Creías," a traditional *ranchera*-type song that showcased Selena's full vocal range and had her spitting out lyrics with the gritty passion of a Lucha Villa, emoting with a complete lack of restraint. EMI decided a south of the border press tour would be timely, including a high-profile meet-and-greet conference with music media types in Monterrey. Mexico, Behar noted, was two and a half times the size of the U.S.

Latin market. Abraham was nervous, and so was Selena. Would her Spanish get her through? Would she be able to communicate with Mexicans without having the image of Tejanos as hayseed *pochos* entering their minds?

The contingent she was facing may have been *puro* Mexicano instead of Texas-Mexicans, but to Selena they looked like the radio, television, newspaper, and magazine people back home. They were just looking for a story. Selena gave them one. The smile was just the beginning. One by one, she hugged every one of the thirty-five press representatives in attendance. Then she opened the session for questions.

She was a refreshing change from the usual Mexicana star, who was fair-skinned, blond-haired, and green-eyed. Selena was one of their own, brown and proud and unapologetically Latin. She played her cards right. The next day, one newspaper hailed her as *"una artista del pueblo,"* an artist of the people.

Selena got off easy. She dodged the language bullet. Her Spanish had been stilted, tentative, and grammatically imprecise, but no one that she'd hugged dared to call her on it. When she returned to Corpus Christi, though, Selena agreed with Abraham that it was a good time to take a crash course in the mother tongue and learn to speak it properly. She wasn't some *pocho* from Texas. She was Selena. For several months, she spent extended periods in Monterrey and Mexico City, learning to speak the language the way it was meant to be spoken. The next time she went south, she wouldn't just knock on the door, she'd kick it down. She did exactly that when Los Dinos played in La Feria de Nuevo Leon on September 17, 1993, in front of seventy thousand, then returned on October 5. Almost overnight, Selena became the biggest Tejano act in Mexico.

The English crossover was about a year away, Selena told one reporter. Making an album in English was more than just a language thing, she was learning. "It's really weird how we work in the English market. Everybody takes a year to record." Her band was much more efficient. A.B. could crank out hits on demand, which is why he was originally scheduled to co-produce the album. "What my brother does is arrange and produce all my material and write. And we practice in the house. And we go into the studio and we have the music sequenced, so that way we have the timing perfect and then everybody goes in and lays their parts. It goes a lot faster. So we record in maybe three or four days, the music tracks. Then I go back and do my vocals. So it gets out in a month and a half to two months, by the time they press it. So I would say three months.

"We usually go by a song title that's on the album that comes at the last part. You know, usually people work around the name of the album. We don't do it like that. I guess we kind of do things backwards. But who's laying down the rules?"

She didn't expect to change her personality just because she was singing a different language. "It'll be my style," she promised. "I'm not one to sing about songs that go into detail about sexual things. That's not for me. I think everything should be tasteful. That's what we're going to project on the English album." First there was the rest of the world to conquer. "I know that with this Spanish-international thing and English, it is just the beginning. It is like we are starting all over again," she said. "But we have more on our résumé, a little bit more experience to help us out."

A larger issue was whether the record company understood. Mitchell Lee, the first A & R (artist and repertoire) rep to get his hands on the project at SBK Records, an EMI-affiliated label, understood that singing in English came naturally to Selena. Getting the right producer, the right songs, was A & R's job. So was selling the act to the record company. To Lee's dismay, few understood what kind of act it was to begin with. "Those idiots. I had to take them to Las Vegas to hear her. They didn't get her. Nobody got her. They thought she was a Tex-Mex singer. I had to pay to jam it down everybody's throats."

The only rules were family rules, set up under the banner of Five Candle Productions. Abraham was *el patrón*. He, too, had made the transition to the big time. But he had to step out of the creative loop to take care of business. "Before, my dad had a lot of say-so in the songs and music," Selena said. "And now I guess since my brother has proven himself, he's able to handle everything on his own."

A.B. had set up his own production and publishing companies. For composing purposes, he had brought in Pete Astudillo as collaborator. Ricky Vela, the one non-blood who made the trip from hard times to the big time, programmed the keyboards and sequenced the computers. "But my brother is like the boss, you know," Selena said.

In addition to drumming, Suzette handled the merchandise, ordering, printing, and selling T-shirts, ball caps, and beer-can coolers emblazoned with the Selena y los Dinos logo.

Selena was the star. But she was finding a life for herself away from the microphone, too. "Me, I'm in charge of the uniforms and outfits," she said proudly. "I design clothes and jewelry on the side. So we make our own things, which I love to do. I love shiny things and I love clothing. I was telling a friend of mine the other day, . . . I know this sounds stupid, but whenever I finish putting crystals on a jacket I can just sit there and play with it in the light, the sparkles. Oh, that's so stupid. But anyway, I like shiny things and I make jewelry. Well, I have my own business and I have a mail-order catalogue coming out soon. So I do that in my time off. I make belts and all that junk."

Looking back, she was relieved to see where the whole family had been and where they were going. "I lost a lot out of my teenagehood, but I have gained a lot, too," she said. "I can't really say that I lost because I got ahead of everyone as far as career and being more mature about business, even though I didn't know what the heck was going on. Thank goodness we stuck to it because we have come a long way, you know. Really and truly, I can't imagine myself having an everyday job and going into an office. I love business. I have my own business aside from singing, but I can't picture myself going to the same place every day. I don't know—it would be kind of a drag to me, I guess because I have gotten so used to traveling now. When I have the chance to relax, I am real hyper and ready to go.''

She admitted to being superstitious about performing. ''I don't really believe in all that, but I don't like to go out and see the band that is going to perform before me because, I don't know, it seems to have an effect on me. Whether they are good or not, I get this feeling like, I'm nervous now. I don't know, for some reason I get nervous before I perform. So I've learned to just stay away.''

Amidst the heady rush of recognition and the spreading popularity, Abraham kept the loyal fans happy while making his wallet fatter. The dance-hall and club circuit was just a phone call away. In November, Selena y los Dinos passed through the Brazosport area, their old stomping grounds. After one show, Abraham Quintanilla walked into the Denny's on Highway 332 and saw a familiar face: Rena Dearman, the original keyboardist for Selena y los Dinos. Rena had divorced her husband, Rodney Pyeatt, and was back in showbiz, performing with her country band Painted Desert. She'd just gotten off a gig at Kick's Club in Freeport when she spotted her old mentor. They exchanged smiles and hugs.

''Where's Selena?'' Rena asked.

''Next door. We're staying at La Quinta. She's with her husband, Chris.'' Abraham roused his brood and summoned them over to the restaurant. Rena was thrilled to see them all again. But she was particularly taken with Selena. The years on the road hadn't affected her one bit, or so it seemed. ''Selena hadn't changed,'' Dearman said. ''She was the little girl I remembered. She had that same bubbly attitude. She was always smiling, even when she didn't have to.''

A.B. asked Rena about her own music, and at his request she later sent him some material she'd written. The band was going into the studio again soon and needed songs. A.B. called her. He was really into "I'll Be All Right." If everything worked out, it would be included on the next album, *Amor Prohibido*. Unfortunately, a record company rep rejected the composition. "I'll Be All Right" didn't fit the mood of the album. Still, it was a good song, A.B. told her. Maybe it would wind up on the next Spanish-language album, which was due out in late 1995, sometime after Selena finished her crossover English-language pop album. Dearman had plenty of reason to believe they thought it had potential, since a few months later, A.B. and Selena sang their arrangement of her song to her after a gig in Houston.

Shortly before Christmas, San Antonio photographer John Dyer received a telephone call from the art director of *Más* magazine, a slick national start-up funded by Mexican magnate Emilio Azcarraga aimed at an audience fluent in Spanish and familiar with *People* magazine. "They were doing a cover story on Selena and wanted me to shoot a spread on her. I hadn't heard of her before then. The art director came down. He began to get involved in the shoot. He started talking about me getting her with a dominatrix look because she had these tight leather pants and a bustier on," Dyer said.

"Selena was involved with the whole shoot, with the stylist, with the makeup assistant, everyone. Her mom sat outside the whole day and didn't say a word.

"The only hitch was the makeup. It was hard, in my opinion, like women on the Mexican soap operas who paint their own eyebrows. She insisted on doing real black eyebrows, pancake makeup, the whole bit. She didn't want to hear it. She said, 'If I change my makeup, my dad is gonna be furious.' Otherwise, she was great, real up and bouncy. We did half a dozen set-ups and she never acted like I was taking advantage of her. She wasn't cynical, standoffish, or haughty; not what you'd expect from someone of her stature."

Several weeks earlier, San Antonio writer Joseph Har-

mes conducted the interview with Selena for the same
Más magazine spread that John Dyer was photographing.
The conversation was one of the most honest and insightful discussions Selena ever had with a writer. Even if she
conversed in the grammatically corrupted patois of a
Valley Girl, Selena was painfully direct about her career,
her personal life, the dad-and-daughter relationship, and
how all the roles intertwined. Speaking about when she
was misquoted: "Sometimes it makes you look really bad,
you know. I've had that happen to me a lot. And then I
get chewed out," she said. Later on, the subject came up
again. "Yeah, my dad gets after me because, like I said,
I talk a lot. And I've learned now not to open up to just
anybody. I befriend anybody and sometimes that person
can be somebody really bad. You meet people on the
road, you don't know how they are, you know? They can
be dressed nice and be really nice to you but they turn
around and they'll say bad things about you, and that's
what I mean. You can get hurt a lot that way."

She admitted to Harmes the need to be more wary.
Maybe it was because her father sheltered her and protected her so zealously. Maybe it was simply her nature.
Whatever it was, Selena's openness may have been an
asset onstage and dealing with her public, but away from
the public eye, that quality became a liability. "I've been
hurt a lot in the past by friends, you know. I get taken
advantage of real easy in the sense that—it can be anything. How can I say it? I trust too easily. That's my
problem. And I end up getting hurt in the long run. This
happened to me a lot. I'm so stupid. But you try to help
somebody out and you think you are doing okay and in
the long run you're the one who's going to be losing out.
Not that I'm saying that you shouldn't help people out.
But it's just—it's kind of hard to explain 'cause you don't
know the situation, you know what I mean? But I'm sure
you can understand, in a way."

Selena discussed a number of other subjects with Harmes. She told him she was driven by design. The house
she moved into with Chris at 705 Bloomington, next door

to Abraham, was also the home of Fashions by Selena. "Well, that kind of is my hobby. Since I enjoy it so much, I'm not really doing it for the money. I love clothing. You should see my closet, oh my God."

She avoided talking about her religious beliefs. "I'd rather not answer. You know, because I don't answer any political questions or religious. I'm Jewish. No—just joking. No, everybody seems to know now in the business that we've made it a rule because we've had some problems in the past," she said cryptically. "We stay away from political or any religious [issues] because, you know, we are here to sing music. And it can create problems, put it that way. Everybody has their differences in religion and politics and those seem to be really touchy situations for everyone."

Her favorite foods were thin-crust pepperoni pizza from Pizza Hut, and arroz con pollo. She ate out a lot. ("You're not home long enough to cook the food before it goes bad. Believe me, I've had so many bread loaves that have gone green that I don't even bother with that anymore.") Her favorite colors were purple and black. She had a black Pomeranian named Pebbles, black carpet, and black furniture. Her bed had an aquarium for a headboard, though she encountered difficulties keeping the tank stocked. ("We had some saltwater fish but they all died.") She had a pet python. Chris was teaching her how to ride his Ninja Kawasaki 250cc motorcycle. ("He wanted to show me first how to change gears. So, later on down the road, I'll be cruising on a Harley, hopefully.") She had tried bungee jumping. ("I'll never do that again. They dared me to do it. And when you dare me, you better watch out.") She felt like the baby in the family. ("I'm older now, and I hope I act a little more mature. We pull our own weight. I'm spoiled in the sense that now I get what I want, but it's because I work for it. It's not because anyone hands it to me. I think it would be pretty sad if I had people giving me things when I ask for it, just because. Then I would consider myself spoiled. But I work for what I have now.")

She showed Harmes photos of her with heroes such as Luis Miguel, Gloria Estefan, and Vicente Fernandez, and espoused the family-style method of working entertainment, quoting the cliché, "The family that plays together, stays together," then adding, "I've been able to see a lot with the family."

When Harmes asked her who Selena really was, she told him, "It's kind of hard for anyone to interview a person and get to know them on a personal basis. You understand what I'm telling you? In other words, what I'm telling you right now is probably what I want you to know about me. It's like you don't know me on a personal basis. Um, really I would want people to know that I think I am a very kindhearted person. Um, I don't like to hurt people's feelings. If I do, it's not intentionally. I'm sincere and very honest. And I feel that nowadays a lot of people have lost that, but I think that starts in the home. My parents have taught me that. Being fair with people."

As always, Selena accentuated the positive. Her star was rising. The organization was expanding. Album sales and concert tickets were zooming skyward. One of the most promising signs, she thought, was the new fan club: "The president is doing exceptionally well. And it's so funny how we met her, because there's this girl that kept on telling her, 'You've got to go see this group, you've got to go see this group. They're great.' And she said, 'No, no, no.' Anyway, she ended up going and she liked the group to the point where she was overwhelmed. She was moved. And she said, 'Hey, you know, I want to do something for these guys.' "

The woman wasn't the first to hatch the idea, just the most convincing, as Selena saw it. "She approached my father and said that she wanted to open a fan club. And we have had a lot of people approach. Fan clubs can ruin you if you don't have people who take care of it, in the sense that [they could think], 'Well, we didn't get this and we paid our money.' You know, people can get upset and they'll get turned off. So to this day, they have collected, just in the San Antonio area, over fifteen hundred members, which is good. They are the largest fan club in San Antonio. And this is not including members from Washington and California. So she's doing good. And what they do is very organized. They have two kinds of membership. One that you pay for: you get two T-shirts, posters, and all these different kinds of paraphernalia, and you get a membership card, your ID card. And there's another membership where you don't have to pay anything but you get an agenda of all the places where we're going to be at. There's interviews with each band member, there's puzzles that have to do with the band. And it's really neat. They keep up with everything. Every month a newsletter goes out.''

The fan club president Selena talked about to Joseph Harmes was Yolanda Saldivar, who had become part of the Selena family, especially whenever Selena was booked in San Antonio, Yolanda's hometown. She was a tiny thing, less than five feet tall, but Selena thought she was cute as a button, so cute she called her Buffy—the nickname Yolanda's family had given her, short for buffalo. Above all, Yolanda was reliable. She was someone you could depend on. She was taking care of business.

Yolanda Saldivar had led a lonely, anonymous life before she entered Selena's world. She was born on September 19, 1960, in San Antonio, to Juanita and Frank Saldivar. Her father supported the family as the headwaiter at Jacala, a popular Mexican restaurant on the west side of the city where he had been serving the enchilada plates and filling iced-tea glasses for forty years. Even as an adult, Yolanda lived at the Saldivar family compound, south of the city limits on Martinez-Losoya Road, near Mitchell Lake. The country domicile consisted of four frame houses and a trailer on six acres of land shaded by mesquite and pecan trees and protected by barbed-wire fencing around the perimeter.

Yolanda led a gypsy-like existence during her school years, transferring three times in elementary school in the historically poor and underfunded Edgewood school district; she began ninth grade at Kennedy High in the

Edgewood district, then transferred to Holmes, then Jay
high schools in the Northside district, and finally graduated from McCollom High in Harlandale school district,
on San Antonio's mostly Hispanic south side, in 1979,
where she had been in the Reserve Officers' Training
Corps. Few classmates could recall Saldivar, but her fellow students at McCollom included future Tejano stars
Ram Herrera, who graduated in 1978, and Emilio Navaira,
from the class of '80.

After graduation, she continued her studies at San Antonio College and then Palo Alto College while living at
home, the site of frequent informal family gatherings, barbecues, and occasional dances. She supported her studies
over a five-year period with a series of day jobs. One of
her employers was Dr. Faustino Gómez, a dermatologist
who sued Saldivar for $9,200 that he said she stole from
him in 1983. The lawsuit was eventually settled out of
court. On December 10, 1990, Saldivar had earned
enough credits to receive a nursing degree from the University of Texas Health Science Center. Two weeks later,
she began work as a graduate nurse at Medical Center
Hospital. In March of the following year, she received her
license as a registered nurse from the Texas Board of
Nurse Examiners. But within two months, Yolanda was
back in court again, when the Texas Guaranteed Student
Loan Corporation obtained a Travis County court judgment in Austin against her for failing to repay a student
loan of $5,361. At the time, she had switched jobs and
was working as a nurse at St. Luke's Lutheran Hospital.
She held down other nursing jobs at Hospice San Antonio
and the San Antonio State Chest Hospital over the next
four years, but her career in health care mattered to her
less and less. Yolanda had found something much more
rewarding. She had found the world of show business
right there in San Antonio, in the form of Tejano music.

Her first brush with fame was Shelly Lares, the young
Tejana singer whom Saldivar approached early in 1991.
If Lares agreed, Saldivar would start and operate her fan
club. She was turned down by Lares and her father, Fred,

who managed her. "We wanted to keep it in the family because that's how we do it," Lares said. Yolanda then approached Suzette Quintanilla, who was in charge of merchandising for Selena y los Dinos. Yolanda had known of Selena long enough to have once confided to a co-worker that she used to hate Selena "for always winning in the Tejano Music Awards."

But after seeing her perform and getting hooked on the song "Baila Esta Cumbia," Yolanda saw her in a different light. Suzette arranged for Yolanda to meet Abraham and receive his blessing to start a fan club. Abraham authorized the nurse to form and oversee the Selena *club de admiradores*, with Yolanda as president, beginning in late 1991. Her efforts were exemplary. She handled the mailings, sent out newsletters and T-shirts in exchange for the twenty-dollar membership fee, and organized events and parties for Selena in San Antonio and Corpus Christi. She called radio stations on Selena's behalf and alerted fans to upcoming personal appearances. In less than four years, she built a membership base of almost five thousand fans.

Though Yolanda was eleven years older than Selena and her short, squat form was Selena's physical opposite, they realized they had much in common after spending time together at Suzette's wedding to Billy Ariaga in September 1993, where Selena was maid of honor and Yolanda was a bridesmaid. Both were loners. Selena didn't have much of a life outside of show business; Yolanda never had much of a life, period. The relationship that formed was built on that bond. The demands on Selena's time were relentless. Abraham and the rest of the family were actually relieved that Selena had someone to help her out. Suzette was busy with the merchandising and welcomed Yolanda's interest. A.B. had immersed himself so deeply in songwriting, producing, and publishing that he was like a brother from another planet. Abraham was consumed with orchestrating the whole show. Selena, who had found refuge in designing clothes, needed a person like Yolanda to lend a hand, and welcomed her presence.

Selena didn't just want someone to help. She needed

someone to lean on. Her life was stressful enough. The only time she really felt free was onstage. "I like performing because I get to pretend to be someone else," she said. "I get to let loose." Now her passion for fashion was turning into reality in the form of a design business, and she had plans for starting a chain of boutiques. Yolanda could help take up the slack.

Not everyone was quite as enamored of Yolanda as Selena was, though.

"Yolanda was always very possessive," observed Albert Dávila of KEDA-AM radio in San Antonio, one of the stations that Yolanda kept in touch with on behalf of the fan club for updates on Selena's live gigs and record releases. "She'd keep you away. Selena was possessed by her. One of our employees went to [Yolanda's] house to pick up some materials and freaked out because one room had an altar, candles, everything. It was a Selena shrine."

The Selena y los Dinos road brigade now swelled to three vehicles carrying sixteen people and state-of-the-art production gear, a contingent that impressed the more than three thousand hometown fans who packed into the Memorial Coliseum in Corpus on February 7, 1993. The free concert was recorded and released in the summer as *Selena Live*, her fourth album for Capitol-EMI Latin, which had shortened its name to EMI Latin. Filling the hall was a foregone conclusion. By playing to the hometown crowd Abraham was guaranteeing record sales.

As René Cabrera noted in his "Tejano Journal" for the *Caller-Times*, "You have to go back to June 18, 1979, to find the last time a major Tejano entertainer scored a big hit with a live recording at the Coliseum. That was Little Joe with his *Live for Schlitz* recording for Freddie Records. Freddie is still making bank deposits with music that was recorded that night."

Freddie Martínez was banking chump change compared to what this concert would generate. Tickets were given away for the event at the request of city officials. Once again, the P. T. Barnum in Abraham couldn't resist tweaking the city for their concerns. "They were scared that there was going to be a riot or something." He smiled contentedly. "The only way we could have had more people here was to have lined up chairs from the front to the back, and we didn't want to do that." The venue was set up to accommodate dancers. Otherwise it wouldn't have been a real Tejano deal.

Following the Corpus homecoming concert, Selena shared a bill with David Lee Garza at the Houston Livestock Show and Rodeo in the Astrodome, an event that drew tens of thousands every night over its two-week run, mostly people who came to see name entertainers and not the stock of rodeo animals or the cowboys who tried to tame them. The crowd was almost sixty thousand, a figure no Tejano act booked at the rodeo had achieved before. Some of the count could be chalked up to the growing popularity of Tejano music, which was getting hotter and hotter. But the real draw was Selena, Tejano's siren and most glittering jewel. Nothing could stop her. Not even a know-nothing video director. Filming their second video, "La Llamada," at a beach house in Long Beach, California (their first video, "La Carcacha," was filmed in Monterrey the previous year), Selena was shocked when she arrived at the set to find actors dressed in the Mexican cowboy look popularized by *banda* music, a retro roots sound popular in the Mexican interior and on the west coast. The director had confused Los Dinos for a Mexican band.

Tejanos had their own cowboy style that fans in western shops and convenience stores across Texas were alerted to, thanks to the poster that Coca-Cola and Tony Lama Boots created of Selena and her labelmate Emilio Navaira. They were wearing matching black hats and black-leather duster coats to promote a contest for a free trip to the 1993 TMA awards at the San Antonio Convention Center Arena. The lucky winners would watch the twenty-one-year-old Selena take home Female Vocalist of the Year and Female Entertainer of the Year honors once again, as well as Album of the Year honors for *Entre a Mi Mundo*.

In May, her appearance at the prestigious Festival Acapulco won her critical acclaim as the only and absolute queen of the festival.

When *Selena Live* reached the stores in late spring, it served notice that Selena was the hottest act in Tejano (the words *Los Dinos* appeared only on the musician credits again), although in a contradictory declaration, the music was described on the cassette exterior cover as "International/Mexican." Whatever it was, the music created at the concert in Corpus revealed that Los Dinos could still do the homeboy stuff right on the button, evidenced by "Qué Creías," a lowdown *ranchera* adorned by David Lee Garza's soulful accordion and Selena's scorching vocals, all sass and fire. The band proved they could manufacture formula sentimentality by strolling agreeably behind Pete Astudillo's lead vocal on "Perdóname." But it was on "La Carcacha" that Los Dinos rose to the occasion by rocking the house with dynamics and production values equal to any contemporary act's in this part of the planet. Just as the studio version on *Entre a Mi Mundo* suggested a crossover into the rock or funk idioms, the power *cumbia* recorded live did not require language skills or familiarity with Latin ways for listeners to work up a sweat. This was no surprise, given all the rhythm and bombast. The keyboard lines were fattened into a salsa-tinged wall of sound by Ricky Vela and David Lee Garza again lent street credibility and a touch of the blues to his squeezebox instrumental break. Selena's duet with Emilio Navaira, "Tú Robaste Mi Corazón" (You Stole My Heart), was as close to English pop as it got on the album. Sung in Spanish, the pleasant ballad was made to be a duet, and it reached number five on the Hot Latin Tracks chart, even though it was more harmless than inspiring. The album reached number one on the *Billboard* Mexican Regional chart, making three albums in a row for the girl from Lake Jackson. But charts told only half the story. Creatively, Selena, her brother, and their band were peaking.

In late September, the family formalized their growing

empire when A.B. registered Q Productions as an assumed name with the state of Texas to be run as a partnership. A year and a half later, Abraham, Jr., would sign similar papers, essentially taking over the business while A.B. shifted his interests to his Phat Kat Groove production company.

A return booking on Johnny Canales's show, taped at the Bayfront Convention Center in Corpus, drew an overflow audience. Selena was dressing the band in their coolest duds yet—matching black pants, black vests, and white shirts. She owned the stage now, and acted like she knew it while maintaining a modicum of composure, casually chatting up Johnny *en Español*. This time he didn't kid her about her Spanish because she had mastered speaking *la idioma*.

Canales nonetheless shared with the audience another moment of embarrassment for Selena, recalling a show they did together in Caldwell, Idaho, with Jamie y los Chamachos. Canales had walked onto Selena's bus after the show to find her sitting on the floor, eating potted meat out of a can.

"What are you doing?" he had asked her.

"Eating," Selena had said with a full mouth, looking up at him.

After relating that story, Canales declared with certainty, "With crowds like tonight, you'll be eating steak pretty soon. Round steak, at least."

Selena shrugged and smiled. "I don't want to get used to the good life." She furrowed her brow. "Round steak. What's that?" she asked Canales.

"Bologna." He cackled, knowing he'd pulled one off on her.

Selena laughed along with Johnny at the punchline. She was nothing if not a trouper.

Behind the scenes, the crossover wasn't selling as easily as the Q clan or EMI Latin had anticipated. Selena's entertainment attorney, Stephen J. Finfer, recalled the difficulty he and José Behar encountered. "I believe there were many options, but it was very tough. At certain stages, we were both mystified by the inability for some people to recognize her true potential.''

The general market, the English-language record business, didn't know what to make of her. She sold records, sure, with sales in the solid six figures. But this Spanish business was a whole other world. A major label hadn't signed a name Spanish act to sing in English since Julio Iglesias ten years ago, and everything he touched went gold, platinum, or better.

By the fall of 1993, however, Finfer had his deal. It was an in-house arrangement with SBK. SBK, said Finfer, ''was willing to spend whatever it took to make a great record for her.''

In November 1993, Selena y los Dinos were formally signed to SBK Records for their English-language record. The strategy had already been pretty well set by the time Charles Koppelman affixed his signature to the contract. SBK had already signed Jon Secada and Puerto Rico's Barrio Boyzz to contracts.

Daniel Glass, the CEO of the EMI Records Group, was not shy about hyping the deal to *Billboard*. ''I don't like to compare artists, but Selena is the closest artist I've got to Madonna. She has that same control, and I love artists that know where they want to go and how to get there. She's definitely a pop star.

''What's more, it's rare to find an artist so self-contained and well organized. She has been touring for ten years with her own sponsor [Coca-Cola], entourage, bus, and eight trucks carrying her sound and light equipment.''

Nancy Brennan, the A & R vice president spearheading the project, admitted that before attending a showcase in Las Vegas, ''I had never heard of Tejano music, but I was just so impressed seeing this girl up there onstage. I think she has every element for international success: an amazing voice, a phenomenal stage presence, gorgeous looks, and a great personality.''

For her part, Selena promised to be true to those who

had brought her to the dance. "Just because we signed a contract with a worldwide English company, that doesn't mean we're going to leave our base. I think a lot of people that have supported us would be very disappointed if we were just to turn our backs and go on to something else."

All the record company needed to do was connect the artist to the marketplace. José Behar, the EMI Latin president who'd signed her to his company four years earlier, had always said he'd done so to cross Selena over to the English market. "I never in my wildest dreams thought she would be such a big Latin act." As he'd once explained to Manolo Gonzalez, his man in San Antonio, the mission had always been clear: "We've got to Anglicize this."

Behar was referring to both the music and the method of distribution. Up until that point, even the major labels like EMI channeled their Spanish-language product separately, through independent distributors who traditionally worked the Latin audience in the U.S. Behar knew that for a crossover to work effectively, the distribution needed to be integrated and handled by the same people who moved all those millions of units by artists such as Whitney Houston, Paula Abdul, Gloria Estefan, and Jon Secada. That meant educating distributors. They needed to understand that despite the ethnicity of the artist and the material, the number of units sold transcended language and culture. An album with Selena's name on it should be handled no differently than product by any other artist. Distributors in the Southwest didn't have to be educated, because groups like Mazz, La Mafia, Selena y los Dinos, and Emilio Navaira y Grupo Rio were moving almost fifty thousand units apiece in the Texas region.

Gonzalez and Behar agreed that Texas was the place for crossing over, not Miami or Los Angeles. "I don't see it happening anywhere else," Gonzalez said, noting that the nature of Tejano life was to assimilate.

From where the Quintanillas sat, though, there wasn't any rush. Selena's one-off Spanish duet with the Barrio Boyzz, "Dondequiera que Estés," strengthened her fan support in Puerto Rico and Central America. The Boyzz appreciated Selena's inclusion of Bobby Brown's material in her live sets and liked her bubbly personality. "She made fun of our New York accent, trying to imitate it," said Freddie Correa. "She called one of the band '*chuleta* lips.' " At home, with Selena, La Mafia, and Emilio as headliners, Tejano had moved into giant-size venues such as San Antonio's Alamodome, Dallas's Texas Stadium, and Houston's Astrodome, although no venue attracted crowds as large as the ninety thousand plus who were turning out to hear Tejano acts on the package show bills in Monterrey, Nuevo Leon, where Mazz, La Sombra, and La Mafia were making huge inroads. Industry growth was once again going through the roof. Tejano 107, the first FM Tejano format in town, retained its position as the most listened to radio station in San Antonio. The Dallas-Fort Worth area got its first Tejano-formatted FM signal, Kick 108. Another major label, Arista, had set up shop in Texas to tap into the Tejano scene.

Sitting onboard their home on wheels outside the Escape Club in Austin, A.B. complained to a visitor that the quality of songs being sent to Selena for the ballyhooed crossover were not what they were cracked up to be. He could do a better job than these so-called star producers and songwriters. Abraham nodded gruffly. "Take a look around," he said. "This is a nice bus. Look inside the club. The place is packed. We don't need [the English-language pop audience]."

The whole Tejano scene had changed before everyone's eyes in five short years. The old circuit of dance halls, dance-hall promoters, and tie-ins with local radio stations was dead or dying. The Astrodome, the Alamodome, Texas Stadium, and the Summit, where the mega acts played, were the venues of the future. That was their destiny.

But in order to play the same places as the white acts, the bands had to do business with the white promoters who controlled the venues. By banding the Tejano bands together, Abraham tried to break that monopoly. Pace

Concerts, the promoters who controlled the majority of the arena, amphitheater, and stadium concert action in Texas, had finally taken an interest in Tejano and proposed a showcase package show at the Astrohall, adjacent to the Houston Astrodome. But when the offers went out to the big groups that Pace wanted on the bill, Abraham called for a walkout. Pace's guarantees were an insult. The gringos paid gringo bands twice as much as they were contracting the Tejano acts for, and they were bringing in Mexican acts and treating them like Madonna while treating the Tejanos like stepchildren. Selena, Mazz, Mafia, Emilio, Ram Herrera—they could all make better money booking their own shows, Abraham believed. They were hot on the radio, hot in the record racks, and these gringo promoters were trying to use them. "We already own Houston," said Abe. "Why do we need them?"

How could he blow off Pace? another manager objected. They had a lock on all the big rooms. They were merely testing the waters. If they made money on this venture, Pace would pay the Tejano bands as much or more than the Anglo acts the next time around.

Abraham was unmoved and led the walkout, the rebel bands promoting their own show on the same day in Houston. Pace took a bath in red ink. Abe chalked up a victory for *la raza*. They didn't need the Man running their show. They could do it by themselves.

"It was classic Quintanilla. He stuck to his guns," marveled one booking agent who'd dealt with him.

Principle was sometimes more important than money. During Fiesta, San Antonio's big annual citywide spring party, Abraham turned down an offer to play a sanctioned event with a guaranteed audience of thousands because he suspected that the white country music acts booked for the same event were getting paid considerably more than he was being offered for Selena. (He suspected correctly.) Instead, he set up a concert for Selena y los Dinos in Rosedale Park that drew a paltry five hundred fans. This would have been economic suicide if not for the corporate bailout by Coke, who picked up the concert tab. Performance fees were escalating upward of fifteen thousand dollars a night, thanks to Coca-Cola's sponsorship. "I know a guy who wanted to give her thirty thousand dollars for one night, to play at his daughter's fifteenth, but Abe wouldn't take it because it would break part of the contract with Coke," said former roadie Rubén García.

Selena was becoming a trademark as valuable and easily identifiable as Coke. She was the premier act in Tejano and the biggest musical entertainment act in Texas. Like most great artists, her life played out in her music, a fantasy version of the teenage years she was denied. The tale of boy meets girl that she was never able to enjoy herself became the stuff her music was made of. It was a simple process. A.B. asked her what she wanted him to write about, she told him, and he did. Typically, the story lines followed lives Selena had never had, such as the tale of barrio teen romance in "La Carcacha." Selena was a singer's singer and a total entertainer. More important, especially in the eyes of young girls, she was a walking, talking Barbie. She invited young girls to share in the fantasy world she had created for herself, dressing herself up in imaginative doll-like outfits adorned with baubles and beads, a different costume almost every performance. Depending on her mood and the whims of design, she was *la sirena*, the Mexican siren with cinnamon skin, arched eyebrows, and a painted face; or the sultry temptress, who tantalized the men and boys by exposing her bare midriff and accentuating her breasts with bustiers and her *nalgas* with tight-fitting pants; or the independent businesswoman who sublimated her sexuality to emphasize mind over body. The challenge facing Selena was, in her words, "trying to maintain the level of success" that she and her family and the whole organization had created. She had gotten so big that she inspired rumors about her life, and tales of *la envidia*. Could she handle the whispers about why there had been no announcement about Selena getting married? Where were the wedding pictures? Could she ignore the second-guessing from the audience as to why she referred to Chris as "my love on the bus'' when she introduced her brother and sister by name during concerts? How could she square her desire to be a young independent Latina woman driven to succeed in the world of fashion with her real-life position as part of the family unit in which she was merely a partner in the enterprise of music? If she really was in control of her destiny, it was just a matter of time before she made the determination that when all was said and done, Father didn't know best. She did.

5
New Frontera

O N JANUARY 27. 1994. SELENA'S biggest dream came true, a dream that ironically had nothing to do with show business and everything to do with her interest in fashion. It was the opening of the Selena, Etc., salon and boutique at 4926 Everhart, a fifties-vintage frame home that had been converted to commercial use after Corpus Christi's biggest shopping centers were built nearby. The shop was everything a girl with an eye for beauty could want, where high-dollar designer fashions—from the creative imagination of one Selena Q. Perez—and personal-care services were the main attractions. Nothing delighted Selena as much as her fashion and design work. The bag full of costume jewelry, glue, pliers, and metal was never far from her reach. On the road, off the road, she was always working on belts, earrings, jackets, stage gear, and casual wear.

The fashion game fired her up. Marcella noted that opening up a place of her own had been a dream of Selena's since she was a little girl. "She can do whatever she sets her mind to." Selena put it another way. "I want to do something outside of the music business to see whether I'm *un poquito inteligente,*" Selena said. Her entrée was Martin Gómez, a fashion designer from the Rio Grande Valley. Martin had her figured out. Selena looked up to Martin because he had a degree in fashion design. Martin was charmed by Selena because her heart was in the right place, even though she had little background in formal design training and she lacked business acumen. Before she started her business, he said later, Selena would go to Victoria's Secret and buy a bra for thirty dollars and glue on baubles, then sell the finished product for twenty dollars. Martin taught her to make them for ten dollars and sell them for fifty.

Her nonperforming interests were so time-consuming that she was more than happy to delegate some responsibilities to Yolanda Saldivar. For three years, she'd done an excellent job with the fan club, boosting membership to more than four thousand, organizing special events, helping Selena deal with admirers at public events, all the while earning the trust of Selena and her family as no outsider ever had. Yolanda impressed everyone with her commitment and passion. Over the past year Yolanda and Selena had become close friends. So when the announcement was made that Selena was designating Yolanda manager of her clothing boutiques in Corpus Christi and San Antonio, signing Yolanda on as the registered agent when Selena registered the company at the Bexar County courthouse, no one was surprised.

They shared the common bond of being bent on promoting the name *Selena*. They had become so tight that in late 1993 Yolanda quit her nursing job to move to Corpus, to be closer to Selena. "She just inspired me with her talent, her motivation," Saldivar told the Dallas *Morning News*. "She gives her whole to you." Yolanda's devotion was unfailing, bordering on the obsessive. Her bedroom at her parents' house in south San Antonio was covered with Selena posters and pictures, burning votive candles, and a library of Selena videos on the shelves to entertain guests, who were often given Selena water bottles or bumper stickers as a memento of their visit.

Being part of Selena's organization gave Yolanda a

sense of worth she'd never had. Her position made her a very important person. If someone wanted to get to Selena, he'd often have to go through Yolanda. She knew well enough when to be discreet and when to divulge personal information, such as Selena's phone and beeper numbers. She was more than willing to accommodate Selena at all times, whether it was helping to direct traffic backstage, give her a comforting neck massage, or assist her in selecting her stage wardrobe. The brush with celebrity was a heady experience for the ex-ROTC woman who knew too well what it was like to be a wallflower. "God, if only I was like Selena," she once cooed to a boutique employee.

In exchange for her services, Yolanda won a free ticket to the high life in the form of the American Express card that Selena had given her to conduct company business. With it, she could rent Lincoln Town Cars and entertain associates in fancy restaurants. She traveled to Mexico and carried two cellular phones. She bought Ellen Tracy designer jackets and took them to Selena's design house to be altered.

Yolanda derived her power from Selena. Selena got Yolanda's undying support. Others might have seen it differently, but the two developed a strong personal and professional relationship. Yolanda called her *m'ija*, my daughter. Selena called her Buffy; she was her buffer between the rest of the world and her. Yolanda wanted only the best for her boss, once mentioning her wistful desire to buy her a chair made of crystal. But such a gift was so impractical, an employee told her. And if one existed, why, it must cost at least $100,000.

"I have it," Yolanda replied, straightfaced.

The Selena, Etc., shop that opened in Corpus Christi and the one that opened eight months later in San Antonio were the only projects in Selena's life that weren't controlled by her father, or so Selena believed. If she couldn't be there to run things, Yolanda, her loyal assistant, would take care of it. She was there when Selena needed her, helping out, of course, but also boosting Selena's confidence as a businesswoman and a person.

On several occasions, Selena talked about wanting to take Yolanda on the road with her, but she didn't receive much encouragement. Both Manolo Gonzalez and José Behar at EMI Latin recommended that Abraham hire a professional to support Selena on tour. Yolanda may have been loyal, they said, but she didn't have the skills required for heavy-duty road work. Gómez didn't think she had the skills for retail, either.

The relationship started falling apart as soon as Yolanda became a business associate. One of the first things she did in the office was trade desks with Gómez without asking. His was much bigger, and she needed it to run the company. "I never got along with her from the beginning," Gómez told Cristina Saralegui. "She was always perfect when Selena was around, but when she was gone, she treated everyone terribly.

"Everything was great at first. Working with Selena was great. But when things got busy, [Selena] said that we would have to get somebody to manage the place. Yolanda couldn't do anything."

The music part of Selena's life was taking on worldly dimensions, with Los Dinos making their debuts in New York, Los Angeles, Argentina, and Puerto Rico. It didn't matter where they went, Selena knew how to read the audience, doing merengues in the Dominican Republic, going crazy with *cumbias* and *charangas* in Colombia, and playing that good old country music and American pop when she went back to places like Lake Jackson.

Off the road, she focused on her clothesline and boutique projects while keeping her 34–24–36 figure and her *pompas* trim. In her spare time she shopped. From her house on Bloomington, it was a quick hop down Old Brownsville Road or West Point to the expressway and the retail wonderland crowded alongside it. The Wal-Mart was the beginning of a five-mile-long shopping tour, followed by the K-mart, various power centers anchored by Target, Bookstop, Builder's Square, Circuit City, and Craig's Record Factory on the south side of the freeway, and the promised land of consumer consumption across South Padre Island Drive via Staples—the Padre Staples Mall, which was adjacent to Raintree Plaza and Sunrise Mall. If there was any single reason for downtown Corpus to be so dead, Padre Staples and the surrounding environs was it.

And now Selena had one of the swankiest stores in the 'hood.

"I decided to blaze new paths in the world of fashion," she said. "Also, I don't think it's good to have your money squirreled away in a bank, not doing anybody any good. You have to work and create jobs for people. For that reason, what I earn with my concerts, I like to invest in my stores. Also, I've always had a passion for fashion. For this reason, these shops are my dream come true. I hope to grow as an *empresaria*."

The boutique on Everhart was both a business and a plaything. Whenever Selena needed pampering, she'd bop over to the shop for a manicure, a facial, or a new hairdo. She loved showing up at the shop *sans* makeup, her hair mussed up, and wearing jeans. No one recognized her in the shop without her bustier and game face. She derived great pleasure from watching customers ogle the pictures of her, listening to them ask employees what Selena was really like.

Chris and Selena hosted barbecues for the band and crew in the yard. But it was the simple pleasures that they enjoyed most. "For me, an ideal day is when I'm in jeans around my house. I like to clean my own house. I clean the walls, mop the floor, wash the car, and wash the dog. I make up my bed and I even cook sometimes, but the truth is, I'm not too good at it. But, well, that's why they invented home pizza delivery. Fortunately, I have a husband who isn't all macho and helps me with the household chores."

With endorsements, performance fees, and record royalties, her whole family appeared to be walking in high cotton, able to afford luxuries never before imagined. For Selena, that meant a sporty black BMW (which was stolen, dumped in the ocean, and later replaced by a red Porsche Targa), a motorcycle, an aquarium headboard for her bedroom, more Fabergé eggs for her collection, and the latest production gear, instruments, and accessories for her band. Those trappings lent credibility to her image as a role model, a position she used to visit schools and urge students to get an education and to warn them about the pitfalls of drugs and alcohol. "Everyone wanted to be like Selena," said Jessica Benítez, a longtime friend. "Everyone wanted to be the kind of daughter she was, the kind of wife, singer, performer, and person she was. She expressed confidence in herself and in her heritage."

She also apparently couldn't be stopped. Her second Astrodome rodeo appearance, on February 28, 1994, with Ram Herrera, drew a crowd in excess of sixty thousand people, establishing another record for a Tejano act. Two days later, in Los Angeles, she won a Grammy award for Best Mexican-American album for the *Live* album, although Selena acted more like a fan than an award winner, snapping photographs of stars.

In March, she topped *Billboard*'s Hot Latin Tracks chart for the second time. Again, the achievement was accomplished as a duet partner, this time with the Barrio Boyzz, the popular new harmony group signed to SBK, Selena's record label for the projected English-language crossover. The song "Dondequiera que Estés" stayed at the top of the chart for more than a month.

On March 13, she practically owned the Tejano Music Awards. The event, which had moved from the San Antonio Convention Center Arena into the newly completed Alamodome, attracted an audience of more than twenty-five thousand Tejano aficionados to a star-studded evening that included a performance by Selena y los Dinos and numerous trips for her to the podium to accept awards for Female Vocalist, Female Entertainer, Best International Artist, and Album of the Year.

Pete Astudillo was leaving Selena's band to go solo, opening shows with his band Oxygeno for Los Dinos. But his presence was still felt on *Amor Prohibido*, Selena's fifth album for EMI Latin, which was released in April. The album, which was recorded at Manny Guerra's studio in San Antonio and engineered by Manny's house engineer, Brian "Red" Moore, covered the waterfront with the stuff of which a supergroup is made, touching all the right bases and moving writer Ramiro Burr to declare her "the artist to watch in the 90s." The album alternately rocked, sizzled, and simmered while paying just enough lip service to roots to maintain a sense of balance. The most compelling tunes were the ones aimed at the Spanish-international market: "Techno Cumbia," which honored the most popular rhythm coursing through the Latin music world while updating it with vocal samples, second line drumming from New Orleans, and horn charts inspired by soca from the Caribbean; "Amor Prohibido," a perfect pop *cumbia* with a descending keyboard hook (the song was inspired by Selena's grandmother and grandfather, whose romance defied the boundaries between separate stratas of society in Mexico); and "Bidi Bidi Bom Bom," the second song with Selena's name listed as a composer, which matched nonsensical lyrics about a boy who makes a girl's heart go *thump-thump-thump* with a catchy, instantly hummable melody. Young rockers could identify with "Fotos y Recuerdos" (Pictures and Memories), which took the melody of the New Wave act the Pretenders, with Chris Perez's guitar lead emulating the style of the deceased Pretender James Honeyman-Scott, and cobbled it onto Spanish lyrics written by Ricky Vela.

The two nods to the past were "No Me Queda Más," a Ricky Vela original that riffed off romantic boleros popular for decades on both sides of the border and showcased Selena's vocal range and control; and "Tus Deprecios," a collaboration by A.B. Quintanilla and Ricky Vela that was the album's one nod to conjunto, where Tejano music came from, with Johnny Sáenz's trilling accordion serving as the song's signature.

The album's contemporary outlook revealed the growing generational split in Tejano. "You have to cater to today's Tejano," contended Ramon Hernandez. "It's a more sophisticated Hispanic now. We don't have to dig into our origins or roots."

Sales were unprecedented. The album lingered at the top of *Billboard*'s Latin top-fifty album charts at the number-one or number-two position for the rest of the year. By December, it was certified quadruple platinum, which in the Tejano field translated to four hundred thousand units sold, a figure exceeded only by La Mafia. She was the real deal now, with a full-blown stage show that featured a full-time conga man, Art Meza, two keyboards, and two vocal harmonists and dancers, Rock 'n' Roll James and Don Shelton. Chris put some sonic bite in Los Dinos' sound, lifting them out of the wimpiness that detractors blamed on the polka and Latin pop in general and putting them on equal footing with the best rock ensembles in the United States. He had finally come to be accepted by Selena's family, and even partied with Abraham. His leads were part of the package.

At the *Billboard* Latin Music Awards in Miami, held May 18, Selena won the best regional-Mexican album category for *Selena Live*, as well as best regional-Mexican female artist. On the following day, at the Premio lo Nuestro a la Musica Latina awards ceremonies, also in Miami, she walked away with Best Female Vocalist in the regional-Mexican category. In late May, the title track from *Amor Prohibido* hovered at number three on the Hot Latin Tracks chart in *Billboard* and the band was headlining a big show at Randy's Ballroom in San Antonio.

In Los Angeles, Dawn Soler was dreaming of Selena. Soler, a senior vice president at PolyGram Music, had heard about her from a colleague, was impressed with her music, and recommended her to Toby Emmerich, the executive vice president of music at New Line Cinema. Emmerich was looking for someone to sing traditional Mexican songs with a mariachi for a new film he was working on, starring Marlon Brando, Faye Dunaway, and Johnny Depp. Even though Selena was hardly experienced in that musical form, she again rose to the occasion, filming a cameo and recording what was asked for. "She just came on the set and made friends of everyone," Soler recalled. "She talked with Brando for an hour and then sang beautifully in a style that wasn't hers."

José Hernández, the director of Mariachi del Sol de México, who had backed Selena, came away impressed. He led the top mariachi in L.A., which helped land him a gig as musical director for pop singer Linda Ronstadt's mariachi tribute, *Canciones de Mi Padre*. Dawn Soler had tracked down Hernández and helped get his mariachi signed for the music in the movie. In March, Hernández found a young female vocalist named Nydia Rojas in Los Angeles to record scratch tracks for the movie. Three months later, he was introduced to Selena, who'd been contracted to sing and appear as a guest artist. They would film two scenes at the Biltmore Hotel in Los Angeles, with Selena lip-synching to the scratch tracks of the other vocalist while she and the mariachi band pretended to be playing on a balcony above the restaurant where Johnny Depp's character was in the process of seducing a beautiful young woman. The band and the singer were both decked out in *ranchera* outfits, Selena the picture of a Mexican songbird, all ruffles and flourishes.

The voice Selena was singing along with haunted her. It was really good. "How old is this singer?" she asked Hernández.

"Fourteen," he replied.

A look of shock and intimidation swept over her face. "Oh my God, she's got a *huge* voice." Almost as big as Selena's own. One evening during the shoot Selena and Chris drove to El Monte, where Hernández ran the Cielito Lindo supper club where the featured entertainment was the Mariachi del Sol. Alvaro Torres, with whom Selena had had an international hit on the duet "Buenos Amigos," was there with his wife enjoying dinner when he spied Selena and her husband walking in. Torres got up to sing with the mariachi, then invited Selena to sing.

"She was all nervous because she said she didn't know

a mariachi song all the way through," José Hernández said.

But Selena faked it so well, threading her way through "Tú Sólo Tú," she brought the house down before sitting down to enjoy her meal with Chris.

Back on the set, Hernández and Selena filmed another scene in which they and the mariachi musicians surround the table where Marlon Brando's character is dining with his wife, played by Faye Dunaway, in the same restaurant, when Brando impulsively waxes romantic. On the set, Hernández was also introduced to Selena's personal assistant, Yolanda Saldivar. "She seemed like a person who was there totally to help with anything Selena needed," he recalled.

Although Yolanda accompanied Selena to Los Angeles, both José Behar and Manolo Gonzalez advised against bringing her on the road. Neither Selena nor Yolanda protested too loudly. The Corpus boutique was up and running, and in September, the second Selena, Etc., salon and boutique opened in San Antonio. The store, at 3703 Broadway, was in one of the chichiest retail strips in the city, on the edge of Brackenridge Park and a stone's throw from the Witte Museum. The music successes were shared with the family; the shops were hers and hers alone. Both Selena and her manager had their hands full.

She didn't let on when dealing with the public. She showed the sort of blissful ignorance that made her life seem effortless in many respects. Albert Huerta, the attorney and business manager of Johnny Canales, cornered Selena during a taping of the *Johnny Canales Show*. It was another packed house at the Bayfront, and Huerta couldn't believe that a homegirl was responsible for the crowd.

"Selena," he said backstage, "you haven't been recognized in Corpus Christi. Why don't we present a special appreciation concert at Johnnyland [Canales's outdoor music stage on the edge of Corpus]. I can arrange for the city council to recognize you, give you the key to the city."

She smiled vacantly at Huerta. "I like it." She sighed. "But talk to my dad."

Her dad, her dad, it was always her dad. She was a full-grown adult now, but she always deferred to Dad. It was part of the deal—all for one, one for all—but sometimes it felt stifling. Thank goodness she had her design house and boutiques. Dad had no say in that part of her world.

On one occasion, Selena confided to Manolo Gonzalez, EMI's chief in San Antonio, about feeling constrained by her father's overprotectiveness, that it felt like he was cramping her style. Gonzalez sat her down and tried to comfort her.

"Selena, think of a beautiful little bird in a golden cage, trying to get out," he told her. "And there's this big old cat, licking his chops, crouched below the cage, waiting to eat her up. The bird just wants to get out. It doesn't know there's a cat down there. But there's someone watching over her, just in case."

Selena lit up and reached across the table to hug Gonzalez. "You got it, Manolo."

On June 11, *Amor Prohibido* knocked Gloria Estefan's *Mi Tierra* from the top of the *Billboard* Latin 50, after that album had spent forty-eight weeks atop the chart. On the previous week, the single "Amor Prohibido" hit number one on the Hot Latin Tracks chart, where it stayed for nine weeks. The video, in which Selena wore Chris's shirts, was filmed at Joshua Tree monument in the desert of Southern California. That was followed by a four-day video shoot for "No Me Queda Más," shot on location with the San Antonio Symphony by Sean Roberts. A film of the making of the video captured Selena being powdered between scenes and saying, "They're putting *más* powder on me because I have very oily skin. That's why we're coming out with the Selena line of makeup, ha ha ha."

On July 28, Selena y los Dinos played the Mosquito Festival in Clute, near Lake Jackson, in front of an enthusiastic crowd of ten thousand. It was a triumphant return of the whole Quintanilla family to their old stomping grounds, fresh on the heels of appearances at Houston's International Ballroom and the Acapulco Festival '94 in June, which was broadcast worldwide on Spanish television. Everyone turned out to see and hear the little L.J. girl who had gone from singing in her daddy's restaurant to singing in domed stadiums. But for thirteen-year-old Maricela García, it was more than that. The blind girl knew many of Selena's songs by heart and competed in talent contests singing her music. Before the show, Maricela said, "I can't see her, but I want to touch her." Selena got the message and came out to meet the girl, taking her hand and letting her feel the texture of the black leather motorcycle jacket she was wearing.

For one old friend, Meredith Lynn Cappel, it was a renewal of a friendship that had broken off years ago. "A friend of mine who's from Mexico saw her on Univisión and she told me about this girl named Selena," Cappel said. "I couldn't believe it. We hadn't spoken in all those years." The Selena she saw on the stage was nothing like the girl who was her closest pal in elementary school. The outfits she wore were almost embarrassingly provocative. The music she performed was different from the music Meredith had heard her sing before. After the concert, Meredith Lynn worked her way toward the stage, where she handed Suzette snapshots taken of Selena and herself as children. "Please, I've got to see her, just to say hi." Suzette had heard the line before on many occasions, but this time she believed it. "Wow, you really do know her."

Suzette took her hand and guided her to the touring bus parked behind the stage, leaving Meredith's husband and daughter trapped behind in a sea of fans. It was a strange sensation for Meredith Lynn. Never before had she seen so many Mexicans at a single gathering. But she was determined to say hello and ran the gauntlet of security guards, backstage passes, and controlled access areas to do so.

Just as she was about to board the bus, the door opened and Selena jumped out excitedly to give Meredith Lynn a long hug.

"My best friend! My best friend!" Selena yelled for Marcella to come quick. "Mama, Mama, don't you remember my best friend from third grade?" The two sat down at a table and commenced to yak about old times.

"She remembered so much more than me," Meredith Lynn said. "I was just in a daze. My best friend from third grade and here she is this grown woman, all foo-fooed up, and I kept saying to myself, 'I don't know this Selena.' "

"Tell me about your music," Cappel asked.

"No, no, I don't want to bore you with all of that," Selena said. She was more interested in hearing about what had happened with all the kids in the old neighborhood.

"It was like another life she had," remembered Meredith Lynn. "It's really neat how down-to-earth she was and how she didn't forget her friends. She grew up with parents that were struggling, just like everybody else. We wore the same clothes every day—I guess we were in the lower class. We had so much in common. Our birthdays were a day apart. Same background. She didn't take that for granted."

"I can't believe you're the same person as on TV," Meredith Lynn said over and over.

Selena just laughed and laughed.

The laughter continued as Meredith Lynn's photographs of little Selena the tomboy were passed around to family, band, and crew. Selena introduced her mother, Marcella, and her husband, Chris. Meredith Lynn was nonplussed.

"My first impression was, 'You're married?' " she said. "I was looking at him and he was just not the person I would have thought she would hook up with. He was just a regular old guy, same age as all of us. I wasn't impressed with him, but I didn't have any negative thoughts, either. He just laid back on the couch and was laughing at the pictures just like any other Joe. I guess I shouldn't have expected her to marry some big fancy TV star.''

Reminiscing, Selena told Meredith Lynn she still had the stuffed koala bear she'd given her for her ninth birthday. Meredith Lynn told Selena she'd been a cheerleader in eighth grade.

"Oh, you're so lucky!" Selena responded.

"I think she missed her high school," Meredith Lynn said afterward. "I just assumed that she was the most beautiful, popular girl in her school and I guess it just never happened. I wish that I had shut up and found out what she had done in high school, but somehow I don't think she wanted to talk about it. If Selena had stayed in Lake Jackson, she probably would have been our class president. But even if she didn't pursue her career, I think someone would have found her. I don't think there's anything else she could have done but sing. I've never in my life heard someone sing as beautifully as she does.

"It just struck me funny that she was on all these Mexican stations and she did Mexican-speaking songs, because I know she wasn't raised Mexican. But she never talked about her music beyond my asking her about those songs—she told me 'Bidi Bidi Bom Bom' was about a schoolgirl crush and every time the guy would walk by her heart would palpitate, *bidi bidi bom bom*. I told her I wished she'd sing it so most of us would understand it.

"I asked her about the music awards and she was just like, 'Let's talk about us, let's talk about what we did as kids.' It wasn't important; she was so down-to-earth. She didn't let it go to her head and brag. I guess that's why everybody likes her so much. Her concert was so upbeat—old people, young people, everybody was dancing. It's so easy to like her music because it makes you feel so good. She really put on a show."

Meredith Lynn finally found her husband and daughter and introduced them to Selena, then tried to let Selena get back to business. "You've got all these people to see. We have to go so you can attend to your fans."

"Please don't go," Selena begged.

Selena passed along her addresses, her phone and pager numbers, everything, so she could renew her friendship.

The next day they talked on the phone, and again a few weeks later. Selena told about getting mobbed at a local mall that day—"I can't believe anybody would recognize me down here!" she exclaimed to Meredith Lynn—where she bought a set of cow-patterned dishes, and she talked about her dream of building a big house out in the country, a white house with a white fence, with horses and cows. "You'll have to come visit me and our kids will grow up together."

The renewal of an old friendship made the day-to-day exploits of the career girl a little easier to handle, especially the occasional rough bumps. San Antonio photographer John Dyer had Selena booked for another photo shoot for *Texas Monthly* a month after Mosquito Fest. Fitting it into her schedule was almost impossible. She arrived at the studio practically panting, coming off three days of doing commercials in San Antonio and on her way to Corpus Christi the next day, then on to New York. The most she could give Dyer was two hours. But despite the fatigue and the rushed pace, when Dyer opened the shutter, Selena gave him what he asked for.

"Her dad was there," Dyer said. "He was cool. He was friendly. He didn't come in throwing his weight around. We had a little bit of a problem with makeup again. She showed up with makeup already on and I asked if we could take it off. She shook her head. She said, 'No way.' She was very conscious of her stage image.

"I intentionally wanted to do something contemplative, not smiling or mugging. But I think I set the scene a little too quietly and she let down and let the fatigue get her."

After the shoot, Abraham approached Dyer away from everyone else. "I was standing there watching you and you didn't make her smile," he said.

In August, shortly after Selena hosted a charity softball game against disc jockeys in San Antonio, the Los Angeles *Times* recognized the growing clout of Tejano music in Southern California with a three-page feature story. The coverage preceded a concert in which she was co-billed with the Barrio Boyzz at the Universal Amphitheater; the event filled three-quarters of the house and was highlighted by José Behar presenting Selena and Abraham with a platinum record for *Amor Prohibido*. L.A. harbored the largest Hispanic population in the United States, but Tejano acts had yet to make inroads. There might have been enclaves of Mexican-Americans with Texas ties scattered throughout Southern California, but if a Spanish song wasn't a hit in Mexico, it wouldn't be a hit in Los Angeles. The current flavor appealing to Mexican tastes in California was a quirky sound called *banda*, a hyperspeed send-up of traditional Mexican brass bands from the thirties that included a tuba to hold down the rhythm. The sound bore a striking resemblance to British ska music and had very little in common with Tejano. Strange as it seems, Selena had an easier time getting airplay in Miami than in L.A. Sooner or later, though, she'd break into L.A., even if it meant coming in the back door through Mexico.

At the Universal Amphitheater show, writer Greg Barrios hooked up with Selena again. He hadn't seen her perform in eight years and was struck by how much had changed. "It was all very orchestrated, very different. Before the show, she was ensconced in the inner sanctum, lots of security, and I had to be pushed through all that. There were a lot of people in there, and finally I was introduced. We talked for ten minutes at the most, and half of that was picture-taking. Then I went outside and there were all the band members—no one knew them in Los Angeles, they were nobodies. I recognized A.B. and we had a long talk; I told him when I knew him, asked him about the English-language album and how he was going to do it, about what he was going to do and what he wasn't going to do because he was in competition with other producers. Then I found the sister and we talked about Texas, and Crystal City, and the Spinach Festival, and when she'd been there last.

"Lurking in the corner of the room is this guy with curly hair who is slowly getting very drunk and hanging around with another guy, sixteen or seventeen years old, who is also getting pretty drunk."

Barrios approached the curly-haired kid. "Are you Chris?" he asked.

"Yeah," Chris replied bashfully.

"I loved your guitar solos on the last album," Barrios told him.

Chris lit up and smiled.

"It was like you had given him an injection of vitamins, bringing him out of that depressive mood," Barrios said. "And then we found out we had gone to the same high school and he opened up, talked about his relationship with his wife and where he stood."

Afterward, a friend that Barrios had brought along said the writing was on the wall. "I don't see this marriage lasting more than one year."

"You're absolutely right," Barrios concurred.

The Universal concert was an eye-opener for Barrios. "I couldn't get over how powerful her voice was. It was no longer a little-girl-sounding voice. She did this fabulous thing with a young man and practically seduced him onstage. It was a little more like Julie London—it wasn't trashy, it wasn't bad-girl, it was tease. It was a song where you've got this in-between thing between the man and woman about love and relationship, and she comes on, answering it, saying, Who needs these men? She was dominating and the crowd loved it. One of the back-up singers was one of the Barrio Boyzz, Freddie Correa, who told me backstage that he was going to do a solo album and A.B. was going to produce it." The show closed with an encore of two songs from the set list, "Bidi Bidi Bom Bom" and "Amor Prohibido."

The recognition kept coming. The September issue of *Texas Monthly* magazine cited Selena as one of the twenty most important Texans of 1994. Coca-Cola honored her with a limited-edition eight-ounce commemorative contour bottle of Coca-Cola with Selena's signature and a label stating 5 AÑOS CONTIGO . . . SIEMPRE SELENA, SIEMPRE COCA-COLA (Five Years with You . . . Always Selena, Always Coca-Cola). Forty-nine hundred cases of bottles were produced and distributed throughout Texas and New Mexico in October, and they sold out almost instantly. She had a deal with the Dep Corporation to shill for their Agree Shampoo and contracted to do commercials for Southwestern Bell's Call Notes voice-mail system.

At a flea market in San Antonio, Abraham ran into his old Lake Jackson acquaintance Primo Ledesma, the disc jockey who had played Selena's first record. He could see that Abraham was finally enjoying the spoils from pushing his kids into music. Selena, as ever, was his pride and joy. "He was telling me about a deal he had cut for her to have one of the lead roles in *Dos Mujeres, un Camino* [a popular *telenovela* in Mexico], worth something like twenty million. But that didn't work out, I don't know why. I heard it had something to do with Erik Estrada, something like he didn't like the idea of having her as a wife." (Selena did film a cameo in Monterrey in the spring of 1994 that lasted two episodes. She had romantic scenes with the handsome *regiomontano* Ramiro Delgado, from the popular music group Bronco, and her leather-clad derriere was prominently shown climbing over a railing at a rodeo arena. She was also negotiating to be one of the stars in a new *telenovela* produced by Emilio Larrosa, scheduled to begin airing in the fall of 1995.) "He told me about the Coca-Cola deal. She would get twenty thousand just to walk across a room and say, 'I like Coke,' or whatever, for a Coke commercial."

The Coke connection had in many respects been more important in developing the band than EMI Latin was. The financial and tour support made her a recognizable face in Latino communities in the United States. The image sold, too. So well that the bottler kept her signed and working even after 1992, when Coke strategists dropped celebrities from the ad campaigns, keeping only Selena,

Elton John for Diet Coke, and Christopher Cross for Sprite. Hispanic marketing worked differently from Anglo marketing. And the marketing folks at Coke felt she was a valuable commodity. "We didn't want to step away from someone so successful. So instead of shooting commercials we shifted emphasis to posters and point-of-sale displays," said Coke's Diana Garza. "Where it was different was where her star started to rise. She would cause a stir whenever she'd show up for a Coca-Cola road trip. People from other parts of the country were asking for her."

The buzz on Tejano was spreading fast. Two new syndicated television programs, *Puro Tejano* and *Tejano Country*, joined the blitz, showcasing music videos and reaching an international audience with broadcasts in almost every major market in the United States and numerous foreign countries. But Selena was already two steps ahead, having cracked the international market in a big way and on her own terms, finally without a famous duet partner. The vehicle was "Bidi Bidi Bom Bom," whose catchy title lyrics made for a song hook that grabbed and wouldn't let go. The song zoomed up the Latin charts domestically and abroad so convincingly that Abraham insisted to Manuel Dávila it was going to be a crossover hit on its own, even if it wasn't in English. He cited Z-95, the English-language pop station in Corpus, which was playing the song in heavy rotation.

"You're wrong," Dávila countered. "It's a hit, but it's not a crossover hit. Not yet. Z-95's audience is seventy percent Hispanic. It's in KZFM's interest to play it. Now, if WFIL in Philadelphia is playing it, you're telling me something. When it's in the Anglo radio station's best interest, then it's a crossover."

The fall marked a further increase in momentum, after the second Selena, Etc., boutique opened, on Broadway in San Antonio in September. There was a brief promotional tour of Mexico. She was hailed as *la reina tejana* upon her arrival in Vera Cruz, where she was front-page news, and "Bidi Bidi Bom Bom" inundated the airwaves.

There was also a major concert appearance at the state fair in Dallas, with the up-and-coming act La Diferenzia. Despite Selena's high profile, news coverage of the state fair event focused on the opening act. Abraham was so furious about being upstaged he took it out on promoter Glenn Smith, who was putting together a Cinco de Mayo bill for the following May at Sea World in San Antonio. Emilio and La Diferenzia had already been agreed upon to share the bill, but Abraham told Smith that the deal was off and that his daughter wouldn't perform if La Diferenzia played the show. Smith protested, but Abraham remained adamant. If Sea World wanted his daughter to perform, it would be without La Diferenzia. No one was going to upstage Abraham's Selena.

Coinciding with her expanding fashion empire, the menagerie at her home had grown considerably, with a miniature Doberman, a husky, and two mastiffs joining Pebbles the Pomeranian in the Perez household. The small pool built in the yard was as much for the animals as it was for Chris and Selena. But the house was still owned by Abraham, and living next door to Selena's parents was cramping their style. They had made enough money. They were around family enough on the road. It was time to start looking for a place of their own. Someday in the not-too-distant future, Selena and Chris would be heads of their own household.

In September, Abraham finally got serious about getting the band out of his house and upgrading the whole operation. Doing business with two answering machines wasn't cutting it anymore. With increasing frequency, callers to either number couldn't leave messages because both machines were already filled to capacity with messages regarding Los Dinos business. As one employee saw it, "He had an arena act and he was still treating it like a weekend dance-hall band."

Eddie's Paint and Body Shop, at 5410 Leopard, was designated the new home of Q Productions, Q Studios, and Selena's Design House. A more anonymous location couldn't have been selected. A metal-sided building on an industrial strip adjacent to the Greyhound R.V. and trailer park, across the street from a café and topless bar, the new headquarters would not be confused with Music Row. But it satisfied the Quintanillas' requirements just fine. It wasn't the outside they were concerned about.

Eddie Quintanilla directed construction of the new Q empire facilities. He embarked on a crash course in building studios by studying copies of *Mix* magazine and learning about acoustics at the library. A thirty-two-track Pro Tascam automated studio console with twenty-four-track head stacks, one of only a handful that existed, was purchased from Hermes Music, which operated music stores in the Valley and San Antonio. A studio engineer, Ron Loccarini, was brought in to help put the studio together. Although Eddie had not been versed in the nuances of studio construction, Loccarini was impressed with what had been done. He would merely add icing to the cake.

"I want the best," Abraham said. "Can you do it?"

Loccarini signed on and started wiring the entire studio.

"He let me buy every piece of equipment to make it the best facility around," he recalled. "He spent over $130,000 just on effects and microphones." The gear included Summit tube preamps, Focusrite preamps and EQ, Lexicon 480L Reverb, Genelec 1038 A monitors that cost $10,000 apiece, a pair of 1031A studio reference nearfield monitors, valued at $14,000 apiece, and a centerpiece 1959 Neumann tube vocal microphone, priced at $4,500.

It was a mad dash buying and setting up the equipment and testing and analyzing the room's acoustics. Two days before Thanksgiving, the groundwork paid off when José Hernández, the director of Mariachi del Sol de México, flew to Corpus to oversee Selena's vocal overdubs at the new Q-Zone Studios. With Yolanda by her side, making sure she had everything she needed, including her Slim-Fast diet drink, Selena christened the state-of-the-art facilities with music as down-home as it got in Corpus. She might have been hesitant, knowing as little as she did about *rancheras*, but she had an innate feeling for what Hernández called the most passionate of all Latin styles, the Mexican version of singing the blues. "When I heard her voice, I couldn't believe the wide range of styles she could cover," he said. "Linda [Ronstadt] has a very strong voice, but Selena has this certain feeling about her. Personally, I thought she captured the soul of the music. I'm sure she had heard these songs before." The experience jazzed her to the point that she told Hernández she wanted to do an album of nothing but mariachi someday. "Amalia Mendoza's songs would fit you perfect," he told her.

Initially, Hernández thought his biggest challenge of the sessions would be making sure Selena's Spanish pronunciation was on the money. The record company had leaned on Selena before to sing proper Spanish, a problem common to many Tejanos, whose casual Spanish was considered rather crude compared with the Spanish spoken in the interior of Mexico. Then religion entered the picture in the form of a disagreement about lyrics. Selena was overdubbing vocals for "Siempre Hace Frío," a song that the movie soundtrack producers had requested be added. Once again, Hernández had Nydia Rojas do the scratch vocal track, which he brought with him to Corpus Christi.

Abraham objected. "Selena can't sing that song," he told Hernández. Their contract was for only four songs, and this addition would make it five, he pointed out.

Hernández assured him that the technicality would be taken care of.

"That isn't the problem," Abraham replied. "There's certain words in there that are against her beliefs." He cited the word *adore*. There was also a problem with the phrase—roughly translated—"If he doesn't come back, kill me, sky, eat me, dirt, take me, Jesus."

"She can't do it. José, you gotta understand."

Hernández removed *adore* and replaced "take me, Jesus" with the line, "I want to die."

That led to hours of deep discussion with Abraham about God, Jesus, and religion. "Hey, *compadre*, bring me the Bible," he shouted out. With the Good Book in hand, Abraham began to talk theology.

"He was trying to convince me there was no Holy Spirit, that Jesus is just a teacher," said Hernández, himself a born-again Christian. "He said, 'Before you get out of here, I'm gonna convert you.' He was trying to explain his beliefs and what he thinks about life after death, who he thinks Jesus was. It was really deep. A lot of people see him as a hard business guy, but I know how strong his beliefs are—so strong he tried to convince me."

Hernández left Corpus believing the same things he had when he arrived. But he also realized that both Abraham and Selena shared a deep spirituality he'd rarely seen before. Neither was a member of the Jehovah's Witnesses. As long as Selena pranced around the stage in clothes that were provocative and revealing, she couldn't be accepted into the faith. Bustiers and bare midriffs did not qualify as the sort of modest dress required of women of the church. But that didn't stop them from believing God's kingdom was an actual government ruling in heaven that would soon return to earth to bring back the original state of paradise. The world as it was known would soon end in "great tribulation," with wickedness and suffering ended forever. Only the chosen 144,000 would be taken to heaven with God, according to the Bible, their spirit bodies resurrected in order to live there. Eternal life required obedience to Jehovah and faith in Jesus' sacrifice. Meanwhile, on earth, they believed the Bible set the moral standards.

Membership in the sect numbered more than four million worldwide, with new members recruited through the Bibles that the Jehovah's Witnesses paid for and distributed, and through the *Watchtower*, a periodical with a circulation of fifteen million that was sometimes sold door-to-door or on the streets. Each Kingdom Hall of the faith was presided over by elders, male members who, after meeting certain qualifications, worked as a whole. The Quintanillas believed in all this and weren't shy about saying so whenever someone asked.

• • • •

After the overdubbing for the mariachi scenes in *Don Juan de Marco* was finished, Selena hit the road again. Touring had become more comfortable over the years. With Abe focusing more and more on business affairs, he traveled less and less with the band, which loosened up the organization. Still, one-nighters were tough to endure. She performed at a festival in Monterrey filmed by the *Siempre en Domingo* variety show, the most-watched television program in Latin America. But it was the performance she had the following week in San Antonio that filled her with more butterflies and apprehension than she had had since Papa Gayo's. Her apprehension in taking the stage at HemisFair Arena had nothing to do with the small turnout—under three thousand—and everything to do with the knowledge that she wasn't just doing a concert, she was headlining a fashion show featuring her design line. The event was the kickoff of the first Tejano Music and Media Conference, held at the Institute of Texan Cultures. In a newspaper review the next day, fashion writer Rose Mary Budge described Selena as "cool, calm, and collected modeling a sensational ivory-brocade gown." Selena described herself otherwise during a backstage interview, telling Budge, "I'm always scared to death when I walk down the runway. I mean, what if I trip, or stumble or something. So I always walk just as fast as I can, to get it over with. It's completely different when I'm singing—I'm never nervous then."

Selena was up-front with Budge about her passion. "I probably would have been a designer if I hadn't gone into entertaining. I've always loved fashion. It was my dream to produce a line of clothing like this, but I was always too busy. Then I met Martin and everything clicked," she said, referring to Martin Gómez, the San Antonio designer she partnered with. The seventy creations, priced from $30 to $1,500, all bore conspicuous labels that read "Designed by Martin Gómez, Exclusively for Selena."

Budge noted that while Selena was known for her bustiers and outfits so tight they looked like they'd been painted on, her line had something for everyone, including modest and practical pieces. "But glitz and glamour haven't been forgotten. They were evident on the runway, especially when skin-tight gold and silver evening gowns stepped into the spotlight. The models had to take tiny steps and walk like vamps—and the crowd loved every minute.

"Especially pretty on the runway were silk-organza palazzo pants with a sheer matching jacket in a dark-floral print. The jacket floated over a black bra. A silver jacket and sexy, short skirt also got wolf whistles and cheers from the crowd, as did a high-necked black dress that turned out to be backless.

"Their new line is a hit," Budge concluded.

After the fashion show ended, Selena again took the stage, this time with Los Dinos, following opening sets by Culturas and the Barrio Boyzz. The concert attendance was a disappointing 2,500 but the band still delivered, as Ramiro Burr noted: "Although Selena gets all the credit, her success is owed partly to her brother A.B. Quintanilla, who writes some of her songs and has, in recent years, curbed the band's tendency to go overboard with synthesizers." The fashion show was a big boost for both boutiques, since neither was doing much business.

Some longtime Selena acquaintances took umbrage at what they perceived as Yolanda Saldivar's obsession to control who saw Selena and who didn't. "She's weird . . . don't pay any attention to her," Selena told one friend. No one complained too loudly, though, until financial discrepancies with both the fan club and the struggling boutiques surfaced. After medical insurance for stylists and clerks at the Selena, Etc., boutiques had been canceled in the fall, employees questioned the way finances were being handled. Saldivar brushed them off. She'd take care of it, she assured them.

In January 1995, Selena's attractive cousin Debra Ramírez moved from Lake Jackson to work in the boutiques and help Selena prepare for expanding the fashion venture into Mexico. Ramírez quit after a week. She didn't like what she saw. "I wasn't happy with my business arrangements. I wasn't happy with the way things were set up. I had told Yolanda I didn't feel the girls were professional. I noticed they didn't report all their sales for a particular day. I told Yolanda and she told me that it wasn't any of my business. She said, 'I'll take care of that.' ''

One employee Yolanda continued to clash against was Martin Gómez, the designer who actually dreamed up the original fashions that bore Selena's name. Martin thought Yolanda was mismanaging affairs from the start, and the animosity between Yolanda and Gómez grew especially hostile when Selena's fashions were being shown. Bills weren't being paid. Martin accused Yolanda of mutilating or destroying some of his original creations.

Yolanda managed by intimidation. She told the Mexican national seamstresses at the design house they could either leave or side with her. Feeling surrounded by loyalists, Yolanda approached employees in December to donate to the fund she was collecting to buy Selena a gift. Laurie Rothe, an employee at Selena, Etc., in Corpus, called up a local jeweler named Phillip Randolph and told him all the people who worked for Selena wanted to chip in and buy her a ring. A few weeks later, Rothe and Yolanda Saldivar walked up the stairs to Randolph's Custom Jewelers, a second-floor shop at the corner of McArdle and Airline, near the malls in south Corpus Christi. They told him they wanted to commission a ring for Selena. But not just any ring. They wanted an egg-shaped stone, set on a band. Selena collected handcrafted egg designs, a hobby that friends attributed to her birthdate on Easter Sunday in 1971. Randolph gently protested against setting the stone in the band. ''Let me do it as a little footstool and make it look like a pleated cushion, and I'll just drop the egg on there and then cover it with diamonds.'' The design centerpiece would be a white-gold-encrusted egg surrounded by fifty-two little diamonds, totaling about 1.5 carats, set on a fourteen-carat-gold ring. The letter S would be incorporated into the design three times on each side.

Yolanda and Laurie liked the idea. Yolanda returned a

week later, wearing blue jeans and driving a white Cadillac. Randolph gave her a wax design of what the ring would look like, not asking for his usual deposit. "It was for Selena, I thought it would be cool," he said. She kept the wax a little more than a week, taking it to San Antonio to show the employees what it would look like. Randolph began to fret that Saldivar had taken the wax to another jeweler so she could get a better price.

But when she returned to the jeweler on December 28, he knew he had a customer. He quoted her a price, believed to be about $3,000. Cost, he observed, did not seem to be a factor. She left a deposit this time, paying for it with her American Express gold card, with her name embossed above SELENA, ETC., INC.

Two weeks later, when the ring was ready, Yolanda returned in the Cadillac. Her passenger, Selena, waited in the car while her assistant finished business inside. Again Yolanda paid the bill, this time with an American Express card with her name embossed above SELENA'S DESIGN HOUSE.

"She sort of made that a point, not to let Selena know how much it cost and how it was paid for," Randolph said.

As he gazed out the window of the store, he saw Yolanda bring the ring to Selena. "When a woman's hand starts shaking, you know you have done it right. That means they are real nervous and they like it." But the ring didn't fit. Selena, wearing a sweatsuit and running shoes, accompanied Yolanda back upstairs to the shop. Randolph kissed her hand when they met.

"I am proud to meet you." He smiled graciously.

Selena smiled back. She looked around the shop and spied the Fabergé egg book Randolph had been looking through for design ideas.

"Is that my book?" she asked Yolanda.

"No, that's his," Yolanda replied.

"I have the same book," she told Randolph. She proceeded to look over the merchandise in the jewelry cases for the next ten minutes as Randolph sized the ring for her right index finger. "She said everybody would see it because she held the microphone with [that hand] during her performances." The cases were open and jewelry was left for them to check out while Randolph resized the ring. "I was never thinking that somebody might steal something," he said. "It probably wasn't real wise, but nothing was missing." Selena left the store wearing the ring, promising Randolph she'd be back.

Daddy's girl was showing signs of being as shrewd, independent, and street-smart as her father. In a quest to expand her fashion empire, she met Leonard Wong, a San Antonio native of Chinese and Mexican descent, while shooting a commercial for Agree Shampoo.

Wong ran Synergy, Inc., a company he set up to market products by direct sales to the Hispanic community. Inspired by Amway, Avon, and Mary Kay, Wong's Primavida line of shampoos, toothpastes, laundry detergent, skin cream, and other personal-care, cosmetics, and cleaning products were specifically tailored and formulated for Latins, to be sold by Hispanic individuals trying to supplement their incomes.

But Selena came to Wong not because of his sales methods or products but for his reputation for mixing scents. She wanted him to create a perfume with her name on it, though the sales concept appealed to her, too. Selling Selena perfume through Wong's Synergy network was the perfect way to reach her target audience while also helping people earn some extra cash.

" 'How do we go about this?' " Wong recalls her asking. "She told me what she wanted to do. Her two goals were to come out with an English album and to come out with a fragrance, a perfume."

Wong showed Selena a fragrance genealogy chart that is the guide to the first level of formulating a product.

"Don't you worry about a thing." He smiled. "I can make it smell like *menudo*, I can make it smell like *chorizo con huevos*"—sausage and eggs.

"I want a perfume like me," Selena said. "I want a perfume that's strong and yet weak."

The fragrance she was after fell in the fresh-to-floral range, a strong, elegant scent, a descendant by way of Chloë, Charlie, and Giorgio of a classic French scent called Quelques Fleurs. It was in the neighborhood of aldehydic and sweet, with a faint trace of spicy. "We zoned right in on the fresh-to-floral range and then we tried mixing just a little bit of the oriental, as in Shalimar and Opium, to give it more strength," Wong said. The project took the better part of a year, as Wong sent her samples on the road, met her in her shop in Corpus, and stayed in touch by telephone.

Selena would call back with her reaction. "Leonard, this stuff smells like an old lady." "Leonard, this one is too sweet."

Their relationship grew stronger. Wong lined up investors prepared to write checks totaling two million dollars to launch the perfume while Selena took great interest in Wong's sales program. "Selena was very excited about it because she could see that it is a wonderful way to distribute products very inexpensively and to help poor people." She invited Wong and his wife to her fashion shows and signed autographs and T-shirts for them.

Throughout their discussions, she made it very clear to Wong that the venture was hers and hers alone. "Leonard," Selena said, "this is my project. There is no one else involved with me. It isn't a family project, it isn't a corporate project. It's mine."

That made Selena's introduction of Yolanda Saldivar all the more mysterious to Wong. "It was kind of awkward when Yolanda came by herself," Wong said. "We were always like, 'Why?' "

Selena ran her affairs hands-on, trying to oversee personally every detail. She interviewed prospective boutique employees before they were hired. When she was running late to one such interview in San Antonio, she telephoned the interviewee several times on her way, apologizing for her tardiness in such a reassuring manner that the person she was interviewing was no longer nervous by the time Selena arrived.

She could afford to pay attention to detail. Thanks to Abraham's taking care of band business, Selena focused more and more on her beauty line and keeping the boutiques going. Though she made it clear to people like Wong that when it came to fashion, she was running the show, she immediately deferred to Dad when music was involved. He was smart, he knew the players, he knew the moves, he protected her—maybe too much sometimes, but he protected her, even though the job was threatening to overwhelm him. "We were getting calls from Mexico, Puerto Rico, Miami," said Jimmy González, who'd been brought over from La Mafia's organization to manage Q Productions. "Eddie, Abraham, and I would sit at the end of the evening, looking at each other and saying, 'How are we going to handle it?' "

Sometimes Selena protected Abraham. When she and Chris began to talk about moving out of Molina, Abraham took her to Manuel Dávila's house in Ingleside, on Corpus Christi Bay. The Dávilas were happy to show their honored guest around their Mediterranean-style home, especially since Manuel and Abraham went way back.

"She was dressed real attractively, she had on a nice dress, she had her makeup on all nice, she was being reserved like she always was," Dávila said. But he could tell she was getting incensed over the way Dávila was talking to his old music *compadre*.

"I said something to him like, 'You're fat, you're ugly.' All of a sudden, she changed. She was this little girl, very proper. 'Ah, Mr. Dávila, this is my father you're talking about.' "

The last piece of the studio puzzle fell into place after Christmas. Ron Loccarini, the acting studio engineer, was encountering problems operating the console. He spoke English and the bands were singing in Spanish. A.B. was producing a band called Eclipse, whose singer was having difficulties phrasing correctly. "The kid wasn't getting it right," said Loccarini. "I could see A.B. was getting ir-ritated, really upset, with the communication breakdown" between studio engineer and singer.

The next day A.B. took his complaint to Abraham, who took Loccarini aside, told him no offense intended, paid him three weeks' severance pay, and hugged him good-bye. Brian "Red" Moore was brought in from Manny Music in San Antonio. Moore knew Selena y los Dinos intimately, since he'd engineered several sessions on the band before. More importantly, Red was fluent in Spanish. He could tell the players when they were on the money grammatically and when they were butchering the lan-guage like *pochos*. Initially, Moore expressed no interest in leaving San Antonio for Corpus, but when he got a look at what Eddie Quintanilla had put together, he changed his mind and assumed the role of house engineer at Q-Zone studios.

For the year, Selena y los Dinos had grossed more than five million dollars. Tejano music sales in general for 1994 exceeded twenty million. Spanish radio gross ex-penditures for 1994 were $226.7 million in the United States. Predictions abounded that 1995 was the year that Tejano would break into the mainstream. *Billboard*'s end of the year tally ranked "Amor Prohibido" as the number one on the Hot Latin Track chart for 1994, *Amor Prohi-bido* as top Mexican-regional album, and Selena as top Mexican-regional Latin artist. Meanwhile, recording for her English-language pop crossover was under way, using a scattershot method of pairing her with several different producers.

There was also a new man in Selena's life whom she'd met him in September 1994. His name was Ricardo Mar-tínez, a plastic surgeon in Monterrey who'd done liposuc-tion on Isaac, Abraham's youngest brother and the band's crew chief, Suzette, and finally Selena. Ricardo, like Chris, wore his hair in a ponytail. He retained a hand-some, youthful appearance despite the fact that he was in his fifties. But unlike Chris, or Selena's family, or Yolanda, Martínez was sophisticated, cultured, and refined, a result of his upbringing and his profession. He was precisely the sort of Mexicano who contrasted with the Tejano *pocho* stereotype. To Selena, Martínez epitomized the qualities she sought to emulate. Material wealth, name recognition, platinum records weren't enough. Selena had been trained all her life to improve herself, to do better. The music, important as it might have been, wasn't as important to Selena as it used to be. She was tired of the road, the one-nighters, the grind in general. Her obsession was to succeed in the fashion business, and she was convinced the expansion into Mexico was the key. She met the good doctor on one of those business trips to Monterrey, and felt an immediate kinship with him. Outwardly, their relationship was that of a student and a professor. Selena could confide in Ricardo in a way she couldn't to Yolanda, much less to Chris or anyone in the family. He knew so much, he was so full of wisdom, that she could tell him how she really felt, revealing feelings she had previously saved exclusively for the diary she carried with her.

She told him she loved her husband but the relationship had hit some rough spots. She even told him about the birth control implant she was using, implying that a family was not in her immediate future. In fact, Ricardo sensed Selena was going through a period of great sadness. She talked about problems she was having with her dad. Abraham had always been opposed to Selena opening a business in Mexico. "I think her father controlled all her money," Martínez said later. "If her father didn't agree with her, I imagine that she wasn't going to be able to get all the money she needed." The doctor also observed that Selena's relationship with Yolanda was beginning to deteriorate. "I at first saw a normal relationship between a boss and an employee, although they were, at the same time, very close. Yolanda wasn't afraid to give her opinion about every song, about whether it suited Selena or not. Later, I saw something cooler in their relationship."

Ricardo had great affection for Selena, her openness

and her desire to better herself. He admired her innocence and tendency to be trusting in spite of the line of work she was in. If he hadn't had a wife and children, he would have succumbed to the obvious temptation of intimacy. Instead, he portrayed himself as her friend, confidant, doctor, and financial adviser.

By simply being there, Martínez became an indirect threat to Yolanda, Abraham, and anyone else who got their power, influence, and paychecks from Selena. If Selena listened to the doctor and followed her own heart instead of trying to please those who depended on her for their financial security, they'd be out of jobs. Martínez could blow the whole thing.

She was the sex bomb, the all-American girl, and everything in between. She was a public figure. She was so well known at the Corpus Christi airport that baggage handlers had a running bet on whether or not she'd make a flight, since she was always the last one to arrive. To make matters worse—or more amusing, depending on whose perspective it was—she wouldn't let the road crew take her bags in advance, so it was standard operating procedure for her to speed up to the loading area with ten to fifteen pieces of luggage piled into her red Porsche.

In January, she headlined the Teach the Children festival in the Mercado in San Antonio. The show funded a nonprofit program to provide school supplies to needy kids. She also attended the grand opening of a new Hard Rock Cafe on the Riverwalk in San Antonio and joined other special guest musicians, including Freddy Fender, Doug Sahm and Augie Meyers from the Texas Tornados, and members of the seventies rock band Cheap Trick, on the old rock-and-roll classic "C.C. Rider." She improvised on it deftly, although Fender sensed it was a work she was unfamiliar with.

There was a brief detour into the world of art rock. Her introduction was a phone call from David Byrne, a New York singer, songwriter, and guitarist. He'd built a strong international following, first as the leader of the Talking

Heads, an intelligent, edge-rattling rock-and-roll band that sold on a mass scale in spite of itself, and later as a solo artist with myriad interests in the world's more exotic beats, rhythms, and melodies, particularly those of Latin-American origin. During the months of November and December 1993, Byrne had been holed up at the Clinton Studios in New York, putting together tracks for the album *david byrne* on his luaka-bop custom label. He and the core of the band—bassist Paul Socolow, drummer Todd Turkisher, and percussionist Valerie Naranjo—were riffing off a tape loop of a drum sound when they came up with a cardboard sound. The song they recorded, "God's Child," didn't make the final list of songs that made it on to the album, but Byrne hadn't forgotten it when he was approached by people putting together the soundtrack for a film about to come out. He liked the premise of *Don Juan de Marco* and the pairing of Johnny Depp and Marlon Brando. Perhaps the song would go well in the film. The Hollywood folks listened, liked it. Maybe to spice it up, Selena could overdub something on the song, it was suggested. She's got some tunes in the movie and makes an appearance.

Selena intrigued Byrne. A convert to Latin music, he'd known of her for several years. When he was attempting to revive an original play by artist Terry Allen, called *Juárez*, Byrne and Allen both thought of Selena as a perfect fit for one of the play's characters. He liked her *cumbias*, which had a definite mainstream pop approach but somehow retained some integrity and sense of rhythm.

Byrne sent tapes to Q Productions. Then he called Selena. They introduced themselves over the phone and got down to work.

"I figured the movie people wouldn't know exactly how to describe it, so I talked to her and said, 'Do whatever you want,'" Byrne said. "'You don't have to squeeze around my voice, you can take my voice out in places, you can loop sections, if you want to improvise in one area.' In other words, I encouraged her to take some liberties with the song. 'Do what you want,'" he instructed her. " 'You can sing over my voice. Anything.' "

She did just that, repeating Byrne's lines in Spanish and transforming the exotic piece into an impassioned demonstration of *la castigadora* style, unleashing a hell-scorched voice filled with equal parts scorn and lust. In the process the song became "God's Child (*Baila Conmigo*)." The lady just wanted to dance.

Byrne remixed the tape with Selena's vocal. "I thought it sounded great." He sent it back to the movie people, who did not share his opinion.

"They went, 'Well, gee, half of it's in Spanish now. We thought it was going to be a single.' I said, 'Well, hey, she often does sing in Spanish, ya know. Not that that's all she does, but, yeah, she's known for singing in Spanish.'

"It was a music coordinator, or something like that. This was a mixture of movie people and record company people, so communication was getting a bit weird. You never know if someone would report something if it was their idea, or somebody else's idea, or some committee's idea. It was that kind of Hollywood *moosh*: nobody wants to take blame but everybody wants to take credit.

"Anyway, I thought it sounded great. I played it for people, I was really thrilled. I called her office and told the people there I thought it sounded really good, I'm really happy with it. We'll see what happens. The next thing in line was they still loved the song (I don't know if it was the movie people or record company people or whatever) but there was still talk about doing it as a single. So then naturally there was talk about doing it as a video. We even knocked around contracts with Tim Pope, who's a pretty well known video director. It was within a couple of days of the video going into production that I got word that the whole record was being dropped because Bryan Adams had decided to write a song for this movie. And he has and had a track record of writing hits. I thought, This sucks, but sure enough his song was a number-one song. So who am I to say?' "

At least Byrne was in good company: a planned duet between Michael Stipe of R.E.M. and Tori Amos was also dumped, along with several tracks Selena had recorded with José Hernandez.

Celebrating their own *quinceañera*, the Tejano Music Awards preceded their February 11 event with a fifteen-week series of hour-long radio programs showcasing nominees, which was carried by 115 stations nationally, continuing after the awards as the "Pura Onda" weekly music magazine with a top-ten countdown of the hottest hits.

Selena appeared as a presenter and awards recipient at the awards show in the Alamodome, which drew a crowd of some twenty-five thousand, slightly lower than initial projections. The show marked the first time in three years that all the major Tejano labels were participating in the event, although Little Joe and La Mafia still declined to participate. For Selena, who walked away with six awards, including Female Entertainer for the seventh consecutive year and Song of the Year for "Bidi Bidi Bom Bom," the night was marred by a mixup at the podium. Presenter Raul Yzaguirre mistakenly read Shelly Lares's name off a television monitor as the winner of the Tejano Crossover award, although Selena's name was the one engraved on the trophy.

Following a lengthy break in the show, it was announced that Selena actually won the category, causing her to break into tears and refuse to accept the award despite the urgings of José Behar. The next day, Fred Lares, Shelly's manager and father, demanded an apology from the Texas Talent Music Association, sponsors of the awards show. On Monday, the TTMA issued one.

One month later, the organizers took their show on the road, presenting the Tejano Music Showcase at Bally's Jubilee Theater in Las Vegas, starring Culturas, Stephanie Lynn and High Energy, Fandango USA, Oscar G, David Lee Garza, Ricardo Castillón of La Diferenzia, Jay Perez, Roberto Pulido, Emilio and Raulito Navaira, and Joe López of Mazz. If Tejano could sell in Vegas, it could sell anywhere.

February also marked an appearance by Los Dinos at the Viña del Mar festival in Chile and a monumental gig at the Houston Livestock Show and Rodeo with Emilio, which drew more than 61,000, breaking the Tejano Night attendance records that Selena had established the previous two years and ranking second behind Garth Brooks in all-time attendance for a Dome concert.

She also returned to the Grammy Awards at the Shrine Auditorium in Los Angeles. Cameron Randle, Emilio's old co-manager and now the chief of Arista Texas, a new label in the Tejano field, ran into her in the lobby. His new act, La Diferenzia, had been nominated for best Mexican-American album, competing against Selena's *Amor Prohibido*, among other nominees. Though they were both beaten by Latin pop warhorse Vicki Carr, a San Antonio resident, both Randle and Selena were giddy over being at the Grammys.

"We had a standing joke that we could not be seen together or her label would have a heart attack," he said. "So when I saw her, I said I wouldn't be responsible for Manolo [Gonzalez] having a heart attack. At that very moment, I saw Manolo. So did she. So she reached over and gave me a kiss on the cheek.

"When we announced the official roster of Arista Texas in San Antonio in January 1994, a woman asked why I hadn't signed a female. That kept me lying awake in bed at night before I figured out that I hadn't signed a female yet because Selena set such a high standard. But the night after the Grammys, I auditioned two singers in Los Angeles and I signed them both. Selena had everything to do with it." One of them was named Nydia Rojas, the fourteen-year-old girl who sang the scratch tracks with Mariachi del Sol that Selena had overdubbed. After the Grammys, Selena stayed in L.A. another day to cut the track "A Boy Like That" for a *West Side Story* tribute album.

•   •   •   •

The retail trade was less promising. The boutiques were struggling to make ends meet. No matter how charismatic its owner, sales weren't paying for the overhead. Staff at both stores had been reduced from thirty-eight to fourteen employees, largely because Yolanda fired anyone she didn't like. But the stores were almost insignificant. Selena and Yolanda were hatching a much, much bigger plan to mass-merchandise Selena's fashion line to retailers in Mexico. In reality, the boutiques were two vanity projects, since the number of buyers of high fashion in Corpus and San Antonio was extremely limited. And though the designs bore Selena's name, the creations came from patterns cut by Martin Gómez.

The growing mutterings over whether Yolanda was juggling the books to keep the operations above water or whether she was stealing to maintain a lifestyle that kept up with Selena's merely made matters worse. How could you confront Selena with suspicions when she was the one who had handpicked Yolanda to take care of business? Yolanda was her eyes and ears. Selena told everybody that. If anyone told Selena that Yolanda was skimming, kiting, or stealing, Selena might believe Yolanda instead. Gómez's complaints found their way instead to Abraham, in December of 1994. The boutiques might have been Selena's deal, but Abraham did not hesitate to protect his daughter's interests, even if his daughter was in denial about the woman who was running the shops.

Selena had no reason to suspect Yolanda. Yolanda wouldn't do anything to jeopardize her position or betray Selena, especially after she had presented Selena with the beautiful diamond-encrusted-egg ring. That didn't stop her father-manager from passing along the accusations to his daughter.

"Dad, you think all people are bad," she told him. It was true. That's what he always said. How was this any different? She just didn't see it that way. How could Yolanda be doing all these bad things when she was working so hard? Yolanda wouldn't have been helping to plan the

Monterrey fashion empire if she was trying to ruin her.

Martin Gómez, the designer who was the real artisan in the Selena, Etc., empire, tried to confront Selena. Yolanda was bad news, he said.

"You're exaggerating," Selena replied, brushing him off.

Yolanda pledged her loyalty time and again, even as Abraham's accusations were becoming more pointed. Abraham, Suzette, and Selena had a meeting with Yolanda on March 9. Abraham presented Yolanda with the inconsistencies. Where had the money gone? "She just looked [at me], she didn't have an answer to any of the questions," Abraham said. He told her he was going to pursue the matter legally. Yolanda had no response. Suzette gave her a piece of her mind: "I got up and I got close to Yolanda and got into her face and said she was a liar and a thief."

The next morning Abraham got a call from his brother Eddie. Yolanda had shown up at Q Productions with Laurie Rothe from the Corpus boutique. Abraham drove over to the Leopard Street studio and informed Yolanda she was no longer welcome on the premises. That same day, after a heated conversation on the phone, Selena told Chris, "I can't trust her anymore." Chris felt the same way. "There were a lot of things out that weren't accounted for and we couldn't get an explanation we were satisfied with." But Selena couldn't let Yolanda go, either. Yolanda was the one with all the contacts in Monterrey. Yolanda was crucial if the fashion line was going to take off. She was needed to make sure the *fábrica* was cranking out the clothing line in time for the winter buying season and that the investors had been lined up. Besides, there were still bank records, statements, and financial records to retrieve from Yolanda before taxes could be prepared.

Yolanda got the message. On the day after she was banned from Q Productions, she drove to A Place to Shoot, Inc., a full-service gun shop and range house near the Saldivar home in south San Antonio. A facility that variously described itself as "One Stop for All Your Shooting Needs" and "The Best Doggone Shooting Range in Texas," A Place to Shoot had what Yolanda was looking for. After examining the merchandise she selected a Taurus 45 snub-nosed .38-caliber revolver, telling the clerk she was an in-home nurse caring for terminally ill patients and had been threatened by a patient's relative. Before she could actually take the weapon home, she had to clear a background check by the Bexar County sheriff's department. On March 13, she picked up the gun and had family attorney Richard Garza draw up a letter of resignation. But two days later, Yolanda returned the Taurus, saying her father had given her a .22 pistol.

The following week, Yolanda's name was removed as a legal signator for boutique and design house checks. But she was kept on. It was far from over. Yolanda called Irene Herrera, the current fan-club president, in an attempt to retrieve the financial records. If she could just stay away from Abraham, maybe everything would work out. Yolanda was still stopping in to check with Leonard Wong about Selena's perfume scent. She was still in charge of the Mexico expansion, which included a boutique in Monterrey and a mass-produced fashion line. Even when the two boutiques in Texas were barely staying afloat, Yolanda kept pushing to expand into Mexico. A showing for her winter line, all designs by Martin Gómez, was scheduled for buyers for all of Mexico's biggest department stores, and half the numbers had already been presold.

On Monday, March 26, Yolanda returned to A Place to Shoot and repurchased the .38. She then drove to Monterrey with her sister Virginia Mendoza to work on Selena's plans. Selena was enjoying strong fan interest and record sales in the northern Mexico region, and establishing a physical presence was important. Selena and Yolanda had been taking more and more trips south to Monterrey, Mexico's industrial capital, less than three hours by car from the Texas-Mexico border. Compared to San Antonio, much less to Corpus Christi, the city of two and a half million was a wealthy, sophisticated urban center with its own sense of fashion and flair. Unlike in the rest of Mexico, Selena was already recognized as a star there, largely through her *telenovela* appearances and concerts with such well-known national bands as Bronco.

This trip, though, raised the question of who exactly Yolanda was working for. Ostensibly she had been raising investment money for the Selena Mexico fashion line, but she tried to clean out several bank accounts on which she was authorized to sign. One suspicious bank teller alerted Selena. Yolanda and Selena spoke on the phone, and Selena asked her to bring the bank statements, her cellular phone, and the missing perfume sample back to Corpus. On March 29, while in Monterrey, Yolanda called Dr. Martínez at his office and talked to his secretary. She had been raped and papers had been stolen, she told the secretary. She was in hiding. When informed of Yolanda's message, Martínez shrugged it off. He didn't believe her. He knew that Selena's family didn't approve of Selena and Yolanda's relationship, though he had no idea how deep their mistrust had become. In fact, it was all over but the crying. Selena and Yolanda's business relationship, as well as their personal relationship, was ending.

The whole affair was too confusing for Selena to sort out. Yolanda had been her best friend and most trusted adviser, but she'd been dropping the ball. What about the accusations that she'd been skimming? Whom could she trust anymore? How would she make ends meet for the boutiques?

The perfume was the last straw. Several weeks earlier, Selena and Yolanda had met with Leonard Wong at a Denny's in Corpus to tell Wong the latest scent he'd blended was perfect. Wong said he would send some samples by overnight delivery to her. But Selena still hadn't gotten the perfume.

When Wong told her over the phone he'd shipped the sample two weeks earlier, her voice changed. Wong could tell she was upset.

"Well, Yolanda must have it. Yolanda is in Mexico

right now, but as soon as she gets back, I'll get it from her.''

Wong told her he'd tried to call Yolanda nine or ten times, but she'd never returned his calls.

Selena's dad must have been right. He kept going on and on about how Yolanda was bad for her. Her dad was her dad; he knew best. It had always been that way. But the design house, the boutiques, and Yolanda were her domain. Selena was as stubborn as Abraham was when it came to doing things her way, but she couldn't ignore what Abraham was saying, even though he thought everyone was out to take advantage of her.

Why did it always have to come to this? Selena wondered. Why did Abraham's obsession with power and control, orchestrating the family, living his life through the band, have to get in the way of her business? Why did someone like Yolanda, whom she trusted, have to be just as obsessed, so obsessed that she would turn on her? Whenever Abraham wanted to exert control over others, he would threaten to withhold access to the band. Whenever Yolanda wanted to exert control over others, she would threaten dismissal from the fan club or boutique or imply that she would deny access to Selena. In that respect, both of them treated her like a commodity. But there was a real person inside that shiny exterior and no one could control her. Not Abraham, not Yolanda. They were mere adjuncts, accessories to the show. Selena controlled their destinies; it wasn't the other way around.

Earlier that month, on March 7, two days before Yolanda was confronted by Abe, Selena, and Suzette, Selena had sat in the Q Productions office surrounded by family and friends, listening to a vocal track she'd finished for producer Guy Roche and Nancy Brennan, the A & R vice president of SBK Records. The song, "Dreaming of You," was one of the selections intended for the crossover album. The sound of her voice singing the chorus "and I'm dreaming, dreaming of you" filled the room, overlaid with Selena whispering, *"Mi corazón,* my love . . ."

"You like it?" Roche asked Brennan.

"Yeah, I like that," Brennan said, adding the caveat, "I wouldn't want it on every track, but it's cool."

The crossover was a mixed bag. Selena wanted to go for it, regardless of the strings attached. As José Behar would note, she wasn't making the transition as a Tejano music artist. "She acquiesced to the market's needs rather than the market acquiescing to her." From the family's standpoint, there was no rush. She'd just sold out the Astrodome and album sales continued to zoom skyward on the Spanish-language product she was turning out.

In addition, there was the whole artistic process of watering down Selena's Latin-ness. To accomplish this, EMI brass spared no expense in trying out producers—Keith Thomas, whose clients included Amy Grant, Whitney Houston, and Vanessa Williams; Guy Roche, who did Celine Dion, Michael Bolton, Cher, and Expose; and Rhett Lawrence, the svengali behind Mariah Carey and Paula Abdul.

The prospect of going mainstream excited Selena, but so did the prospect of her fashion line in Mexico. But first, duty called.

Al Aguilar, of Sosa, Bromley, Aguilar, and Associates, was one of a hundred thousand or so Selena fans who gathered at Calle Ocho, part of the Carnival Miami that Selena headlined on March 11. Coca-Cola had sponsored a *Sigue Selena a Miami* contest to see Selena at the event, with Selena commemorative bottles awarded as second prize. Backstage, Aguilar was pleased to see that despite all the fanfare, the Corpus Christi girl had somehow managed to maintain her down-to-earth levelheadedness. "I don't think there has ever been a celebrity contract with the Coca-Cola system that has endured the length of time that we had with Selena," he said. "They're usually one-year deals. But Selena was enduring. She had those unique traits, all of the qualities that we wanted, that Coca-Cola wanted. She represented good. No matter where I was or where I saw her—she would be in a crowd of people or she would be backstage surrounded by a whole bunch of folks—and if I walked into the room she would stand up and come over and shake my hand and hug me and say, 'Mr. Aguilar, it is so wonderful to see you again.' With stars, it's usually just the absolute opposite: they are the center of the universe.''

After Al and Selena casually conversed about the new album-in-progress and made small talk, Selena walked out onto the stage to face a sea of people who'd been patiently waiting through intermittent rain showers, ready to sing along to her lyrics. They knew Selena was it, even though they were not Mexican-Americans from South Texas but Cubans, Nicaraguans, Puerto Ricans, and Caribbean Latinos. Selena had transcended Tejano.

''I had this enormous sense of pride that here's one of us from South Texas making it here in this other region of the country where historically our Mexican-American culture and music has not transcended very well. Amongst all of these other international Latin groups, she was *the* star, and they loved her,'' Al Aguilar said. ''I had a sense of what she always gave me; she always made me feel young, she always made me feel happy, she always made me feel proud of my culture and my roots. She was a youthful representation of what Hispanic America is all about and what it wants to be.''

It was a brave new world and Selena was defining it. Aguilar put it in marketing terms. ''Not being able to speak any Spanish or understand or appreciate the language or the culture, that's not cool anymore. What's cool is being able to enjoy the best of both worlds. I want to have my cake and eat it, too. I want the very best that America has to offer. I want the best of what the Hispanic world has to offer.''

She was *la onda. La onda* was Selena.

Five days later she was back in San Antonio for the umpteenth time, doing a show at Tejano Rodeo the same as she'd been doing shows for the past fifteen years. The contradiction of the international superstar doing another

Tejano club gig was a classic example of cognitive dissonance: when two beliefs are held that conflict with each other, one tries to believe them both and make them both true, despite the fact that if one is true, the other can't be. Reconciling the conflicts was becoming more and more difficult for Selena.

6

Black Friday

O N THURSDAY, MARCH 30, 1995, Selena phoned Leonard Wong again.

"How are the kids?" she asked, making small talk.
"Leonard, you make it sound like so much fun to have
kids. I can't wait to have my own."

Wong told her he'd arranged for a meeting on the following Thursday with the people from New York who
were going to show Selena the perfume bottle they'd designed from her sketches. He also made sure she'd talked
to Yolanda about the perfume sample. Selena said she
would pick it up from her that night or the following day.

The schedule over the coming weeks would be hectic.
There was a concert at the Sports Arena in Los Angeles
on Saturday, and she'd promised Jacob Avila, a nine-year-
old neighbor, lunch at McDonald's on Sunday for helping
her look for her missing dog, even though she'd already
given her helpers cupcakes and autographed photos
when the dog returned to the house. The film she had a
cameo in, *Don Juan de Marco*, was opening next week.
Two big Cinco de Mayo concerts were booked for early
May, one a Coke-sponsored event in Chicago, the other
a spectacular at Sea World in San Antonio. There were

more songs to try out for the English album.

She'd found a smart pair of shoes at Mangel's downtown for only seven dollars and picked up a pair of in-line skates to take to California. Maybe she'd have time to hit the beach at Venice or do the Palisades by Santa Monica, she hoped. It was a glorious time of year to be at home in Corpus. The rains and warming weather greened up the whole countryside, the days were warm, the nights pleasantly cool, and the muggy heat of summer was still weeks away.

As much as she was trying to accomplish, Selena did not hesitate to put it all on hold to spend most of the afternoon having lunch with her mom. "My foot was swollen—I'd broken my ankle," Marcella said. "But I wanted to spend time with her." Marcella and Selena passed four hours at the Olive Garden restaurant on S.P.I.D. During their long conversation, Selena told Marcie about a previous visit to the same place. She'd seen a little old lady eating by herself and felt sorry for her. Selena paid for the woman's meal but told the waiter not to let the lady know. "I want you to give her one of those little cakes you give people on their birthdays. Put it in a bag so she can take it home." Marcella felt so proud of her daughter; she was so giving, so generous with her love, as well as with her material wealth. Show business could be such a competitive, down-and-dirty endeavor, people crawling over each other in pursuit of riches and recognition but her daughter rose above the fray. Her goodness neutralized all the unsavory aspects of making music for a living. On the way home, as Selena was zipping in and out of traffic, singing at the top of her voice, her mother leaned over to her and spoke into her ear. "I love you."

Selena looked back and smiled. "I love you too, Mama."

There was still the Yolanda problem hanging over her head. Selena wanted to resolve it once and for all. Dad kept saying it was time to get the books straight. The businesses may have been hers, but he still had an interest in her finances, and he didn't like what he saw. The shops were losing money, the ledgers weren't balanced, Dad kept hounding Selena, and Yolanda was dodging both of them.

On Thursday evening, March 30, it was Selena's turn to dodge. Yolanda had dropped her sister off in San Antonio and borrowed her nephew's truck to drive to Corpus Christi, where she checked into the Days Inn and called Selena's beeper. Selena answered her from the boutique. She had spent three hours getting a manicure and pedicure. Selena told Celia Solís that she was going to fire Yolanda as soon as she got some missing financial records from her. Then she cooked marinated baked black-fin shark for Chris—his favorite dish—and his father, Gilbert, who was visiting at the house, taking her own sweet time. Around 11 P.M. she phoned Yolanda. She'd be coming by, but she couldn't stay. She just needed those bank statements to prepare taxes. She woke up Chris, who'd dozed off, and he drove her over to the Days Inn. Selena had Chris wait outside in the truck while she met with Yolanda for twenty minutes. Their conversation was formal yet cordial. No matter what the circumstances were, Selena still appreciated all the things Yolanda had done for her over the years. But back in the truck, Selena noticed that some bank records she'd requested from Yolanda were still missing.

"When we got home, we looked through the stuff and she was upset," Chris related. "She didn't call Yolanda and tell her. Yolanda paged her. It was my decision that she call Yolanda. Now Yolanda wanted to be taken to the hospital. [Selena] didn't want to go back [that night]. I told her to tell Yolanda that it was too late, and that's what she did."

Selena was clearly upset. She'd been taken advantage of. She called Martínez to talk about the supposed rape and find out if Yolanda had given the papers to him. Yolanda had told Selena the same story she'd told Martínez: she'd been raped, she was hiding at the Days Inn in

Corpus, and she had the papers Selena wanted. Martínez advised her not to go back alone, to take someone with her. But as bad as she felt toward Yolanda, Selena couldn't help but sympathize when Yolanda told her the assault story. Someone had abducted her, pulled her out of her car, she had related.

But Chris was right; it was too late to deal with Yolanda now. It could wait until tomorrow. She was glad he was there for her. Before going to bed, they expressed their love for each other.

Friday, March 31, began as a cool, cloudy day. Selena rose at 7:30, dressed in her workout sweats, and tried to tiptoe out of the house. But just as she opened the bedroom door in the pale light of the new day to walk down the hallway, Chris's father opened the door of his bedroom, frightening Selena.

"You scared me to death!" she cried.

She took the Chevy truck because it was blocking the Porsche and tooled up Navigation Boulevard to the Days Inn, phoning Yolanda in advance. At the motel, Yolanda was upset, nervous.

"What happened? What's wrong?" asked Selena.

It was in Monterrey, Yolanda said. Someone tried to grab her while she was in her car and rape her. Selena took pity. Here Yolanda was, her world crashing around her, with no one to give her comfort. Selena escorted her to the truck and drove her to Doctors Regional Medical Center. If she'd been raped, she needed medical attention. At the hospital, the circumstances grew stranger and stranger as Yolanda was examined. The results were inconclusive, two nurses informed Selena.

Selena put her finger to her lips and asked the nurses to be quiet. She didn't want Yolanda to hear.

This wasn't adding up. Had Yolanda played her last sympathy card, thinking Selena was a pushover? Had she been had again? The nurses said Yolanda would have to go to San Antonio for the vaginal exam, since that was her legal residence.

"Yolanda, I'm taking you back," Selena said.

Dad was right about Yolanda, she'd been taking advantage of her, earning her trust only to betray it. She'd withheld papers, made up stories about being raped, kept talking about Abraham this and Abraham that. "Maybe we should just stay apart for a while so my dad won't get mad," Selena had told her.

The cellular phone rang in the truck. It was Chris. Abraham was looking for her, he said. Had she forgotten the session at the studio? Selena had been recording vocal tracks for her projected English-language crossover. The session was supposed to start at 10 A.M. A.B. and Suzette were waiting for her, which was nothing unusual. Selena lived on Selena time, which more often than not meant she was late.

"Oh no, I forgot!" Selena told Chris. There was one last bit of business to take care of and she'd be there.

Back in room 158, Yolanda and Selena exchanged harsh words about the way finances had been handled. Selena emptied a satchel full of bank statements onto the motel bed. Then she began to remove the egg-shaped ring Yolanda had given her on behalf of the boutique employees.

Even Selena was against her now.

A flash of metal caught Selena's eye. Yolanda had a gun. She was pointing it at her own head. Then the gun turned.

Selena turned in a panic to run. The gun went off. A bullet struck Selena in the right shoulder as she ran.

Selena managed to open the door and run out toward the swimming pool. Yolanda ran behind her, holding the weapon as if she was going to fire a second shot.

Selena ran past the palm-shaded swimming pool toward the parking lot, then down a walkway between the office and restaurant and a wing of rooms. She collapsed outside the motel's entrance. The bullet had severed an artery, and her blood splattered on a planter box near the door.

It was 11:49 A.M. when Selena ran into the lobby,

bleeding to death, still clutching the egg-shaped ring in her hand.

"Help me, help me, I've been shot," she called out.

She tried to push open the lobby door, then pulled it open and ran in, collapsing again.

Shawna Vela and Rubén DeLeon, two employees at the motel, tried to stanch the blood spurting from the wound and make her comfortable. "Who shot you?" they asked frantically.

"Yolanda," Selena said, closing her eyes, a faraway squawk of a seagull fading into silence in the gray, drizzling light.

The call to 911 from Barbara Schultz, the Days Inn manager, was quick and to the point.

> Schultz: We have a woman ran in the lobby said she's been shot. She's laying on the floor. There's blood.
> 911: Okay, how old is she?
> Schultz: She looks about twenty.
> 911: She's in the lobby right now?
> Schultz: Yes, ma'am, she just passed out.

An EMS ambulance arrived within three minutes and Selena was rushed to Memorial Medical Center, arriving at high noon. Marcella was called at home while emergency room doctors worked furiously to save her daughter. Abraham, Suzette, and A.B. were at the studio when Abe's sister-in-law called to say there had been an accident involving Selena. After they reached the hospital, the emergency room surgeon emerged to talk to Abraham, telling him he'd administered four units of blood. No, no, no, Abraham interrupted. Selena wouldn't want that. Only God can be the source of life-giving blood, that's what Witnesses believed. The surgeon shook his head. It was too late, he told Abraham. Selena had died at 1:05 P.M., Central Standard Time, ten days before her twenty-fourth birthday. The cause of death was internal bleeding and cardiac arrest.

• • •

At the Days Inn, Yolanda briefly paced outside room 158, holding the gun in her right hand. She went inside the room and then reemerged with the gun wrapped in a cloth. She walked quickly to the parking lot and jumped into the red extended-cab GMC pickup she had driven to Corpus from San Antonio, started the truck, revved the engine, and with tires squealing, raced around the parking lot toward the motel entrance. She then pulled into a space on the north side of the building, rolled up the tinted windows, locked the doors, and put the gun barrel to her temple, threatening to kill herself as police approached the vehicle. The Corpus police were more than willing to wait her out, sending in a SWAT team, a hostage negotiation team, and blockading the area with patrol cars.

The details trickled in. "We knew about it first," said Manuel Dávila, Jr., general manager of Beso 94 in Corpus. "A guy that works for me on weekends, one of those weekend warriors, works at the hospital. He called and said, 'Selena's been brought in here, she's been shot.' I waited for someone [else] to say it had been done. I knew it was true. My guy called [back] from the hospital. He said she was gone. We knew it. But we couldn't release it."

There was nothing else to say.

One Corpus Christi detective heard on the police scanner that Emilio Navaira had been caught in midembrace with Selena by his wife, Cindy, who did the deed in a fit of jealousy. The rumor was picked up by several radio stations. Though it was eventually disproved, the damage was done. Cindy Navaira was so shaken she had to be taken to a hospital.

Danny Noyola, the principal at West Oso High School, near the Molina neighborhood Selena lived in, broke in on the intercom with the news after rumors had circulated around school. When he finished, he closed his office door and cried. The already dark day turned darker. The whole neighborhood felt close to Selena, but Noyola had been closer. He'd coached Selena in eighth grade, her last year in public school and believed Selena could have been a great painter or an athlete. She'd performed at a Favorites Dance for her would-have-been classmates. She'd been an inspiration to the school and the neighborhood. What made it worse was that the first West Oso Greats Weekend had been scheduled to begin that night. The new stadium was being dedicated. Ricky Vela's parents were setting up a booth at the career fair to show the video interview that Ricky's sister, a Vassar graduate, had done with Selena. One sixteen-year-old West Oso student, Mark González, was not surprised at the emotional reaction. "People around here, we don't really make it that big in life. She was an inspiration. She was cool."

José Hernández was driving around Phoenix after playing a gig the night before when his wife called him on his cellular phone. Johnny Canales was waiting to board a plane at the Corpus Christi airport on his way to Eagle Pass, where he was getting married.

Ramon Hernandez was at home in San Antonio when two faxes came over the machine from friends in Corpus. One read, "Guess what? Selena's been shot. And do you know who did it? Emilio's wife." He went to eat at Barnacle Bill's, up the street on Southwest Military Drive, where he saw Manny Guerra and Pete Rodríguez, Manny's director of promotion, standing in line.

"Did you hear about Selena?" Manny asked.

Ramon nodded quietly.

"Do you know who did it?"

"No. I've heard it was Emilio's wife," Hernandez said.

"What?" Manny said with surprise.

"Well, you know how it is in this business." Hernandez shrugged.

They sat at separate tables and quietly ate their meals.

After lunch, Hernandez turned on channel 41. Monica Navarro broke into regular programming to say that Selena had died.

"I don't recall many people crying," Hernandez said. "I recall looks of shock and disbelief. I don't think it hit people until a day or two later."

The original Los Dinos with Abraham Quintanilla at top right.
(Hispanic American Entertainment Archives)

The tomboy from Lake Jackson hanging out in the neighborhood.
(Meredith Lynn Cappel)

Mrs. Pérez's third-grade class at O. M. Roberts Elementary. Selena is fourth from left, front row.

Selena y Los Dinos, circa 1986, pose for promotional photograph. Clockwise: A. B. Quintanilla III, Ricky Vela, Roger García, Selena, and Suzette Quintanilla.
(Hispanic American Entertainment Archives)

Fourteen-year-old Selena poses with her father, Abraham, in the Corpus Christi backyard of Rosalia Hernandez, the photographer's mother. The occasion was Selena's first photo shoot for publicity stills.
(Ramon Hernandez)

Selena at sweet sixteen smiles for the camera at a photo shoot for Manny Guerra's GP records on the heels of winning her first award at the Tejano Music Awards in San Antonio.
(Ramon Hernandez)

"...And the winner is": Selena is recognized at the 1988 Tejano Music Awards in San Antonio.
(Ramon Hernandez)

The glamorous life of a singing star on the road, 1988.
(Ramon Hernandez)

Selena relaxes before taking the stage at the Hispanic State Fair held at La Villita in San Antonio, August 1989.
(Ramon Hernandez)

Husband and wife at work. Selena struts while Chris plays guitar.
(Al Rendon/LGI)

Chris Perez holds up his new wife at Caesar's Palace during a BILLBOARD magazine awards show in June 1992.
(Ramon Hernandez)

Los Dinos at the top of their game. This photograph was taken in February 1993, the day after the Coliseum concert in Corpus Christi that was recorded and released as SELENA LIVE. Clockwise from left: Ricky Vela, Joe Ojeda, Selena, Suzette, A.B., Chris, and Pete Astudillo. *(Al Rendon/LGI)*

Selena and Yolanda Saldivar pause at a fan club appreciation party at Desperado's Club in San Antonio during the Tejano Music Awards week, 1993. *(Al Rendon/LGI)*

Selena in leather oozes sexuality in this outtake of a photo magazine for MÁZ magazine.
(John Dyer)

Selena grins and bears it, letting her hair down in another outtake from the MÁZ magazine photo session.
(John Dyer)

Thirteen-year-old Marcella García touches the leather jacket of her idol before Los Dinos' triumphant homecoming concert at the Clute Mosquito Festival, July 1994.
(The Brazosport Facts)

Like the flower.
(Scott Newton)

A husband and a mother mourn the loss of their loved one at graveside.
(Wide World Photos)

Fans pay their respects at the Selena, Etc. boutique in San Antonio.
(Wide World Photos)

Some thought the president of Mexico, Carlos Salinas, had been shot. Johnny Pasillas, Emilio's brother-in-law and manager, frantically called radio stations, trying to end the jealous-lover rumor.

Albert Dávila of KEDA-AM in San Antonio heard about it from his brother Manuel in Corpus. "We get calls all the time," he said. "Sunny [Ozuna] dies every six, seven years. This one, though, was different. Manuel, he told me Selena had been shot. It'd been confirmed. We knew about an hour before we broke it. It's not a story you're proud to break. When we did, the phones lit up. Callers said, 'You're lying.' They called KRIO and KXTN, but they hadn't gone on the story yet. We were waiting. 'Who's gonna go on it next?' Twenty-five minutes later, they both went on it. Manuel called back and told me she was dead. He was crying. We were in kind of a daze, but we had to do our thing."

Ramiro Burr, the music writer for the San Antonio *Express-News*, got a call from the EMI Latin offices across town. The woman sitting in the pickup in the parking lot of the Days Inn in Corpus threatening to kill herself was Yolanda Saldivar, a registered nurse who was widely known as Selena's number-one fan.

Leonard Wong was handed a note while in a meeting. "Selena has been shot," it read. When the meeting was over, several employees suggested calling Yolanda to see what had happened. Wong tried dialing her cellular phone number, but all he got was a busy signal. When he heard a few hours later that Yolanda was the one who allegedly did it, he crumpled over. She was the last person he would have suspected. He'd sat with Yolanda and her grandmother and niece at Selena's fashion show. It couldn't be true. But it was.

Meredith Lynn Cappel had just returned from the Wal-Mart to her home in Lake Jackson when her sister called and told her to turn on the television. "I started watching and pacing and then the phone rang off the wall for the next two days. I didn't really get to deal with my feelings then. I started putting videotapes in and taping everything.

I was devastated. I brought my pictures of her to her old house. Channel Eleven was over there. I was in a total daze and they were shoving the microphone into my face and asking me questions. All I could think about was, All her dreams—gone.''

David Byrne, on tour in Japan, read the news in the *International Herald-Tribune*.

"This day will go down as Black Friday," sobbed Rudy Treviño, the director of the Texas Talent Music Association, sponsor of the Tejano Music Awards, where Selena ruled.

San Antonio's major Spanish-language radio stations, including Tejano 107, KXTN-FM, KRIO-FM, and KEDA-AM, interrupted their regular programming. News reports established who Selena was—a twenty-three-year-old Grammy-Award-winning singer who was easily the most popular recording and performing artist in the Tejano music field—and registered varying reactions of shock and disbelief. Anyone but her. Not the good girl, the family girl, the one born to entertain. She was the kind of person who acted in *telenovelas*; she didn't live them. A shooting? No way, especially a shooting involving a jealous woman in a crime of passion.

At a press conference he'd hastily organized while Yolanda held police at bay, Abraham said that his daughter had gone to the Days Inn to fire Saldivar, who was still not being identified by name in media reports. "The reason Selena was at the hotel room was to terminate [the accused's employment], and we believe that's the motive for the shooting," said assistant police chief Ken Bung.

By midafternoon, a line of automobiles began backing up traffic for more than a mile in front of the three Quintanilla homes on Bloomington Street in the neighborhood where gang graffiti and cacti distinguished the blue-collar community from other subdivisions like it across America. Police were called in to direct traffic. Messages of sympathy painted in white shoe polish decorated the windshields of cars and trucks throughout the state:

"Missing My Baby," "Long Live Selena," "The Valley Loves You, Selena." The chain-link fence in front of the three homes had become a shrine festooned with Mylar balloons, inflated pink Easter bunnies, drawings, scribbled notes, posters.

The lead item on national network evening news programs was the end of the major league baseball strike. Thirty minutes later, the death of Selena was the lead item on all the television stations in Corpus Christi, San Antonio, Houston, and the Rio Grande Valley. Two San Antonio network affiliates, KENS and KMOL, sent reporters and remote trucks with satellite uplinks to the scene of the crime. Not surprisingly, the reports on Spanish-language stations KVDA and KWEX, the Telemundo and the Univisión affiliates, were more extensive, including coverage of how the death had affected Latin personalities in Hollywood and Hispanic communities throughout the United States and Mexico. Julio Iglesias interrupted a recording session in Miami for a moment of silence. Celia Cruz called Q Productions to offer condolences. Madonna sent a fax.

Grieving callers read improvised poems on the air. Artists such as Stephani, the All-American Girl, called in to KXTN-FM in San Antonio, talking and crying. Jaime DeAnda, leader of Los Chamacos, telephoned to share a memory of how Selena helped his band get started. Gigs were called off all around Texas, including the Chamacos' show at the Yellow Rose in Corpus, Shelly Lares' dance in Huntsville, and Stefani's engagement in Brownsville. The Houston group La Mafia canceled engagements in Guatemala and flew back to Texas.

While Corpus Christi police held Saldivar at bay, Tejano 107 in San Antonio announced a candlelight vigil at Sunken Gardens for 7 P.M. At Selena, Etc., boutique and salon on Broadway in San Antonio, cars began pulling in to the parking lot, their occupants getting out and milling about on the pavement. A bouquet of flowers was placed in a corner by the entrance to the boutique, along with a picture of Selena and several handwritten notes. Several adults, four teenage girls, three younger boys, and an *abuelita*, a little old grandmother, gathered at the boutique's entrance, studying the flowers, reading the notes, and peering inside at the pictures of Selena interspersed among the expensive designer outfits. Their faces were neither animated nor emotional, but solemn and blank. They just wanted to look. To see. To touch. To personally connect with this dark event.

A note was posted by the door. "Do not put candles too close to flowers. It could cause a fire."

Across Brackenridge Park at Sunken Gardens, the amphitheater was filling up fast, and a steady line of people, from little children to senior citizens, streamed in. Parked in the middle of the stage was a small truck that was the remote studio for KXTN-FM, the station sponsoring the candlelight vigil. (Business still being business, competing Tejano station KRIO-FM staged its own candlelight vigil at South Park Mall.) The event had been haphazardly organized and the assembly was waiting for someone to lead. Two life-size cut-outs of Selena holding a can of Coca-Cola were placed outside the remote studio truck. When station staff began handing out candles, a small stampede broke out in the rush to the stage, and one young girl was pulled crying from the crowd.

The station's morning-drive personality, Jon Ramírez, formally opened the proceedings, telling people the reason they were there was because "somebody stupid had a gun." He shared his memories of Selena—"*Esta amiga*, role model, and one of Tejano's major superstars," is how he described her—and elicited a few laughs when he recalled being taken aback by her physical attractiveness when he met her the first time. ("I said to myself, 'Yes! This lady makes me want to go home and take a cold shower!'") Ramírez also said what almost everyone who'd ever come in contact with Selena already knew: "She never behaved like a superstar."

Fifteen minutes after Ramírez started speaking, the whole slope was dotted with flickering candles. Kids still skittered under parents' legs, as kids tend to do, laughing and giggling, and friends still greeted friends with smiles. But a quiet, respectful serenity prevailed among most of the five thousand in attendance, embodied by the teenage boy and girl—brother and sister? boyfriend and girlfriend?—standing facing the stage, one holding a candle and the other holding a white banner that said HONK IF YOU LOVE SELENA.

Throughout the evening, KXTN's news staff, headed by Mike Pesina, broke into regular programming with live coverage of Yolanda Saldivar's standoff with twenty-five police negotiators and SWAT team members. The station had initially altered its format to an all-Selena weekend, but backed off before the night was done, instead emphasizing at least one Selena song per hour.

Saldivar stayed in the truck for almost ten hours, sometimes crying, sometimes talking to authorities on a cellular phone. Her various conversations during this tense period shed little light on her precise motive—"I had a problem with her and I just got to end it," she told officers—though she indicated there were extenuating circumstances, at least from her point of view. "I loved her. I didn't mean to hurt her," she cried at one point. The blame was not hers, she insisted. It was Abraham's fault. "Her father hates me. Her father is responsible for this. He made me shoot her." On another occasion, she reiterated the sentiment, saying, "Her father came between us." She was obviously feeling remorse, crying, "Forgive me, God, for what I did." She knew the consequences of her actions, acknowledging, "I did something very bad and I disgraced my family."

Finally, just before 9:30 P.M., with a light rain falling, Yolanda surrendered and was hustled away as the crowd of several hundred who had gathered across the street behind police lines to watch the standoff cheered.

At least one burden had been lifted.

"I think she just got tired," said Corpus Christi police chief Henry Garrett. Bond was set the next morning at $100,000 though district attorney Carlos Valdez was able to raise the amount to $500,000 several days later, after the Nueces County jail was deluged with death threats. Rumors were flying fast that some toughs were taking up collections to make bond for Saldivar so they could kill her. Even in prison, she was as good as dead. The Mexican Mafia, the dominant gang in the Texas penal system, supposedly had a price on her head. Whoever did the deed would be a hero among *la gente*.

Within twenty minutes of her surrender, Saldivar was taken downtown to the police station, fingerprinted, photographed, and then brought to a room where she began talking to police detectives Paul Rivera and Ray Rivera (no relation). At Paul Rivera's request, she was observed through a one-way mirror by Texas Ranger Robert Garza. Paul Rivera, who'd been investigating homicides since 1978, informed Saldivar of her right to a lawyer, which Saldivar waived. He then began dictating notes onto a tape recorder. Afterward, at 11:20 P.M., a secretary typed up the statement from the recording. Paul Rivera showed Saldivar the typed two-and-a-half page statement; she made corrections on dates and her sister's age, and then signed it, at 11:45 P.M.

The statement read:

My name is Yolanda Saldivar. I am 34 years old, born 09–19–60. I have been working for Selena, Etc. in Corpus Christi since about July of 1994. I was hired initially to travel with her as her chaperon. For the first two months everything was fine, but later I started doing payroll and keeping her books.

At first there were thirty-eight employees with the company, and in the last few months the company was going down and it went to fourteen employees. Selena Quintanilla told me that her business was going down and I know she was paying a clothes designer $3,000 a month. Her father's name is Abraham Quintanilla, and he did not agree with me working with the company. During the first week of February of this year, 1995, her father told Selena that I was a lesbian while we were in Miami, Florida. Her father also told her that

I was stealing money from the company. Her father, Abraham Quintanilla, was putting a lot of pressure on Selena, and Selena suggested that we stay away from each other so her father wouldn't get mad.

On 03/27/95, which was a Monday, I drove to Monterrey, Mexico, with my sister, Virginia Mendoza, who is forty-five years old. I stayed there Monday, Tuesday, and Wednesday, and I kept in contact with Selena. On Wednesday, 03/29/95, I talked to Selena from Monterrey, Mexico, and she told me to bring some bank statements and some other papers and a cellular phone that she needed. The next day, 03/30/95, I came to Corpus Christi around 7:30 P.M. in my nephew's red 1994 GMC truck. My nephew's name is Charles Ruiz. I came to Corpus and I checked in to the Days Inn Motel on Navigation in room 158. I paged Selena some time between 7:00 and 7:30, about eight times, and she returned my call around 11:00 P.M. A short time later she came into the room and talked to me for about ten minutes. She told me that her husband, Christopher, was outside waiting in his car.

Selena took the bank statements and files that I had brought from Monterrey. Before she left I told her that a man had opened my car door in Monterrey and tried to rape me, and I showed her some bruises on my arms and neck. The next day, 03/31/95, Selena called me around 8:30 A.M., while I was asleep, and told me she was coming over to the motel. A short time later, maybe around 9:00 A.M. she came to my room at the Days Inn Motel and she took me to Doctors Regional Hospital on Alameda, where I was treated by a doctor for the bruises that I had on my body. The doctor told me he could not do much because it had happened in Monterrey, Mexico.

As she was driving me back to the motel in her truck, she told me that her father had told her that the papers I had brought from Monterrey were wrong and that her father had said I was a lesbian. I got mad and I told her that I did not want to work for her anymore. We got to the motel and we both went inside the room and we both argued because I wanted to quit working for her. I gave her everything that I had, the cellular phone and the bank files, as we argued.

She started dumping all the files on the bed from the briefcase or handbag that I had. I took a gun from my purse that I had bought about two weeks ago in San Antonio for $250. I bought the pistol at a place named A Place to Shoot, located on Morrison Blvd. in San Antonio. The gun holds five bullets. I took the gun from my purse and Selena started walking toward the door, which was open. I pulled the hammer back and I shot at her as she was walking toward the door, which was open.

Selena took off running and I don't know where she went. I got scared and I got in my truck and drove around the parking lot looking for her. I could not find her and I parked on the other side of the parking lot. A police officer approached my truck and I put the gun to my head. Other police officers arrived and I continued with the pistol to my head for the next ten or twelve hours. I then decided to come out of the truck and give myself up.

I was placed under arrest and I was taken to the Corpus Christi police station where I talked to Sgt. Paul Rivera and Sgt. Ray Rivera, who warned me of my rights. I then gave them this statement, which was true and correct, of my own free will and there was no threats or promises made to me in giving this statement.

Public opinion was already clear. A caller to KXTN-FM in San Antonio voiced what the majority of Selena's fans were feeling: "This lady shouldn't have had the chance to be negotiated with into giving up. Did she give Selena a chance? As [Selena] was running away from her, she shot her in the back. And now the way the judicial system is so screwed up, she'll be walking the streets two or three years from now."

In the confusion at the hospital, the green sweatshirt

Selena had been wearing was inadvertently thrown away in a biohazard waste bag by paramedics. It had been cut off while they had tried to resuscitate her and had been soaked in blood, as were the sheets on the gurney that carried her to the hospital. Her green sweat pants, socks, and shoes were found at the morgue.

Abraham had gone into automatic mode, speaking openly to the press. He tried to make sense out of what happened and rationalize the terrible loss, saying, "I know, I just know she has eternal life. The way I believe, that's not my daughter anymore. My daughter is in God's memory, for the future time when she is resurrected."

On Saturday, the death of Selena Quintanilla Perez was topic A all over Texas, even in corners of the state where no one in the Other Society had ever heard of her. "And I'm from Refugio, I grew up around those people," one Anglo said. The reaction was typical of the majority of Texans, to whom the murder of Selena was just another senseless shooting. To "those people," though—the five million Texans of Mexican descent—the death of Selena was Black Friday, a day of infamy even darker and more evil than the assassination of John F. Kennedy. The reaction was similar to that of fans of Elvis Presley, Stevie Ray Vaughan, and John Lennon when those musical artists suddenly died, only intensified. Texas-Mexicans knew a thing or two about grief and how to express it. Selena was more than just a great entertainer to them. She was a role model, particularly to Hispanic girls; a paragon of the triumvirate virtues of God, family, and home. She was an entertainer who was a millionaire at nineteen, had a positive personality, and talked to kids about staying in school and avoiding drugs; she was a hero to a brown-skinned people who had precious few heroes to claim.

Her music validated the cultural duality of the majority of her fans, proving one could embrace the traditions of the land while being hip, modern, and up-to-date. Like the majority of Texas-Mexicans who have assimilated into the mainstream, Selena's first language was English. By opting to sing in the native language of her parents, she proved that who you are and where your family came from could be sources of pride and not something to be ashamed about.

Saturday editions of the Corpus Christi *Caller-Times* and the San Antonio *Express-News* immediately sold out. A handwritten note affixed to the *Caller-Times* news rack in front of the Days Inn coffee shop explained there were no papers for sale "due to thieves."

That evening, a vigil that drew 1,500 fans was held for Selena at the Bayfront Plaza in Corpus. An announcement was issued stating that a public viewing of the casket would be held at Bayfront Auditorium on the following day.

The sun that rose out of the Corpus Christi Bay on a beautiful cloudless Sunday shone on an orderly line of people that stretched almost a mile in front of the white-washed building where Selena's body lay in state. One hundred forty-three miles to the west, the nine o'clock Sunday morning bilingual service from San Fernando Cathedral in downtown San Antonio that KEDA-AM regularly broadcast turned into an undeclared Selena mass. After a mariachi choir played, the pastor spoke out about what had happened. "It isn't this woman who senselessly killed her," he said. "It is this whole culture of death we're promoting." He criticized the urge to retaliate, the code that says, If you hurt me, I'll have revenge. He urged the congregation to "say no to the spirit of getting even."

By late Sunday morning, a crowd of about one hundred people, almost all of them Hispanic, walked around the grounds of the Days Inn, a relatively new two-story motel building with a limestone block exterior just east of the greyhound race track on Navigation Boulevard. Fans took photographs of other fans in front of the motel marquee, which read, "We Will Miss You, Selena." Others clustered around the lobby entrance—the spot where Selena had collapsed and died—staring blankly at a bouquet of flowers that had been placed in a corner. Still more were posing stoically by the door of room 158, their images recorded by cameras and video recorders held by friends and family members. At the foot of the door was a small bouquet of carnations, some single roses, a pink oleander blossom, a votive candle, and several notes, such as this one: "Selena, I love you and will miss you forever. I will always have you in my heart. Love always, Jessica García."

No one seemed sure where exactly she was shot, whether it was in the room or outside in the courtyard or in the parking lot. But almost everyone knew where she died. Many seemed to be searching for something, anything: evidence, mementos, some kind of answer to a question they didn't quite understand. Several young men hovered around the wooden trash container by the lobby entrance, inspecting every square inch for flecks of dried blood that hadn't been washed off. Two teenage boys wearing Dallas Cowboys jerseys ran their fingers through the thick blades of grass by the walkway between the pool and the lobby, where Selena had stumbled. Near room 158, three boys picked up pieces of wood chips in the flower bed, studying each one carefully for traces of blood.

The motel courtyard had attained the status of Dealey Plaza in Dallas and the Lorraine Motel in Memphis. Two men kneeled at the wooden trash container by the lobby, examining what they thought was a rust-colored puddle that the clean-up crew had missed.

Cars, vans, and pickups slowly circled the motel, as if in a funeral procession, their windshields decorated with messages written in white shoe polish:

"Selena Forever," "Missing My Baby," "From Your Fans in the Valley," "We Love You," "Fotos y Recuerdos," "Del Rio," "H-Town," "Austin," "San Antonio."

A couple miles south on Navigation Boulevard, the convenience store clerk gave directions to the Quintanilla houses on Bloomington. The Molina subdivision had its share of success stories, including doctors, lawyers, teachers, and two professional basketball stars. But no one was a bigger source of pride and joy than Selena, the Molina girl. She grew up in Molina, and she had stayed in Molina.

Traffic was backed up five blocks as motorists waited their turn for a slow cruise by the brick homes. Scores of fans stood numbly gazing at the front of the chain-link fence, which had turned into a canvas of bereavement. Poster boards, banners, photos, flowers, colored ribbons, balloons, and stuffed teddy bears hung on links beneath the flags of the United States, Mexico, and El Salvador. Messages were scribbled and posted in every nook and cranny. One note in particular captured the confusion of many of those gathered on the street and the sidewalk:

"I think the only reason that lady took your life is cuz she's jealous but someone will get her, because you were C.C. Babe! I will miss ya a whole lot. You were my favorite singer and always will be. Love, Valerie Minguera."

The writers of other messages were from Puerto Rico, Dallas, Wisconsin, Deer Park, Laredo, Three Rivers, La Feria, and Molina. There were expressions of sorrow from the Universal Little League and the Leyba family down the street. One note was simply addressed: To: Heaven. From: Houston.

A little toddler stared at a picture of Selena on the fence and gleefully tugged at his mother's skirt. "Look, Mommy. Bidi bidi bom bom."

At the Bayfront Convention Center downtown, the midafternoon line of people wound from the entrance of the building and down the sidewalk along Shoreline Drive. The people were waiting to view the closed casket of Selena, which was surrounded by more than two hundred oversized sprays of flowers, many of them white roses, Selena's favorite. The procession passing the casket was orderly and quiet, though occasional laughs could be heard from the line outside. It was, after all, an ideal Sunday afternoon. One man in a cowboy hat jabbered into his cellular phone. The line had been like this all day. Fans started showing up as early as four A.M. even though the doors hadn't opened until nine that morning.

In the early evening, an hour before the doors were scheduled to close, the calm was broken by a rumor spreading through the crowd: The coffin was empty. At eight P.M., the Quintanilla family allowed the casket to be opened to dispel the rumors. The body was Selena's. Her hands, folded across her chest, clutched a single rose. One of those paying their respects was Albert Dávila, who arrived with a contingent from KEDA around dusk. "We passed about two thousand people waiting in line. Right as we got to the door, that's when they opened the casket. That blew my mind. She looked beautiful. She looked like she was asleep. That kind of helped because I saw her. I was thinking at the time, How did those people feel waiting in line all day and they didn't get to see her? How did they deal with it? They wanted to see her to put some finality to it." By ten o'clock, when the doors of the Bayfront were finally closed, almost sixty thousand people had passed through.

And the veneration was spreading. The majority of cars traveling Interstate 37 between S.A. and Corpus had their headlights on. The morning newscasts reported four thousand people attended a special mass at the Los Angeles Sports Arena, where Selena had been booked to play on Saturday night (although Abraham was upset when he learned the promoter had charged admission to the mass). Vigils were being held across the country. The death of Selena was front-page news in the *New York Times* for two consecutive days and was featured prominently on the British Broadcasting Corporation's world news broadcasts. Record stores were cleaned out of Selena albums within hours, although EMI Latin was in the process of pressing several million copies of CDs and cassettes to meet the expected demand.

Back in Selena's hometown of Lake Jackson, one thousand fans and friends gathered at the municipal park in neighboring Clute, where she'd played at the Mosquito Festival the previous July. A brief mass was led by Father James Lynes and Father Reginald Petrash. "It is hard for us to understand why this happened the way it did,'' Father Jim said. The desire to avenge her death by killing the killer ''was part of the problem'' with violence in the modern world, he said. ''This is someone who was among us for a short time, but who touched us through her music,'' Father Reggie said. ''She was gifted by God with an ability to love a great many people. That love continues in her music and in your hearts. Give thanks to God for the time we had with her.'' Following the mass, a disc jockey played the first track off the *Selena Live* album, moving some in the crowd to raise their candles and sway to the music while others danced.

On Monday, April 3, six hundred invited guests bearing family passes gathered under two canopies at the gravesite for the ten A.M. services, which were broadcast live by San Antonio and Corpus Christi radio and television stations.

A Jehovah's Witness minister, Sam Wax of Lake Jackson, preached his message in English: ''The flower stood here, rooted, facing the weather's full fury. Now here it is, still intact, bowed but unbroken, showing strength that belies the delicacy of its appearance.

''You know, a long time ago, the apostle Paul began by offering hope to all of us [which] is recorded in the book of First Corinthians, chapter fifteen. He spoke about the thousand-year reign of Christ, and he said that in that period of time Christ would bring to nothing the last enemy, Death.

''How is it that Paul could have been so sure that that would have happened? Well, you see, Paul was taught by Christ himself. So in adding to that hope, Paul made this statement concerning Christ in First Corinthians, chapter fifteen, verses twenty-one and twenty-two. He said that since death is through a man, resurrection of the dead is also through a man. For, just as in Adam all are dying, so also in Christ all will be made alive.

''That hope has been held on to for centuries by God-fearing people. Interesting, too, [that] when Christ was on the Earth, in addition to healing many people, he also did something that makes our hopes solid for the future and for the resurrection.''

Wax proceeded through John 5:28, the twenty-first chapter of Revelation, James 1:3, and First Thessalonians 4:13 before he concluded the fifteen-minute service, saying, "Father, we want to thank you for all your tender mercies, and now we ask that you comfort people worldwide who have lost loved ones in death. We ask that you also extend such comfort to the mother and father, sister and brother, the husband of Selena, in order that they might also have hope and also might rise to praise and glorify your great name, the One who has such tender mercies, and the One that feels such pity for us here in this condition that we are in.

"So we praise you, dear Father. We look forward to the fulfillment of all of your promises in the near future, as the Earth will become a beautiful paradise and the dead will rise. These things we pray for and once again praise you, in the name of our Lord and Savior, Jesus Christ, Amen."

At the request of the family, the mourners, who included Roberto Pulido, Laura Canales, Elsa García, Ram Herrera, members of Grupo Mazz and Culturas, David Lee Garza, and Emilio Navaira, placed white roses atop the casket as they filed past. In all, eight thousand flowers were piled two feet high before the coffin was cleared and lowered.

Eddie Quintanilla thanked the crowd, in Spanish, for coming.

The *chop-chop-chop* from the two helicopters hovering overhead during most of the service visibly angered Abraham. A few minutes later, he told someone he wished he had a bazooka.

Chris appeared to take it the hardest, wiping a tear from his eye while clutching a white rose; sitting next to him was Marcella, her hennaed head bowed low, struggling to compose herself.

Following the funeral service, the fans outside the cemetery gates stampeded a man in a van who was trying to give out the carnations, birds of paradise, and white roses left over from the funeral.

Back at the Days Inn, a transformation was under way. In less than twenty-four hours, the facade of room 158 had been turned into a shrine. Messages scribbled with pencils, pens, and markers covered the door, the window, the sidewalk, even the limestone exterior blocks: "With love from all of us in Waco, the Torres Family," "Mondo, Dallas," "We miss you. Vickie Huebner, Beeville," "Florida loves You. Shanna Torres," "You will always live in our hearts. With love from the Ruiz-Menchaca Family, Eagle Pass," "Missing my Baby. Fort Stockton," "So much love from the heart—that was taken from life. Love, Dallas," "Sandy, Rita, Gloria, Irene. Yoakum."

"Tell them Laredo is gonna miss her," a dark-haired man in his twenties said to a person scribbling on a notepad. He introduced himself as David Cárdenas and he said he'd just driven in from Laredo with his wife, Cindy. A short older gentleman in a business suit introduced himself in broken English as Armando Gallegos. He had promoted Selena concerts in Miami and Tampa, he explained in Spanish. Memorial services were being staged in several Florida cities, he said. In Florida, Selena wasn't considered Tejano. *"Ella es una estrella internacional,"* he pronounced somberly. "She's an international star."

A young man in his twenties walked up breathlessly to a sidewalk where the blades of grass were still being examined. He was David Maldonado. He and his wife, Maricela, had just driven thirty hours from Lansing, Michigan. He'd become a fan after seeing Selena y los Dinos perform in Ohio. He apologized for missing the funeral, but he felt relieved that he could now pay his respects. "When we heard the news, we felt like we lost a part of us. She was part of my life," he said.

Four hours after Selena's body had been lowered into the ground, a parade of cars with headlights on circled the Seaside Funeral Home and Memorial Park, just behind Ocean Drive and less than a quarter mile from the Corpus Christi Bay. Her final resting spot was next to a newly planted native mesquite, whose leaves shimmered with the fresh yellow-green color of the new spring. The cemetery remained closed to the public in deference to the Quintanillas as well as two other families who were burying loved ones that day.

Another shrine-in-progress was being assembled on the steps of the Selena, Etc., boutique and salon in Corpus with balloons, posters, and messages. The López family expressed their sentiments here in a handwritten letter posted by the door, concluding their thoughts with the hope, "See you again someday."

At the Quintanilla homes in Molina, the procession of motor vehicles continued, with the tour bus of the band Culturas among the cars and trucks waiting in line as police directed traffic. The number of notes on the fence had doubled overnight and now stretched around the corner onto the wooden fence, placed over faded spray-painted graffiti.

By late afternoon, most of the friends and family who'd stopped by to pay their respects had cleared out of the Q Productions complex on Leopard Street. Abraham was still holding meetings and talking to reporters from television programs, radio stations, and newspapers. A.B. showed one of the Barrio Boyzz around the studio. Eddie Quintanilla regaled visitors with stories about his brother and his family, of growing up in Corpus Christi, and of Abraham's old group Los Dinos, who had loved the street-corner harmonies of doo-wop music and rhythm and blues but who played traditional Tex-Mex fare—polkas and waltzes with Spanish lyrics—to pay the bills. He also remembered the family committing their lives to music, roaring around in that battered blue van, pulling an itty-bitty trailer. "That was a long, long time ago." Eddie smiled.

Abraham Quintanilla, tired and spent, sat in a chair by the mixing board console in the studio control room. He'd just been unusually candid with the reporter from NBC's *Dateline*, saying, "I saw a way to get back into the music world, through my daughter. Maybe I made a ba— a wrong decision, because look what it has se— led to."

Now, while a television cameraman and a sound person packed up their gear, he paused. There was dread in his voice when he spoke about what was to come. When the last person left, when the friends and family had gone, then it would sink in. "When I know she's not here, when I see that empty place, that's when I'm going to start missing her.

"It's a tragic thing that happened. It's a reality."

Firearms, he said, were partly to blame. "We live in a dangerous world. Why make it worse? My God, everyone's armed to the teeth. Anybody is liable to kill you for a minute thing. Look at this lady. If that gun wasn't accessible to her, it wouldn't have turned out the way it did."

Life would go on; so would the music. "I want it to continue. Of course, it would never be the same. There will never be another Selena. But we'll go forward with it."

Were there any lessons people could learn from this?

He paused, his head slumped down. "Parents, it's time to go back to the old-fashioned way of teaching our children," he said. "About morals, about life, about the dangers of life. [Children are] too trusting. They don't think there are bad things out there. I hope that a lot of young people see this and use it as an example to be cautious and not be so ready to trust. As I digest this in my mind, I don't think Selena knew how popular she was getting. I would tell her, '*M'ijita*, don't be going to the store by yourself at night. Don't go to the mall alone. There are people who will kill you for no reason, just because you are famous.'"

He knew all that, but Abraham Quintanilla also recognized the dynamic between his daughter and himself. She listened, but she also had a mind of her own.

"Dad, you think all people are bad. I can take care of myself."

Abraham talked about the band's first tour of Mexico and how she was called a woman of the people. "She never forgot where she came from," he said.

He spoke out against the veneration in progress, shaking his head. "Selena wouldn't want that because she believed worship should only go to the Creator. Just remember her as a good person who loved life. I don't think Selena would be pleased to be part of any form of idolatry."

The seeming perfection was undeniable. Selena left this world forever young, virtuous, happily married; an independent businesswoman, an American girl, and *una mujer* Mexicana who still lived next door to Mom and Dad. In the muted, misty twilight falling at the end of a grim Monday, the veneration continued. Where there had been two floral arrangements three days ago on the steps of the San Antonio boutique, there was now a vast altar. The entire side of the building by the parking lot had been turned into a street cathedral infused with bright colors brimming with life. Every square inch of the boutique's porch was filled with flowers, pictures, posters, and other objects of devotion. A large rendering of the Virgin of Guadalupe bordered with pink crinoline was propped on an easel, surrounded by blow-up Easter bunnies, several T-shirts, a few drawings by children, a low-rider etching, and too many images of Selena to count. Metallic helium-filled balloons, several with the message "We Love You, Selena," floated above the wrought-iron porch railing.

One note begged forgiveness: "Dear Selena, I can't believe you're dead. I'm sorry for what I said about you. I was just mad."

On a narrow perch at the bottom of the railing was another phalanx of flowers. Beneath them, on the asphalt, thirty votive candles in glass holders flickered in the gathering darkness. Standing in a semicircle around the base of this improvised church were three men and ten women holding crucifixes and quietly reciting the Catholic rosary.

The men then began to play the musical instruments they held—a button accordion; an acoustic guitar; and a *bajo quinto*, a ten-string oversized guitar—while the women launched into song, softly raising their voices into one. They sang *"Cuál Grande Es Él?"* (How Great Thou Art), *"¿Te Vas, Angel Mío?"* (Are You Leaving, My Angel?), and *"En Tí y Tus Manos"* (In You and Your Hands).

There was another song where the word *corazón*, the heart, punctuated the chorus, distinguished by a mournful, high-pitched female wail of resignation.

The *bajo* player, Richard Alcorta, said all the musicians and singers were members of the Spanish choir at St. Henry's Catholic church. They frequently sang at funerals, but this occasion was spontaneous. "I didn't know Selena but I wanted to say good-bye," he said.

The day after her burial, a mass at Our Lady of Pilar Church, two blocks from Selena's house in Molina, drew 450 people to the 225-seat church. On the following day, the Quintanillas removed messages, flowers, and candles from the chain-link and wood fences on their property. The Days Inn placed three flip charts on easels—one by the lobby, two by room 158—in hopes of discouraging fans from writing on the walls and doors. Next to each was the message, "Please write your sentiments on the paper so that they may be preserved."

Whether these acts were motivated by religious beliefs, selfishness, or ignorance, they appeared callous in light of all these people who were only trying to pour out their feelings. Couldn't the family see that they weren't the only ones who loved Selena?

7

Dreaming

IN THE WAKE OF SELENA'S death, Corpus Christi practically shut down.

"People weren't shopping. There was nothing going on," said Manuel Dávila. "The stores took a beating. Everything was focused on what happened to this lady in her hometown. Everybody took it like a member of [his] family passing away."

Unusual events and powerful tributes were taking place. Danny Hermosillo, a news reporter for KMOL-TV in San Antonio, told viewers about Jamie Ayala-Jackson of Austin, who had seen a vision of Selena appear on Sunday, April 2, the day that Selena would have celebrated her third wedding anniversary to Chris Perez. The next day, Spanish television talk-show host Cristina devoted her entire program on the Univisión network to Selena. The rival Telemundo network rebroadcast her 1995 Astrodome concert later in the week. On Tuesday, the first *corrido* tribute to Selena debuted on the ten o'clock newscast on KENS-TV in San Antonio. Word had it that maintenance workers at the Days Inn were unable to remove all the bloodstains from the carpet in the lobby. The distinctive outline of Selena's body was still visible. In the week following her death, seven out of every hundred newborns in Santa Clara County, California, were named Selena.

Murals popped up everywhere, including two major ones in Corpus: one at the Las Casuelas Lounge on the west side and another at South Port and Dillon. Freddy Fender, formerly Corpus's highest profile Hispanic celebrity, was amazed at the impact the death had on the entire community. "My family is really troubled by this," he said. "My grandchildren run to the TV whenever anything about Selena is on. I wouldn't be surprised if they name a street after her, or a building."

Leonard Wong, the scent man who was creating Selena's perfume, was feeling troubled. He had a gnawing feeling that the perfume was one of the subjects that came up during the final, fatal argument between Selena and Yolanda. He couldn't get it out of his mind. Then he saw an interview on KMOL-TV between Selena and news anchor Randy Beamer that was being replayed as part of a tribute. At the end of the interview, Selena told Beamer she was coming out with an English album and a new perfume. "It's going to smell like *chorizo con huevos*"— just like sausage and eggs. Wong began sobbing uncontrollably.

Two days after Selena's burial, her murderer had an attorney. Douglas Tinker was appointed by Judge Mike Westergren to defend Yolanda Saldivar. "This is not something that I welcome," he told the Corpus Christi *Caller-Times*. "But it's a duty that I have, that called upon, I represent people accused of a crime. I'm flattered that Judge Westergren thinks that I'm capable of dealing with it." On April 6, a Nueces County grand jury indicted Yolanda Saldivar for the murder of Selena Quintanilla Perez. Saldivar pled not guilty. Six days later Westergren set the trial date for October 9.

After the immediate shock of Selena's death, Abraham and the family came to one conclusion: They must keep the dream alive. The immediate goal was to continue doing what they had been working toward for the past fifteen years as if Selena was still among them.

For the first three days after her death, all Abraham could envision was his little girl of long ago, always singing. "She was a genuinely good person—she was clean, she stood for family. It is comforting to know that people responded to the values we instilled in our child." Chris Perez wouldn't move anything in the house. "I keep thinking about the clothes she wore the day before she died," he later told Joanna Powell of *Good Housekeeping*. "We had just returned from Nashville, and we hadn't unpacked yet. A few days later I was cleaning out our suitcase and I found her sweatsuit in the zipper compartment. It still smelled like her, which freaked me out. I closed it up and moved the bag aside."

Chris was finding it difficult to cope. He tried talking it out, telling Vivienne Heines of the *Caller-Times* about the good times. "She was really, really alive. She was real passionate about everything she said and did. She cried as much as she laughed. I never met a person like that. She got me to open up. I learned from her how to say 'I love you' to my mom and dad when they would call me on the road." He praised his father-in-law, saying, "Abraham—he's being really strong about it. I am not. I still need a little more time."

Chris and Selena were living proof that opposites attract, he said. "She was full of life. I'm more laid-back. She kind of evened things out for us. We never saw ourselves without each other. She was the only one, out of all the people I ever met, who could make me care for how she felt over how I felt." He confided that he hated thinking of her as something he'd won. "A lot of people out there thought that I looked at her like she was a trophy. But I never looked at her like that. She wasn't just the Selena who was up there on the stage, that everybody saw. Or the Selena walking to the bus with her bodyguards. That was part of her, but it wasn't all of her."

Suzette felt responsible. She was the one who had introduced Yolanda to Selena. "One thing that really hurts is that it was a person we knew—and once trusted—who did this. Yolanda was a bridesmaid at my wedding. I look at my wedding pictures and they're bittersweet. There she is along with Selena, who was my maid of honor. But this woman manipulated her way into our circle. Perhaps I kind of blame myself because I'm the one who met Yolanda. She became my friend before she became friends with Selena and Chris.''

Children in particular struggled to understand. If Selena was killed in spite of the exemplary life she lived, who was safe then? "These little kids, their world has really been shaken," said Virginia Mann, a counselor at Seguin Elementary School in McAllen in far South Texas. Preteen girls, in particular, had viewed Selena as a "fairy princess" they could relate to. Her death, Mann said, was "like a fairy tale that had a bad ending. All our fairy tales as children end happily. Their security has been invaded. 'It could happen to Selena, it could happen to me.' It jolts you."

Even Selena's birthday became a source of controversy. The governor declared April 16 Selena Day in Texas, but not everyone got the message. At noon on Easter Sunday, almost one thousand fans gathered at her grave to sing her "Las Mañanitas," the traditional Mexican song of birthday greetings. Some brought guitars, and one girl had a trumpet. Some of those attending came from as far away as California and Mexico. During the impromptu service, Debbie Martin, the vice president of Seaside Funeral Home, walked into the gathering.

"What are you all doing here? You're on private property," she admonished the group. "You don't have permission to be here. The family has not authorized this."

Picnicking on the grounds, a sight not uncommon during the Day of the Dead observances throughout Mexico and the Southwest, was considered inappropriate at Seaside. "We can't have that out at the cemetery," Martin told the *Caller-Times*. Police were called in to control the crowd that had gathered by the gravesite.

On the same day, a crowd of three thousand attended an organized Votive Mass of Resurrection for Selena at the Johnnyland Concert Park, a few miles away. Monsignor Michael Heras, pastor of Our Lady of Perpetual Help, noted the irony of a Catholic service being said for a woman whose family followed the Jehovah's Witness faith. "First of all, we believe that the majority of Selena's fans and admirers are Catholic," Heras said. "And nobody knows what she desired of life in her last few seconds. From what we know, there was an earnest search for meaning in her own life, and only God knows right now where that search ended." The Mariachi Clásico performed; Nelda Cruz Mungía sang "Ave Maria" accompanied by Patricia Furly on harp, and two dozen white doves, donated by Efraín Guerrero, aka Happy De Klown, were set free.

The April 28 fireworks display scheduled for Buccaneer Days in Corpus Christi was reworked to include "Bidi Bidi Bom Bom."

Carloads of fans, the messages on their windshields like badges, headed to Corpus Christi to trace Selena's footsteps and leave their own thoughts behind. "Now you can sing with the angels" had been carved into the bark of the mesquite sapling that had been planted by her graveside before the area was fenced off. The boutique in Corpus reopened on April 20, with Debra Ramírez, a cousin of Selena's, running the place. The stucco exterior was repainted, covering the messages scrawled on the walls, and additional nail technicians and hairstylists had been hired to accommodate the anticipated crowds. Selena's new line of spring fashions, manufactured in Mexico, were due to arrive the following week, but along with the high-dollar designer stock, the store's merchandise now also included Selena T-shirts, Selena caps, and Selena can coolers. Employees were instructed to refrain from speaking to media people at the risk of being fired.

Abraham Quintanilla initially announced that the San Antonio store would be closed, but he changed his mind and reopened the boutique on Broadway a few weeks later, with Chris Perez's sister and her husband managing the store. Although both shops operated pretty much as conventional retail businesses during the week, they became tourist attractions on Saturdays, when visitors would come in to talk about Selena, cry, or leave tokens of their respect and grief. "This place is like a museum . . . it's really neat," one counter employee said. "And lots of men come in, too. This is not just a place for women. On Saturdays we play Selena videos all day and feature her music and tributes to her life. Lots of people come in and it's really like a living museum."

Within six weeks, Abraham filed charges with Corpus Christi police, accusing Yolanda Saldivar of embezzling $30,700 from the Selena fan club over a five-month period, from September 1, 1994, to January 31, 1995. He said he first learned of the discrepancies during the summer of 1994, when several fans complained that they had sent in their money and not received the CD, T-shirt, cap, and autographed poster as promised. That was just the sort of problem that Selena talked about wanting to avoid in an interview three years before; she said that was why Abraham had interviewed several potential fan-club presidents before he hired Yolanda.

Abraham also took a public stand on the issue of guns, while reiterating his philosophy on entertainment and politics. At a press conference that he called, he made this statement:

"People are in a state of wonder, asking, 'What do we do next? What can we do next?' People were waiting for this message—this is our message—Stop the violence in America. No more guns." Still, he made it clear that he wouldn't lobby the state legislature, where a concealed handgun law was in the process of being passed. "I don't want to get involved with politics. This is an emotional issue, not a political issue. I have never been involved in politics and I'm not about to start."

He unveiled the campaign Sosa, Bromley, Aguilar, and Associates had developed for print, television, radio, and billboards, featuring the image of Selena and the slogan "No More Guns. All the Flowers, All the Candles, All the Tears Can't Erase the Pain." Al Aguilar, who directed the campaign, called it "the saddest, most bittersweet piece of work I've ever touched at this agency.''

The press conference presented the incongruous tableau of Abraham standing at the podium in his shades, mambo-print sport shirt and slacks, looking at a wide-screen image of his daughter, who appeared wholly innocent, angelic, and very sexually appealing. A vase of white roses was placed between them.

What was the big deal? many Anglos wondered.

Various letters to the editor of the Brazosport *Facts* during the months of April and May voiced the typical response toward the Other Society. One writer, Marge Proctor, complained about Governor George Bush designating April 16 as Selena Day, taking offense that she would be honored on a day that fell on Easter Sunday. Others shared the sentiment.

Dot Mitchell of Brazoria wrote a letter to the editor of the Brazosport *Facts*, published Friday, May 19, under the heading ''Has Selena Issue Run Its Course?'': ''My heart goes out to the family of Selena. It was a tragic thing as it would be for any family. However, in my opinion, it has been run into the ground. Like another reader, I had never heard of Selena until she was killed. It's also true that her birthday will come on the same day every year and Easter will not, but I believe Easter and what it stands for is more important than Selena Day.

''Just so no one is offended or gets the wrong impression or calls me prejudiced, I grew up in Corpus Christi and went to school with many Mexicans. Many of them were my good friends. They did not mind being called Mexicans because that was their nationality. It was not a put-down or a slanderous word. So let's get on and celebrate life and let Selena rest.''

Mexican-American letter-writers objected vociferously. And one Anglo writer agreed with their objections, saying, ''You and many others have missed the point. The reason the governor set Selena's birthday as Selena Day is because she was our very own, a Texan. This honorable action is not mandatory. It will not harm anyone and is only meant for those that want to honor her life ... The point is, Selena was from our area. I for one am proud of that fact. She touched many of us in a special way. For all of you that didn't know her and want to know what this is all about, I suggest that you purchase some of her latest recordings, and then you too probably will become enchanted by her musical talent. If not, may her memory rest in peace. Let us have our special positive way of honoring her short life. This will not harm anyone. Trust me." It was signed "Elizabeth May, Angleton."

The culture clash was considerably uglier on the national stage. Before Selena had been laid to rest, nationally syndicated radio disc jockey Howard Stern aimed his offbeat brand of satire at her. On his Monday morning program, Stern played Selena's music with the sound of gunshots in the background, uttered the opinion that "Alvin and the Chipmunks have more soul," and stated that "Spanish people have the worst taste in music. They have no depth." Her fans, he continued, "live in refrigerator boxes ... like to make love to a goat ... and like to dance with velvet paintings and eat beans." The remarks thoroughly angered Selena fans. Stern started receiving death threats within minutes. A boycott of advertisers on the Stern show was quickly organized by the National Hispanic Media Coalition. A grocery chain in South Texas pulled all products sold by Stern's advertisers off the shelves, specifically Gatorade sports drink, Heineken and Samuel Adams beer brands, and Slick 50 oil treatment. The Acapulco restaurant in Los Angeles and Pizza Hut pulled advertising from KLSX-FM, which aired Stern's show in Southern California.

Stern's apology, delivered halfheartedly in broken Spanish, only threw gasoline on the fire. "Having to apologize from New York, on the air, the radio, ain't going to fly," said an enraged justice of the peace, Eloy Cano of Harlingen in the Rio Grande Valley. "I really think he should come to Corpus Christi and apologize to Selena's family." And in case Stern took him up, Cano had issued a warrant for Stern's arrest. "I did it for all the Tejano fans," he said. "If they say that he is protected by the First Amendment, they need to come and show me. I'm not going to check the law for them."

On Thursday night, April 27, Stern's sidekick, Robin Quivers, an African-American woman promoting a book about her professional life with Stern, made an appearance on NBC's *Tonight Show*, starring Jay Leno. Asked by Leno about Stern's intolerance toward racial and ethnic groups, Quivers said she chose not to argue with her boss. When another guest on the show, singer Linda Ronstadt, a pop singer of Mexican-American heritage, came on the show, she told Quivers on the air that she was "deeply upset" with her comments. Quivers, she said, was "shilling" for Stern. "As a woman and a Mexican-American, I find him extremely offensive."

To the dismay and bewilderment of Abraham Quintanilla, Jr., a rash of pirated, unauthorized Selena merchandise flooded the streets. Bootleg cassettes were being turned out in Mexico, retailing at flea markets and on the streets for six dollars or less. "We need to somehow educate the public not to buy it because it's a very inferior product," Abraham said. "There's a lot of Judases out there." The sensationalism that Abraham used to complain about to Ramon Hernandez hit home in a most immediate manner: One man was peddling bootleg Selena T-shirts to the crowd who had gathered in front of the Quintanilla homes the day after the shooting. One neighbor complained to police that another freelance vendor was going door-to-door selling pirated Selena cassettes for five dollars. While eating breakfast in a restaurant the day after his daughter was buried, Abraham confronted another street vendor selling bootleg merchandise, seizing his illicit goods and telling him to leave the premises.

His legal representatives at the San Antonio law firm of Oppenheimer, Blend, Harrison, and Tate sent out letters and faxes to suspected merchandisers and photographers, informing them that only Q Productions could lawfully profit from Selena's image under a state law known as the Buddy Holly Act. In the firm's zeal to right wrongs, they sent the missives not just to illegal merchandisers but also to legitimate photographers who owned their photography of Selena. To them, the demands of a complete accounting of photo stock and sales and the request to turn over all Selena negatives to Abraham smacked of arrogance. Abraham even told one photographer whose work had appeared in several magazines following Selena's death that he would "get him."

Abraham was particularly upset by the posters and T-shirts that showed Selena at rest in the open coffin. "When my daughter was first killed, I just didn't have the time to think about what was going on out there," he said. "I had my daughter's death on my mind. Now it just enrages me to know that these people are trying to get rich quick over my daughter's death. They're all just vultures. It's another sad sign of the times. There is no more decency, no more morals."

The complaints indirectly confirmed that finances were tight in the Q empire. When Selena was alive, there was always money coming in, regardless of how difficult it was to get EMI Latin to cough up royalties.

Abraham may have appeared strong and determined in public, but the truth was he was so overextended that he was feeling the pressure to generate as much income as possible.

Some of the problems were resolved when Abraham cut a deal with the H-E-B grocery chain as the official retailer for family-authorized memorabilia and merchandise. Newspaper advertisements that ran in South Texas included this message: "We would like to thank H-E-B for their efforts to bring official Selena merchandise to her fans. A portion of the proceeds will go to the Selena Foundation, set up to educate future Tejano stars." It was signed, "the Quintanilla and Perez families." Merchandise featured in the ad included T-shirts for $10.99 to $12.99 each ("Tell the world of your love for Selena and her music with one of several full-color designs. Assorted styles and sizes"), a limited edition 22 × 28-inch color poster for $4.99, and a Selena magazine, a fifty-two page slick consisting primarily of photographs.

One item not featured at H-E-B was Clint Richmond's *Selena: The Last Song—La Ultima Cancion*, selling for the low price of $4.49, which Abraham had a few weeks earlier dismissed as "a ripoff to the public. It's a compilation of news reports." The paperback biography, published by Pocket Books, was written in two weeks by the freelance journalist from Austin, Texas. Published in early May, it topped the *New York Times* best-seller list for paperbacks for more than a month. The Richmond project, printed in both English and Spanish, was indicative of how the rest of the world was caught unawares by the phenomenon breaking out in Texas. When Richmond's agent, James Hornfischer of the Literary Group International, cut the deal with Pocket Books the week after Selena's death, the publisher anticipated printing 75,000 copies. But by the time the book appeared in stores, the print run had been increased to 560,000 copies.

Selena's death had a far greater impact in the magazine segment of the publishing industry, where the theme was the all-American dream snuffed out. It started when the April 17 edition of *People* magazine featured a split-cover issue: 442,000 copies running Selena's photo and with a six-page spread inside were distributed in Texas, and the rest of the 3.4 million copies sent to the rest of the nation hyped the all-Anglo cast of the television comedy series *Friends*. The Selena cover was an instant sellout around the state when it hit the stands on Monday, April 10. The next day, management at the magazine, who were floored by the phenomenal sales, announced a special-tribute issue to be published on Monday, April 24, the same day copies of *Texas Monthly* with Selena on the cover also hit the newsstands. Anticipation ran so high, there was a line of fans outside of Riverwalk Center in San Antonio waiting for the magazine distributor's truck to arrive at Brentano's bookstore. The seventy-six-page special issue of *People*, which retailed for $3.95, was only the third such commemorative issue the magazine had printed, the others having been devoted to Audrey Hepburn and Jaqueline Kennedy Onassis. That was an instant sellout too for many South Texas retailers, including H-E-B and K-Mart, who limited purchases to one copy per family. Six hundred thousand copies sold out almost immediately, with a second run of 350,000 coming close to a sellout too.

Selena homepages appeared on the World Wide Web of the Internet. One page was posted for the tribute to Selena benefit held at the Astrodome in Houston on Memorial Day. Another was a permanent site (http://www.ondanet.com:1995/tejano/selena.html) created by Selena fan Abel M. Hernández of Dallas. The *Caller-Times* set up a page, too (http://www.wtr.com/cchome/selena.htm). The sites affirmed the Tejano culture's embrace of technology. José Limón, a University of Texas English professor and author of *Dancing with the Devil: Society and Cultural Politics in Mexican American South Texas* (University of Wisconsin Press), which applies an academic analysis to the socio-political world of Texas-Mexicans, applauded Selena's arrival in cyberspace. "What you're witnessing here is an interest in Selena coming from the intelligentsia in Mexican-American life. It's very telling to me that I found out about it from my graduate students. They totally live that life. The Mexican-American community is no longer a community of farm workers. There are people who are intellectually inclined and use computers frequently," he told Jeff Classen of the Corpus Christi *Caller-Times*.

Selena was posthumously given awards at the Univisión network's Premio Lo Nuestro Awards. She won four *Billboard* Latin Music Awards and was inducted into the Latin Music Hall of Fame in Miami, where she had built a respectable following. The Pura Vida Hispanic Music Awards in San Antonio presented Selena y los Dinos awards in the Tejano category for best female singer, best group, best CD, best video (for "Bidi Bidi Bom Bom"), and entertainer of the year. A.B. won best songwriter.

The Memorial Day tribute at the Astrodome in Houston was organized by Tony Cavazos Bruni, a Quintanilla family friend and video producer from Sugarland, and Jim McIngvale, better known as Mattress Mac, the hyperactive pitchman and owner of Gallery Furniture in Houston. The concert was broadcast on a delayed basis by television stations in Houston, Corpus, Dallas–Fort Worth, Austin, San Antonio, and Lubbock. On the bill were Los Agues, the Barrio Boyzz, Graciela Beltran, Elsa García, ex–Dino Pete Astudillo, Roberto Pulido, Alvaro Torres, and home-town headliners La Mafia. The performances were recorded on a thirty-two-track sound board, despite the Dome not being recognized for its acoustic qualities, a fact of which every act on the bill became keenly aware. Most of the entertainers, including twelve-year-old Jennifer Peña, who did a karaoke to "Bidi Bidi Bom Bom," covered Selena's songs, although La Mafia opted to show-case their current hit, "Nadie."

Between the short sets, videos played of Selena singing "No Me Queda Más," "Bidi Bidi Bom Bom," "Como la Flor," "Fotos y Recuerdos," and "Amor Prohibido." The tribute drew 30,800 fans, including a two-hundred-person delegation from Corpus Christi led by Abraham, Marcella, A. B., Suzette, and Chris. The entrance and exit of the family carried all the solemnity of a religious service.

In June, Robert Alaniz, a Corpus Christi native and a vice president at the Hill and Knowlton public relations firm in Los Angeles, initiated an effort to honor Selena with a star on the Hollywood Walk of Fame. In order to do so, he had to persuade Walk of Fame officials to waive the five-year waiting period following a celebrity's death before induction. A letter-writing campaign organized by Alaniz failed to sway Walk of Fame committee chairman Johnny Grant. "It will not change a thing. It's just too bad because people waste time and postage. The committee never sees the letters. There's just nothing we can do about it."

Up the coast, in the Mission district of San Francisco,

La India Bonita bar was drawing crowds to their Selena drag show, believed to be the first of its kind anywhere.

The questions lingered: Why did Yolanda do it? Was it love? Hate? Because she felt trapped? Because the old man threatened to get her? The rumor mill continued to grind. Primo Ledesma of Freeport met a writer from Miami who'd seen the special edition of the Brazosport *Facts* published in early April. "[The writer] said that Miami scandal sheets had written that Yolanda was really Selena's mom and Emilio Navaira's wife had killed her. She wanted me to get a copy of her birth certificate to prove her real parents."

The gossip ranged from semitruths and the plausible to the sensational and outrageous: It was a cocaine deal gone bad. Selena was gay. Chris was gay. Theirs was a marriage of convenience. Chris had signed away all his rights in a prenuptial agreement. Before she died, Selena signed off on a will bequeathing everything to Abraham. Selena had gotten a place on Ocean Drive, where she was living while Chris was living at the house on Bloomington alone. Her red Porsche hadn't been seen parked on Bloomington Street all week before her murder. Yolanda's got something on Abraham.

The most scurrilous was a Mexican magazine article, mentioned on Telemundo newscasts, that reported Quintanilla had kicked Chris Perez out of the home next to his own. Chris called a press conference and sat down with reporters from the Associated Press and the Univisión television network with Abraham at his side. "I consider them my family, my flesh-and-blood family," he told them. "There's nobody out there that I know who can help me deal with this better than they can, and I'd like to be there for them also. We were all together most of the time. Everybody is just kind of sticking together right now."

"Of course it bothers us, because it's a lie," Abraham said. "I know there are more good people than bad. We've had great support from the good people who've felt the loss of Selena. They've helped us in a critical time for the family.''

The public posturing did little to dispel the notion that Chris was an emotional wreck. He was clearly haunted by guilt. What if he'd gone with Selena to the motel? ''She would still be here, and if she wouldn't be here, then neither would I,'' he told *People*. He'd lost thirteen pounds and retreated into himself. He hadn't moved a thing in the house, leaving her makeup and dresses where they were, keeping the sticker ''Selena-n-Chris Forever'' adhered to the bathroom mirror. His father, Gilbert, no longer stayed with him—he'd gone back to San Antonio—but his sister, Patricia Ratcliff, and his mother, Carmen Cadena, still came down from S.A. to cook for him and help him clean house.

But he didn't want to have anything to do with business. Selena left no will, and as her husband, Chris was legally in charge of her estate. But less than two weeks after her death, he waived his rights and designated Abraham as the temporary administrator of Selena's estate, giving him ''the authority to protect Decedent's property, to actively run Decedent's businesses, and to protect the Decedent's name and likeness from unauthorized use and exploitation and to assist the owners in the use and exploitation by the owners of Decedent's likeness and name for the benefit of her estate and her heirs at law.''

On July 10, 1995, Chris, Abraham, Marcella, A.B., and Suzette signed agreements in which Chris made Abraham's temporary administration permanent and divvied up Selena's property. Chris received all of the couple's community property, all of Selena's personal property, and one-half interest in all her real property. Abraham and Marcella each received one-quarter undivided interest in all separate real property. According to the family settlement agreement, Selena transferred certain property rights to Abraham before her death. Most significantly, Chris signed off on all the legal papers waiving his rights without the advice of an attorney.

For someone who was reputedly a millionaire at the

age of nineteen, according to her official biography, Selena's net worth was surprisingly spare. Her personal property included approximately $3,800 in cash; her 1987 Porsche Targa 911, worth $22,400 (though $5,385 was still owed on the car); the 1993 Chevy pickup she and Chris drove, worth $16,000; a $3,250 motorcycle; a $1,000 investment in Selena, Etc.; a $1,000 investment in Selena's design house; her egg collection, worth $3,609; $58,250 of furniture and household effects; clothing and outfits worth $49,830; jewelry valued at $29,250; and $51,000 in musical instruments and equipment. Her real property consisted of the earnest money put down on the country home she and Chris were planning, and the boutique in Corpus, valued at $36,201. Her contract with SBK Records and various receivables comprised the rest of her worth. According to the agreement, Chris was entitled to half of the community property, the total value of which was placed at $326,199.

Selena's real worth, of course, was in the value of her name as a performing artist, which was incalculable.

It couldn't have been any other way, Abraham said. "If I was to die right now, this business would go down to the ground. My family and Chris don't understand the music business like I do," he told the San Antonio *Express-News*.

Such statements made it difficult to sympathize with Abraham. He was the one who had to simultaneously manage the act he had nurtured all his life and cope with the loss of his daughter. No matter what he did, his actions were subject to scrutiny and only fueled the barroom speculation that Abraham had blown it. He was the one who put Yolanda out of kilter by threatening to get her for stealing money from Selena, Yolanda claimed. How could he let *la mosca*, the fly, get into the ointment? If he was really running the show, why did he let his daughter, the franchise, go to the motel alone to see a woman he believed to be a liar and a thief? He blew it by not sending her to the motel with a guard or chaperone, so the barroom talk went. He was on a massive ego trip. Besides, look what he did to his daughter by forcing her to perform in the first place. The girl never had a childhood. If she'd been allowed more freedom, she would never have gone back to the motel by herself. She was so trusting, she might as well have been going on fifteen instead of twenty-four.

Manuel Dávila saw it as a case study in knowing when to let go. "Abraham wanted to control his daughter. But there comes a time when your daughter is a woman and she's no longer your little girl. That's probably what got her killed. She made a horrible, horrible mistake. One that cost her her life. She had all this talent, she could sing, she could act, she's smart, she could manage money, and, being twenty-three years old, she figures everybody loves her. It's just like guys who go to war. The old guys are back in the lines, the young guys are up front; they think they're never going to get killed. I don't think she knew how big she was."

Meanwhile, Marcella remained in the background, quietly grieving, seeking solace by reading Scriptures, answering letters, offering comfort to her family, getting comfort from them. On one of the few occasions when she spoke publicly, she told *People* magazine about her own efforts to heal the pain by meeting young fans who gathered outside the family homes on Bloomington Street. "The moms tell me their kids are having a hard time understanding death. I ask the kids what their favorite song was, how they're doing in school. They tell me they miss Selena, and I tell them we have to pick up the pieces and keep going. Not everyone breaks down at the same time," she said. "When one of us breaks down, the other steps in to comfort. We're always there for each other."

She was right. Whatever tensions had been building during Selena's last days, the family unit was once again tight as a drum. The obvious was rarely talked about among the relatives. It didn't need to be said: Trust someone outside the family and this is what happens. Abraham was still calling the shots. Ironically, he was also the man in the spotlight, the star he'd always dreamed of being.

Abe's maroon-and-silver Lincoln was as recognizable around Corpus as Freddy Fender's restored Triumph. A couple of weeks after Easter, he was in a boisterous mood at La Bahia restaurant in the company of his wife, his parents, and family friends, speaking loud enough for other diners to hear him expound on his new-found celebrity. "I'm so famous," he said, for all to hear, "I couldn't rob a bank if I wanted to."

Before the dirt had been shoveled onto Selena's coffin, Abraham and the Quintanilla kids knew what their mission was. "You have to understand, here you have a person that is of Mexican descent but her culture is American," he said to John Morthland of *Entertainment Weekly*. "She's an American girl who happens to be Spanish. All these years she was recording in Spanish, which was her second language, and she wanted to record in English. The mainstream market was a dream, a goal. When this dream was fixing to be realized, she was cut short. So I don't want to deny my daughter, even though she's dead, that dream she had. Plus, to me, speaking for myself, it's a healing process."

A.B., sitting in at the same interview, said carrying on had become a family mission. "Love was the number-one thing that kept us together. The one thing we shared in common was also the love of music. That's something that's always in your heart and never goes away. It wasn't one of those things where everyone sat down and decided, it was one of those things everyone wanted to do and we knew she would want us to do. After everything happened, we just all went about burying ourselves in our usual everyday activities, not to really think about it that much, even though it does still pop up every day."

Sales of *Amor Prohibido*, which had hovered around six hundred thousand units just before Selena's death, had reached 1.5 million in the span of three months. The album shot to the number-one position on *Billboard*'s Latin chart, and five of Selena's albums were simultaneously on the top-two-hundred chart, an unprecedented achievement for a recording artist who sang in Spanish.

Nancy Brennan, the SBK Records A & R vice president who was going to shepherd the English pop crossover, brought in A.B. to put together the album Selena had been working on. Four crossover cuts had already been recorded in Nashville and Los Angeles—"I Could Fall in Love," "Dreaming of You," "Captive Heart," and "I'm Getting Used to You"—with Selena's vocals overdubbed at the studio in Corpus. There were more English tracks due to be cut with famous producers, as well as a few English tunes that had been written by A.B., Pete, and Ricky that were scheduled to be recorded later in Corpus. In lieu of those, A.B. and Brennan opted to add nine existing selections: "Missing My Baby," "Amor Prohibido," "Tú, Sólo Tú," "El Toro Relajo," "God's Child (Baila Conmigo)," "Wherever You Are," "Como la Flor," "Techno Cumbia," and "Bidi Bidi Bom Bom."

A.B. admitted it was difficult putting the album together. "I produced all of Selena's Latin stuff, all her successful stuff, and I'll never run into a vocalist like her ever again, or have a sister like her," he told *Time* magazine. "That's what gives me an empty feeling—losing her first as a sister and then as a vocalist."

Brennan was more than happy to defer to A.B. She knew the project was in good hands. "Her family members were her best friends. Your legacy is much more protected when your family is in charge of it."

Back home, Suzette Arriaga had assumed control of her late sister's boutiques. "Before, the family didn't have a lot to do with them, businesswise," she told the Corpus Christi *Caller-Times*. "Selena took care of it all." It was for that reason that she had hired Yolanda Saldivar to oversee their operations, Arriaga said. "Those were Selena's babies—her boutiques, her designs, and her perfume line. We always told her the reason she got the boutique was because she wanted to be able to pamper herself at any time without paying for it." Tourists and fans were bringing in steady business. Plans were being made to publish a catalogue of Selena's designs, and four perfume scents bearing Selena's name were being readied for retail.

Chris Perez was still going for days without sleep. A loner by nature, he stayed at home, playing his guitar and watching television. While the rest of the family busied themselves at Q Productions, Chris stayed away. When he showed up unannounced in mid-July, Abraham saw him walking in. "Chris," he called from across the room.

"Abraham," Chris replied, his voice unloading a heavy weight. They almost ran toward each other and hugged in a long embrace.

Some friends wondered if Chris was suicidal. Anticipating the release of *Dreaming of You*, he said, "Some may think it's bittersweet, but it's not sweet at all. It's good the shops are doing good. But of everybody that's alive today, no one would enjoy it as much as she would. Whenever I hear [the new album] on the radio, it hurts. But what's weird is I can come home and play it by myself and everything's all right. I guess, when it's on the radio, they usually give this speech about how she died and I know that thousands of other people are listening to that.

"There's still times that I think she's alive and I can call her or I'm going to have to pick her up from the airport," he told newspaper reporter Karen Lister.

The pace began to intensify in mid-June, as stations throughout South Texas vied to be the first in town to play the new single, "I Could Fall in Love." B-104 in McAllen received a copy on Thursday, June 15, and began airing it every hour on the hour. Music director Jeff "Hitman" Dewitt observed an immediate reaction. "The phones went crazy." The song quickly moved into power rotation on the station. "It [was] the most popular song in the Rio Grande Valley," Dewitt said. Suzy Camacho, at KZFM, the contemporary hits station in Corpus Christi, saw the impact of the crossover instantly, saying, "I'm getting a lot of the English-only listening audience calling up and asking for it. I think it's going to go platinum the first day." Other Texas pop stations added the song, too, as did stations in Southern California and throughout the Southwest and Midwest. Staci Kelly, of KQKQ in Omaha, wasn't sure if it was right for the Cornhusker state, though. "We are not playing it right now, but I think the possibility of us getting into it could very well happen," she said.

Selenamania began in earnest on July 3, the day that the July 10 issue of *People* magazine hit the stands. For the third time in three months, Selena was a *People* cover girl. This time, the focus was the new album. The Los Angeles public relations firm of Rogers & Cowan had been hired to hype the album release to the general-market press. José Behar, president of EMI Latin, was quoted as saying he expected *Dreaming of You* would outsell Selena's past platinum efforts, admitting that much of what he called the "massive buzz" was due to her death. "There's no doubt the tragedy has expedited the process. But she had a massive fan base prior to the tragedy. People don't buy her music because she was on the eleven o'clock news, but because the music is beautiful. And this music stands on its own."

Music columnist Ramiro Burr described the media blitz as "one of the biggest CD promotional campaigns in the history of the Latin music," citing coverage on television's *Today, Turner Entertainment, Good Day L.A.*, and *Entertainment Tonight* as well as press in *Entertainment Weekly, Time,* and *USA Today.* "We owed it to her," said Manolo Gonzalez, the southwest operations chief of EMI Latin. "That was her dream. To us who were close to her, it had to be done. I think her main purpose was to put that album out."

José Behar related to Burr the unprecedented nature of the album's debut. "To the best of my knowledge, it has never been done. But this was a situation that called for it. It is kind of like the tail wagging the dog. The CD is being treated no differently than a Janet Jackson or a George Michael release. There's a big party, she's throwing it, but she's not showing up. And it really sucks. But we have no choice. The more interviews we do, the more focused we get. Because it is our responsibility, and of course that of the family, to carry her legacy and to really bring to the forefront the beautiful gift she left us, which was her music.

"We can't change the tragedy. I wish we could, but we can't. So we now have a very serious responsibility of making sure that we share her music with the world, which is what she wanted most when she was alive. We're going to do everything in our power to make sure that this gets done. We're going to be relentless at retail, at radio, with the media."

Four days before the release date, Abraham was once again surrounded by cameras and microphones, rising to the occasion but complaining all the way. "It's a mad-house around here. It's crazy. I don't know if I can take it," he said in a weary monotone. "There's a camera crew right in front of me, waiting for me to get off the phone. Channel Three is waiting in the next room. *Good Morning America* is going to be here in the studio on Monday."

Across Texas, some of the anticipation of the July 18 release date was spoiled by retailers who jumped the gun. El Norteño Records in San Antonio began selling the al-bum on Friday, July 14. Other S.A. retailers complained that El Norteño had used connections with the Quintanilla clan to get the jump on the competition. Calls to EMI offices in San Antonio complaining of the unfair advan-tage were not returned.

Maldonado Records in Austin's predominantly Mexi-can-American east side started selling on Monday, July 17. Owner Henry Maldonado said he broke the covenant with EMI and put the record on sale after "the word came down from the distributors—start selling." The impetus was the appearance of illicit copies of the album on the streets. "The release was done by the bootleggers every-where this weekend. They were selling bootleg tapes for six bucks, and they sounded terrible." Maldonado said the reaction was unprecedented. "In twenty-eight years, I've never had this excitement about a release." Tower Records in Austin called EMI to complain about Maldonado jumping the gun and asked for permission to sell the album on Monday too, but permission was denied.

San Antonio Tejano radio station KRIO-FM sponsored a Monday-night preview party at the Dallas nightclub, a north-side country-and-western disco that spokesman Mark Easterling admitted doesn't normally play Tejano music. One hundred and fifty fans paid two dollars to hear *Dreaming of You* and receive prizes given away by the station. These people represented the new breed of Selena fan. "I didn't know what to expect when they said she was going to sing English songs. But when I heard 'Dreaming of You,' had I not known that it was Selena, I would never have thought it was a Tejano girl singing," said Isabel Ramírez. Club regular Jeff Curtis and his wife, Lydia, gave it two thumbs up. The crossover worked. "[Before,] the language barrier was always there," Jeff said. "If you didn't tune into Tejano, you never listened. But we always appreciated her clothing and the way she looked onstage. What touched me most was the raw track of 'Dreaming of You,' before it was mixed and made commercial. I always think of her husband when I hear it and I think of her dreaming of him."

In Corpus Christi, Abraham Quintanilla gave the official family endorsement to the album party at the Piranha Room, sponsored by Z-95, which was already featuring Selena in heavy rotation. The preview drew about three hundred fans. By contrast, a crowd of four thousand showed up in the parking lot of Craig's Record Factory on the S.P.I.D. Expressway shopping strip to watch seventy-five girls of all ages compete in Selena sound-alike and look-alike contests. The event, sponsored by Beso 94, the top-rated Tejano radio station in Corpus, even drew Abraham and A.B., who showed up later in the evening; A.B. spoke briefly to the crowd. The promotion paid off. By noon the next day, Craig's had sold half its advance order of eight thousand.

The Record Connection on San Antonio's west side had customers pick numbers and wait in line before opening its doors at one minute past midnight Tuesday morning and immediately sold 250 copies of its thousand-copy preorder. "Everybody bought on the average of two each," said Buddy Ruiz, the store's assistant manager. By Tuesday, El Norteño had almost run out of its second shipment of eight hundred CDs and was opening its third order of five hundred cassettes and five hundred CDs. Tower in Austin opened at 12:01 A.M. and sold out of their preordered stock of 175 copies within thirty minutes. Maldonado's Record Shop in Austin opened at 7 A.M. on Tuesday and depleted the remainder of their initial order within an hour and a half.

In the Rio Grande Valley, retailers faithfully observed the Tuesday release date. "Out of respect to Selena's memory, the family, and at the request of EMI Latin, we did not sell any records prior to the official release date," said Juan Cavazos, owner of Centro Musical R y N in McAllen, where the back wall had been transformed into another Selena shrine. Cavazos's one thousand copies were sold out by Wednesday. Meme's Music and Video in McAllen ordered 450 CDs and 800 cassettes—almost half that number reserved in advance by fans—and opened at 12:01 A.M. Owner Manuel "Meme" Saucedo was sold out by the afternoon and reordered several hundred more copies. "Since 1979 when I began selling records, I have not seen this happen," he said.

Even Howard Stern aired the record on his program, which normally does not feature musical interludes. While the music played, Stern commented "I like it" several times. But when the segment ended, Stern asked cohost Robin Quivers, "Can I take my earplugs out now?"

The National Hispanic Media Coalition reiterated its boycott of Howard Stern's advertisers, and although the League of United Latin American Citizens backed off the boycott demands, LULAC nonetheless petitioned the Federal Communications Commission to cancel the licenses of the two Texas stations that carried Stern's show. "This type of hate show should not be tolerated," LULAC president Belén Robles stated.

By Friday, the sales figures were in. The advance pressing had been 1.5 million units, compared to 900,000 units pressed for the new Paula Abdul album. Still, Manolo Gonzalez of EMI Latin in San Antonio said it wasn't enough. "We'll sell two million to the Tejano audience alone," he predicted. More than 210,000 copies were sold the first day. For the week, the tally was 331,155 copies sold, according to *Billboard*'s SoundScan charting system. That figure was good enough for the album to debut at the number-one position on the following week's *Billboard* top albums chart. It was the first record by a Latin artist to debut at number one, and the second-highest chart debut of the year, behind Michael Jackson's *HIStory*, and second only to Janet Jackson as the fastest-selling record ever by a female artist. In one fell swoop, Whitney, Mariah, Gloria, Madonna, and the rest were left in the dust.

It was a handsome package, with a tasteful soft-focus cover photograph of Selena, although the faded-photograph look made it appear that Selena's skin had been intentionally lightened to a porcelain whiteness in the layout process. It presented the kind of contradictory image that the music on the disc echoed. The initial reaction from the music press was both curious and mixed. Some Latin critics attacked the material she had chosen for the anticipated crossover and complained that the producers made her sound like a plain vanilla pop singer. The message was that the music business was still conducting business as usual, with a callous insensitivity toward the people who buy the music. "Old-style whitewashing remains the method of choice," complained the Miami *Herald*'s Fernando González. "Spanish is used as exotica—a spoken verse here, a whispered word there—to suggest a seductive, nonthreatening otherness. Beyond that, Selena sounds nondescript, a composite of R & B vocal mannerisms." Ramiro Burr of the San Antonio *Express-News* was more evenhanded. "It becomes more apparent that perhaps Selena's natural talent was subdued by the veteran pop producer team . . . in order to make her more acceptable to a mainstream audience. The result is that Selena sounds almost indistinguishable from so many other generic female voices." Salvatore Caputo of the Arizona *Republic* wrote, "Without exception, the Tejano cuts . . . are more fun and interesting than the English cuts. It sends a message that for truly big success, you still need to tone down who you are." The Dallas *Morning News*'s Mario Tarradell resented her being "revamped to sound like one of pop radio's many generic vocalists. The bubbly, effervescent personality, the chica-del-barrio charm so prevalent, has been erased. In its place, we get breathy, lovestruck vocal performances that sound like tepid imitations of Amy Grant or Paula Abdul."

Anglos who had never heard Selena's music were charmed, not so much by the English-language pop songs but by "Amor Prohibido," an old Mexican standard updated to a classic example of world pop music, and "Tú, Sólo Tú," as emotionally soulful as Latin music gets. The Austin *American-Statesman*'s Michael Corcoran praised Selena's ability to take on any kind of song and make it sound good. "She was much better than Madonna or Gloria Estefan, the singers she was compared to, or Paula Abdul. This girl could bury them. She was a very good singer. Like Elvis Presley, Selena had the talent to transcend subpar material."

Peter Watrous, whose obituary of Selena in the New York *Times* was the most heartfelt and explanatory piece written about her, weighed in with a review. The English pop songs were "all competent, but undistinguished. And, oddly enough, the Spanish-language hits, even the lightweight 'Bidi Bidi Bom Bom,' sound better than the English-language tracks. It's the expression of a border culture in the modern age, where musicians can pick and choose what they want to be, how they want to sing. There's a power in the music that isn't so evident in the English-language songs, pieces that could have been sung by anybody, at any place and at any time."

Watrous's analysis was on the mark. Selena covered the waterfront vocally, jumping from soft and fragile to full-tilt boogie to as impassioned and venomous as any Latin female singer could aspire to be.

The dearth of English pop cuts had necessitated the inclusion of Latin material that her crossover album would have omitted had she lived. And it was the Latin influences that showcased Selena's voice at her best and most versatile. It was an unintentional way of introducing the sound of her culture to a mainstream audience, but it worked.

Each of the four English pop numbers sound amazingly close to the artist with whom the respective producer achieved his fame. Keith Thomas put a pallid Amy Grant face on "When I Fall In Love," which is absolutely devoid of an edge or even the slightest hint of the emotion Selena was capable of unleashing. Guy Roche's prescription for "Dreaming of You" was a near-perfect evocation of the pop ballad, and it struck the heart of mainstream America. For the song, Roche had Selena alternately cut back on the power and reduce her voice to a vulnerable level only slightly above speaking volume, and he amped up her throaty, glottal dips à la Madonna. The song wore well over repeated plays, somehow avoiding both burnout and sappiness. By comparison, under Rhett Lawrence's tutelage, "I'm Getting Used to You" actually had some punch to it, qualifying Selena for membership in the New Jill Swing school of soul pop, as did "Captive Heart," in spite of Roche's soulless treatment.

None of the four English-language cuts came close to "Bidi Bidi Bom Bom" for delivering middle-of-the-road pleasure, the kind of catchy tune that little kids could sing along with even if they didn't understand the words. Not without irony, it was only the second song that Selena Q. Perez ever wrote, with Pete Astudillo providing the proper Spanish phrasing.

"Techno Cumbia" had a similar effect. The song may have been laced with such exotica as a reggae toastmaster talking over a teeth-rattling bass line, an electronic mishmash of sampling, and a pan-Caribbean attack that included soca and Hi Life from Trinidad and beyond, and second-line drumming straight out of New Orleans. But the kernel of the song was Top 40, its melody harking back to the nonsensical novelty tune "The Name Game" from the sixties.

The most startling selection on the album was "God's Child," her duet with David Byrne. The rhythm was off-beat, with a quirky marimba lead-in, full of mystery and subterfuge in the tradition of Byrne's work with the Talking Heads. The track, which was edited out of the film *Don Juan de Marco* only to wind up in another movie, *Blue in the Face*, nonetheless breathed fire and ice with Selena doing some impassioned salsified testifying *en español* over Byrne's haunting, almost premonitory lyrics:

> *Who calls this child to walk on her own?*
> *Who leads her on this treacherous road?*

Manolo Gonzalez was pleased. "Selena's album is selling more records than we ever dreamed of," he told Vilma Maldonado of the McAllen *Monitor*. "Selena has broken all records. This has never happened in the history of the recording industry, especially by a Hispanic." Gonzalez anticipated the mixed critical response, especially from the hardcore fans. "This album was done to also target the Anglo market, so you had to make adjustments to serve them better. For those people who had never heard of Selena, we tried to give them an anthology of who she was. So we did it with the songs that brought Selena to the top in the Spanish market and conveyed that, so the Anglo market could understand what made Selena. We always try to come out with a product and hope it will sell. But with Selena, from day one when she was signed in 1989, she has given us one surprise after another." He also indicated there were three to six more English demos Selena had made, which might eventually be released.

A month and a half after *Dreaming of You* was released, Selena's old labelmate and one-time duet partner Emilio Navaira set out to prove to the world that above everything else, Tejano was about assimilation. His crossover was aimed at the Anglo audience too. But where Selena went after the crowd that bought Whitney, Madonna, Mariah, and Gloria, her *compañero*—known simply as Emilio now—was headed for Nashville, hoping to find himself on a first-name basis with Garth, George, Travis, and Vince.

He certainly looked the part. Practically every stitch of clothing was spoken for by endorsees, from his Stetson hat down to his pressed Wrangler jeans that crumpled just so around the tops and backs of his round-toed Tony Lama lizard boots. He sang the part, too, falling somewhere between the full-bodied twang and moan of Johnny Rodríguez, country music's first Mexican-American singing sensation, from the early seventies, and the larruping approach of country's current mega act, Garth Brooks. The marketing wizards who conjured up images for the companies couldn't have dreamed up someone as ready-made for Music City, U.S.A., as Emilio was.

He had been doing the kicker bit since high school. It was part and parcel of his stage show. If you couldn't play country music to dance to in Texas, no matter what kind of music you specialized in, you weren't going to survive very long as a gigging musician. Emilio's fans were Tejanos, and many had been raised on country just as Anglo Texans had. They knew all the dance steps— the two-step, the waltz, the schottisch, the Cotton-Eyed Joe, and they even improvised a few of their own, including the Emilio, a cartoonish sort of bunny hop that the performer and his brother did onstage.

The Nashville crossover put new demands on Emilio. As much as the music stood for family values, as did Tejano, it had become overly obsessive about image in recent years. To better focus on Emilio onstage, his brother Raul, a gentleman of considerable girth, was discreetly repositioned farther back in the shadows, despite Raul's creative contributions and his own popularity on the Tejano circuit. Emilio's Nashville debut album, *Life Is Good*, fit right in with the modern, state-of-the-art country sound, although it seemed watered down compared to the brand of country common to Texas dance halls.

In late June, Navaira dropped in at the EMI Latin offices in San Antonio as part of the preparations for the CD and cassette release. His duties that afternoon included taping video greetings in English to the sales staff and distributors of product for Capitol-Nashville, the recently renamed Nashville division of EMI, and sharing his thoughts with the general public in Spanish about his remembrances of Selena.

He paused afterward to sit with a visiting writer and ponder his relationship. It was built on their mutual professional interests, but evolved into the kind of bond that develops with many people working the *onda* circuit. "We were brothers and sisters," he said. "I'd known her for ten years, back when I was singing with David Lee Garza. We came up together and had the same vision. Both of us being Tex-Mex, we had an advantage, because we can do both Tejano and English-language music. I'm just sorry that she's not here to share all this with me."

One listen to *Life Is Good* (Capitol-Nashville) was all the convincing necessary. Emilio was destined to be a Hat Act. A new phrase was being uttered around Nashville: "*¿Se habla* kicker?"

Two days after the Selena album release, Yolanda Saldivar had her bail lowered from $500,000 to $200,000 by state district judge Mike Westergren. Her attorney, Doug Tinker, nonetheless complained, "It's not going to make a difference. She won't be able to get out. We won't even try to get her out." The judge had previously said he'd consider lowering the bail once Corpus Christi police finished their investigation into allegations that Saldivar embezzled $30,700 from Selena's business accounts, but that investigation was still ongoing. District Attorney Carlos Valdez was against lowering the bail because he felt Saldivar was still a flight risk. Saldivar remained ensconced in a private cell in Nueces County jail, where some guards had given her a nickname: Yoda (in honor of the small extraterrestrial creature from *The Empire Strikes Back*). But as the summer heat began to wane ever so subtly, her presence grew larger and larger.

8

Benediction

ALL SUMMER LONG ABRAHAM HAD talked of a band tribute, which was formally announced in September as Los Dinos' farewell tour, scheduled for the following spring. Afterward, the band would break up, Abraham announced. That was a foregone conclusion. The unanswered question was, Who would fill Selena's role? There was a Puerto Rican girl in Orlando named Cathy Burgos said to be Selena reincarnate. There were sound-alikes and look-alikes aplenty. But trying to take an act like that on the road smacked of imitation; despite Abraham's good intentions, no one could fill the shoes of his daughter. Of all people, he should have known that. Fans didn't pay to see Los Dinos. They paid to see Selena, and Selena wasn't there anymore.

The rumors came faster and became more scurrilous. Most involved sex and drugs. Most of the stories were fashioned from fertile imaginations and boredom; others contained a few grains of truth. The trial would answer some of the questions.

On Monday, July 31, the Univisión network talk show *Cristina* devoted its entire half hour to a Q-and-A with

Abraham, A.B., Suzette, and Chris. Marcella stayed home.

Abraham wore a suit and tie. Chris looked as if all the air had been let out of his tires. His eyes were vacant, his face painted with bewilderment; he evoked more sympathy from the viewers than anyone else on the stage. Cristina Saralegui conducted one-on-one interviews first, asking questions in Spanish. All the kids answered in English, with a translator repeating the answers in Spanish. Abraham's Spanish was somewhat stilted, occasionally lapsing into the English "How do you say?" while searching for the right phrase in Spanish.

Abraham reported that he was dealing with Selena's loss by burying himself in work. The crowd number at the funeral was underestimated, Abraham further said. "There were over seventy-five thousand signatures in the guest book." He was displeased about the T-shirts and posters emblazoned with the picture of Selena lying in the casket. He said that it annoyed him so much, if he had to do it over again, he wouldn't give permission to open it. He had had it opened only because of the rumors that Selena's body wasn't really in there.

Abraham responded to the question asked in cantinas everywhere that summer: Why had he allowed Selena to go by herself to the motel if he knew Yolanda was so dangerous? "I raised them all to be like me; we were chiefs and not Indians. My children are this type of person. They're always at the head of things." In other words, the girl was going to do what she wanted to do. "She likes to take things by the horn and correct them."

Chris described Selena as a volcano. One audience member questioned Abraham about Marcella. "She changed her mind about appearing at the last minute because she was more upset than the rest of us," Abraham said. "She couldn't even hear a Selena song without [falling apart]."

Chris set the scene of Selena's last night: It was tax time, Yolanda had the papers they needed. Selena was in the truck when she noticed papers were missing. Chris told her to wait until they got home. Yolanda was already under suspicion, he said. In her, he saw a nobody, a misfit without friends. Through Selena, she gained power and influence over people. She wasn't Selena's chaperone or confidante, he said. She was just someone hired to run the boutique. Selena's chaperones were her brother and sister, her father and her mother.

Chris hadn't touched a thing at home. All of her shampoo and personal effects were still in place in the bathroom; her clothes were in the closet. Still, he was finally working again. The Selena lines of perfume had to be finished. Two weeks after her death, he called Leonard Wong. "Was it finished?" he asked.

"It was done," Wong told him.

"We still want to go forward with the project, because that's the way Selena would want it," Chris said. But he was not being wholly honest; his heart was broken and no one could fix it.

Salomé Gutiérrez, a San Antonio composer, publisher, and independent record-label entrepreneur, had prepared a collection of *corridos* about Selena for release on his DLB label. The *corrido* tradition was rooted in the use of song to transmit news; it preceded newspapers, radio, and television, and the style had persisted in South Texas long after electronic media became the norm. If an event of importance occurred, a *corridista* inevitably wrote a song interpreting what had happened. In recent years, there had been *corridos* written about kidnapped heiress Patty Hearst; hurricanes that hit the Texas coast; the siege and thwarted jailbreak of notorious drug trafficker Fred Gómez Carrasco; and the attempts of the federal government to close down San Antonio's Kelly Field, the largest employer of Hispanics in the state of Texas. Gutiérrez had himself written many *corridos*. The death of Selena had inspired several composers to put words to music to express their feelings.

Gutiérrez's tribute album was titled *Homenaje a Selena*, Homage to Selena. His own composition, "La Muerte de

Selena," was sung by Beatriz Llamas, who also sang on Juan Obregón's "El Corrido de Selena." Gutiérrez sang lead on the title cut, written by Maximino Chávez. Juan Obregón sang "El Adiós a Selena," written by Juan Mañuel Mújica. Juan García and Loy Serna dueted on "La Tragedia de Selena," written by García. Plácido Salazar wrote and sang "Selena, la Rosa Blanca," and "La Musica y la Muerte," and sang "Triste Final de Selena," a Máximino Chávez original. Francisco Frausto wrote and sang "Selena, Siempre Te Recordaremos." And Eddie Torres sang lead on Máximino Chávez's "Selena, Reina de Texas."

Though a poster was made and products were pressed, the collection never appeared in retail stores. Gutiérrez was intimidated by one of the lawyer's letters sent on behalf of the family threatening legal action for any unauthorized exploitation of Selena's name or image. Fearing harassment, he backed off the project. That didn't prevent Rodven, a label from Los Angeles, from running television advertisements featuring the image of Selena for their collection of Selena tribute songs even though Los Dinos were not included in the selections.

The greatest challenge facing Corpus Christi was coming to grips with its newfound status as a Mecca for pilgrims. Just as the faithful had come to Dallas and Memphis to see where Kennedy, King, and Presley breathed their last, people were coming to Corpus to see where Selena lived, worked, died, and was laid to rest. There was a constant parade of Selena fans, messages written on windshields, the Selena T-shirts, the Selena stickers, Selena memorabilia everywhere. There were thirteen stations airing Spanish-language music now, eleven of them with Tejano-style formats, which meant Selena music in heavy rotation across the dial. The English-language contemporary hits station, Z-95, had joined in the rush, emphasizing her music more than any single artist in the history of the city. Wherever you went, no matter where you looked, something would bring back the shock, the tragedy, and the pain. It wouldn't go away.

By late July, the smiling hosts and hostesses in the Corpus Christi visitors center at 1101 Shoreline had developed a routine response to Selena inquiries. First, a city map was produced, on which the host marked in pen the six major sites—the Seaside Memorial Park cemetery, Selena's home address, the boutique, the Days Inn, the family homes on the 700 block of Bloomington, and the studio and office of Q Productions. The host then produced a photocopied close-up street map for each specific site. The requests had been overwhelming, one hostess told a visitor while urging him to sign the visitor log.

The Days Inn motel was an unwilling participant in the veneration. A sign was posted discouraging people from cruising the parking lot. The fateful room had been painted over and renumbered, with the number plate screwed rather than glued to the door frame in order to thwart souvenir seekers. A twenty-four-hour security team patrolled the premises, chasing off sightseers.

The Quintanillas, on the other hand, were very accommodating. The boutique functioned as the official souvenir shop; business on weekends was often so brisk that timed entries were required to control the number of people in the store. The constant outpouring of emotion became so overwhelming that Suzette Arriaga began working out of her house. "It got hectic, a lot of people coming in and crying and showing their grief and it was hard for me to come in and say, 'Hey, everything's okay.' It depressed me, it really did," she told writer John Morthland. "So now I'm running it, but I don't go in every day. I pop in and get my paperwork, then pop out."

People who called ahead to arrange a visit sometimes had Lee Garza, a Q Productions employee, give them a tour through the recording studio and the business offices, where he showed them various plaques and awards, and perhaps offered a chance to meet someone from the family. Abraham might have been raising hell upstairs in the office cutting deals, but he was a gracious host in the reception area, listening to what visitors had to say, accepting their gifts, and offering words of comfort or advice.

Toward the end of summer, the steady stream of visitors pressing the buzzer at the door to gain entrance to the offices of Q Productions became both flattering and irritating. The family was open to the strangers, but it was getting difficult to get work done. "I don't like turning people down, but we are going to have to do something," Abraham told a reporter for the Corpus Christi *Caller-Times*. In another interview, conducted while five families toured the studios, he admitted, "It's beginning to be hard. I don't know what we're going to do about this." He related how he had taken ten days off and left town. But even in Northern California, they couldn't escape their notoriety. "Everywhere we went, people recognized us. People would come up to us and start crying. That brought everything back. Even by leaving, we couldn't get away from it."

Though the family members tried to answer mail personally at first, the deluge of letters finally forced Abraham to hire a fulfillment company in Las Vegas to send messages of thanks on behalf of the family, along with two Jehovah's Witness tracts addressing the process of grieving.

Suzette, a bubbly, beaming countenance, merrily passed through to give Dad good-natured grief about not reordering T-shirts fast enough. Abraham's brother Eddie fielded merchandising calls and talked about the direction of the next commemorative photomagazine for fans. Selena had gotten them this far, he said, echoing family sentiment, now it was up to them to take it to the next phase. Strangers were besieging Abraham with tapes, CDs, and photos of new talent, and Los Dinos were fixing to crank it up one more time.

Isaac stopped in to check on some equipment then bid adiós to his *papi*, Abraham, Sr., who was sitting next to the receptionist's desk, speaking to a photographer from London *Today*. A.B. occasionally emerged from his mad-scientist routine in the studio with engineer Brian "Red" Moore, where he was finishing the theme to a Mexican *telenovela* called *Pobre Niña Rica*, Poor Little Rich Girl.

Both he and his father and the six other people on staff had plenty to do. Their clients included Jennifer Peña, the engaging twelve-year-old who had lit up the Astrodome during the Selena tribute with her karaoke vocal overdub of "Bidi Bidi Bom Bom"; Pete Astudillo, the former backing vocalist with Selena; Escalofrío; Chikko; Imagen Latina; Las Agues; and Oxýgeno. Abraham's vision had included a one-stop hit factory, providing management and production skills, recording facilities, songs, a booking agency, and marketing services to the acts signed.

"It's becoming sort of like a Graceland here," he told Ramiro Burr. "I don't know. There's people coming in from all over, from South America, from Mexico, from Canada, from everywhere. And if it continues that way, we have talked about maybe building on, maybe an extension. We really haven't sat down and planned things out. Maybe we'll have a section for Selena and another section for the rest of the Tejano artists."

The gravesite at Seaside Memorial Park was cleared daily of flowers and other mementos left by the five hundred or so fans paying respects every week; a temporary fence was erected around the grave to keep the grass from being trampled. By the end of August, the temporary grave marker was replaced by a permanent one, black granite with the word SELENA in the same white script that appears on her albums. A bronze plaque with the image of her face was being cast. A month later the fence came down and the turf was replaced.

The show would go on. "We always talked about it— that if anything happened to any of us, the rest would carry on strong," A.B. Quintanilla told the New York *Daily News*. Chris Perez concurred, making it clear it was an all-for-one, one-for-all proposition. "If one of us is not going to be there, we're not going to do it," he said. The family members were tight, but they were also growing up and spreading their wings. By the end of summer,

A.B. was overseeing completion of his new home, a palatial spread with curved, stainless-steel walls and other custom design features and a spare-no-expense studio, located on nine acres west of the city. He was ready to leave Molina. He wouldn't miss the fans cruising by, the flash-bulbs of their cameras going off at all hours of the night. "I'm not saying it bothers me. All I'm saying is that sometimes I want to have some privacy." The new house and recording gear established physical distance from the rest of the family, and then some.

In his younger sister's absence, A.B. was emerging from Selena's shadow as his own producer, arranger, and chief composer, getting his songs recorded by such main-stream Spanish-speaking artists as Paulina Rubio, Thalia, and Christian Castro, while co-authoring a Tejano hit for Mazz, "Estupido Romantico." If he played his cards right, he would be up there next to Emilio Estefan as a contemporary Latin music producer. "She [Selena] had already told me that I needed to get out there and write for other artists," he said to Ramiro Burr. "But she was in such demand, I was touring so hard, I didn't have time to write. [Now] I'm just sitting here twiddling, so I figure I better busy myself."

The Quintanilla-Perez clan appeared together on August 26, walking the artificial turf of the Alamodome during a special Selena tribute at the halftime of the Governor's Cup exhibition football game between the Houston Oilers and the Dallas Cowboys. The tribute was organized by Cindy Villarreal, the director and choreographer of the Oilers' Derrick Dolls pop squad as well as author of *The Cheerleader's Guide to Life*.

It was getting difficult to tell whether Corpus Christi was turning into the Sparkling Selena City by the Sea or the Sparkling City That Wanted to Forget Selena. On Monday, August 14, a ten-member committee appointed by Mayor Mary Rhodes and Nueces County judge Richard Borchard, offered five recommendations to honor Selena and help the public deal with their grief: a Selena statue near the Bayfront Plaza, overlooking Corpus Christi

Bay; renaming the Bayfront Plaza Auditorium for Selena and dedicating a Selena tile mural on the inside; renaming the Avance Family Center, to be built in Molina, the Selena Family Center; renaming Bloomington Street, where she lived, Selena Drive or Selena Avenue; and placing signs at the city limits identifying Corpus Christi as Selena's hometown.

Committee chairman Jorge Rangel spoke for all committee members when he said, "She illuminated and brightened the lives of everyone she touched. All of us are in love with Selena and hope that these recommendations will help brighten our lives. We are not asking that these recommendations be approved because they are the popular or the political thing to do, but because they are the right thing to do."

Mayor Rhodes concurred. Something had to be done. "The outpouring of grief over Selena's death was greater than anything I've ever seen in this community. People are still coming here from all over the country, state, and world to go by her home, her boutique, her gravesite, because they don't know how to handle their grief."

Reactions to the proposals were swift and vocal. While the neighborhood was almost unanimous in their support of renaming Bloomington, there was a problem: one of the intersecting streets was Yolanda Street. Some neighbors suggested renaming that thoroughfare, too. Concerns were also aired that street signs and signs at the city limits bearing Selena's name would be targets for souvenir-seeking vandals.

The proposal to name the children's center in Molina after Selena was dropped when city staffers determined that by doing so, they might jeopardize efforts to raise funds for the center.

More curious was the response to the *Caller-Times'* Sound Off column. Most people were supportive, but some comments indicated that the city was still divided. There were other celebrities, such as television actor Dabney Coleman, film star Lou Diamond Phillips, and singer Freddy Fender, who deserved recognition too. Renaming the auditorium was too extreme: "After all, we are not talking about a dead war hero, we're not talking about the president of the United States, we are talking about a hometown favorite, okay?"

One writer complained, "Our city is named the 'Body of Christ' and Jesus Christ is not getting as much recognition as Selena. This is not Selenaville. Back off." Another suggested changing the name of Johnnyland Concert Park to Selenaland. Letter-writer Charley Blisset was more blunt. "Forget all the small-time proposals. Why not just change Corpus Christi [to Selena] and be done with it?"

Some objected to honoring Selena at all. One said, "I am against the Selena proposals. She has done nothing for our community except make our kids think they can dress in skimpy clothes. Let's learn to dress like ladies and gentlemen again." A second chimed in, "Most of the proposals are silly. This is a segment of our population desperate for a hero. The family of Selena is making millions of dollars after her death. They should use some of this money to relocate poor Hispanics living near the refineries and name the new neighborhood Selenaville." Another agreed. "She never did anything for this community. She did little things, but what did she ever give us, the people? She didn't give us anything. I don't think it's fair to us, especially people who live on those streets that they would have to go and change, Bloomington Street or Yolanda Street or whatever. I hope that the city council plans on reimbursing everybody for the expenses they are going to have to pay out to change names on legal documents and driver's licenses and so forth."

The Selena phenomenon was threatening to open old wounds between the Anglo and Mexican-American communities. Letters to the editor of the *Caller-Times* complaining of Selena overkill were almost all from writers with Anglo surnames. The opinions exposed the frailties in brown-white relations, which managed to surface every now and then, especially when the parallel universes crossed paths, as they did in the wake of Selena's death.

The reactionary tone of some Anglos rubbed more than a few Mexican-Americans the wrong way. "I'm not sure Corpus appreciated her," said San Antonio *Express News* assistant sports editor David Flores, a C.C. native. "I've heard that from people all over the city, outside of Molina. I was disappointed in the way the Anglo community in Corpus did not express the kind of grief or sorrow you'd expect for a native son or daughter." But Flores stressed that in life, Selena enjoyed the anonymity in her hometown. She could go shopping without getting hassled.

By the time school was back in session, the tourist traffic in Molina had slowed to a car or two puttering through the neighborhood. The only tipoff that the homes on the corner of Archdale and Bloomington were any different from others was the message spray-painted on the driveway and sidewalk: WE LOVE YOU, SELENA.

Abraham had always been there sitting in the hot seat, calling the shots, making the deals, running the show. He was the real man in Selena's life, the behind-the-scenes maestro who orchestrated her career and still conducted the entire production. Now, with the star gone, he'd stepped into the star role, too. The impulse could have been driven by the fact that he couldn't let go of Selena. It also could have been inspired by the high of being the center of attention, the feeling he had back with the original Dinos before reality shook him out of his own crossover dream. For the past twenty years, he'd settled for living that dream through his children, giving them a vision and a sense of purpose. Music beat fishing or golf for a hobby. The kids liked it. He liked it. Who knows? They might all get rich. And they did. All for one, one for all.

But now Abraham appeared to step into the glare of the spotlights all too willingly. How could it be any different? He was the one who had raised her, he was the coach, he was her confidant, he was the one who knew her best. Besides, it was his belief, and that of all the Quintanillas, that Selena would have wanted them to carry on. It was all part of making it. Selena had planted the seed; it was up to them to make it grow, with the work of Los Dinos, all the new bands Abe was signing to his Q custom label and to his management company, and with the various deals that made Selena bigger in death than in life.

And so he spoke to the cameras and microphones, held press conferences, attended tributes, negotiated contracts, all in the name of his dear, departed daughter. But the more he was on screen, the less sympathy he elicited. He constantly decried the abuse of Selena's image by others, apparently not realizing he might have been doing the same thing. It was all a matter of control. Only this time, without Selena in the wings ready to make the public forget his strong-arm method of doing business on her behalf, his arrogance started pissing people off.

It was always other people who were pirating Selena's image and abusing it. Only he could sanction the proper use of her likeness. Only he could profit from her image. He pursued the licensing and exploitation of Selena's image as zealously as he attempted to stop the bootlegging.

Abraham wasn't Selena's father-manager anymore, people said, tongues clucking behind his back. He was Mr. Selena. On camera and in photographs, unsmiling, his eyes hidden behind tinted lenses, he came off as arrogant, bullying, gruff, and crass. Just like a manager should be. But not an artist.

It was like Graceland, as Abraham so keenly perceived it, a machine that kept feeding itself—albeit on a somewhat smaller scale. In at least one respect, he was light-years ahead of Vernon Presley, Elvis's father, in trying to protect the value of his child's name and likeness. It was a valiant if hopeless effort in the Latin end of the music business, where piracy was almost impossible to stop. In the long run, the wholesale abduction of her image into public domain was to the family's benefit, since it spread the reputation of Selena to corners of the world even their marketing people couldn't reach.

What little unreleased music by Selena remained in the

archives was waiting to be remixed, remastered, or enhanced by other singers and musicians through the miracle of electronic reproduction, with Abraham naturally making the decisions.

During the period immediately following Selena's death, Abraham often seemed more obsessed with calling the shots than grieving for his daughter. He tried to cajole the management of KIII-TV in Corpus to give him the video footage of the *Selena Live* concert, offering three hundred dollars for a tape of the performance that won Selena her Grammy award, although the station had several thousand dollars invested in the production. He called Johnny Herrera and demanded the tape Herrera had made in his House of Music record shop when Selena was seven—her very first recording. Herrera responded by calling Abraham *nouveau riche* and refused. He openly criticized Johnny Canales's one-hour tribute to Selena, which included her first appearance on his show, at the age of thirteen. Abraham didn't like Canales's claiming he discovered Selena.

"Abraham thought he was the only one who could feel the grief that he did, because he was her father," said Jimmy González, who managed Q Productions until shortly after Selena's death. "He didn't realize how Selena touched everyone the way she did. He didn't understand how people were just as upset as he was. He didn't understand the pilgrimages or the shrines or anything else."

The greatest vanity was the film deal. In May, the family held a press conference in front of the San Antonio boutique to talk about negotiations, name-dropping Steven Spielberg and Michael Douglas as two among many who had expressed interest. Abraham said his planned autobiography would be part of the deal. By the end of August, Abraham decided instead to stake some of his own money and entered into a joint venture between Q Productions and Esparza-Katz Productions for the official Selena movie bio, rather than sell the rights to her life outright. On August 29, 1995, the lead item on the six o'clock news on channel 6 in Corpus Christi was the announcement of the Selena film deal, specifically that "her life and the role her father played will be in a movie." The director would be Gregory Nava, who directed and co-wrote the films *El Norte* and *Mi Familia.* Esparza-Katz Productions had an impressive track record too, having produced the films *Gettysburg* and *The Milagro Beanfield War.* Abraham Quintanilla, Jr., would be executive producer. Quintanilla would not comment for the record to channel 6 or any other local media, though, because he'd signed a contract with the television program *Entertainment Tonight,* giving that program an exclusive for twenty-four hours.

Being executive producer meant more than just being the movie's financier, in this case. It meant Abraham had control, evidenced by a conversation director Gregory Nava had with one Hollywood film writer after the deal was signed: Nava said he was thinking of telling the story from the father's point of view. Nava was selected after negotiations had broken off with Edward James Olmos, who wanted to produce, direct, and star in the Selena movie. Although Olmos ultimately played Abraham, initially he wasn't really the right type, Abraham told Greg Barrios, a reporter from *Entertainment Weekly.* Abraham's hairline didn't recede as far back as Olmos's did.

Two weeks later, on September 13, Abraham called a press conference at the office of Q Productions to introduce Esparza and Nava. Standing behind a phalanx of microphones and in front of a painting of Selena, he told reporters that his job in the ten-million-dollar movie was to call the shots. "I just give the orders, that's all." If the storyline strayed, as far as he saw it, he'd straighten it out. "Nobody knows more about my daughter and our life than I do," he said. "I just want to make sure that this was not a Hollywood dramatic movie but a true-life story. If they get out of line as far as the story goes, I'll put them back on course." At the same press conference, Abraham introduced author Victor Villaseñor, who was writing an authorized biography, and announced the farewell tour of Los Dinos was being planned for the following spring; Pete Astudillo would be rejoining the band, but not back-up vocalists Don Shelton from Corpus or Freddie Correa, the former lead singer from the Barrio Boyzz, whom A.B. portrayed as relative newcomers to the group.

Two Mexican-born *telenovela* actresses were being mentioned for the lead role: twenty-three-year-old Bibi Gaytán, known as Mexico's Cindy Crawford, who also happened to record for EMI Latin, and twenty-seven-year-old Salma Hayek, who played opposite Antonio Banderas in the highly acclaimed film *Desperado*. But they weren't the only ones in the running.

In late August, Abraham drew stares as he walked the grounds of the Hispanic state fair in San Antonio. It wasn't that he was now an immediately recognizable personality; it was the woman he was with. She looked like Selena and dressed like Selena. Was this some macabre joke? people wondered. It was not. She was Leticia Miller, an actress.

"How do you like her?" he asked an acquaintance he recognized on the fairgrounds. "She's auditioning for the part of Selena in the film." The executive producer was trying out the young girl for the role of his daughter and he was watching people's reactions to gauge her credibility. Jennifer Lopez, from Nava's *Mi Familia*, eventually got the role.

In the midst of announcements for the movie and introductions of the board members of the Selena Foundation (Chris, Abraham, Marcella, Suzette, and A.B.), lawyers representing San Antonio music writer Ramiro Burr filed a suit charging breach of contract. Burr had a one-page agreement designating him as the official biographer of Selena, but Abraham had introduced another author, Victor Villaseñor, as the biographer at the press conference called for the movie. "This book project has nothing to do with Mr. Burr's project," he said in response to the suit. The suit was dropped three weeks later, after Abraham apologized to Burr.

The criticism of Abraham Quintanilla's actions following his daughter's death missed the point in the opinion of his supporters. "It sounds like everybody expects this to be a textbook play," said Rubén Cubillos. "First of all, he should have known how to be a manager. He should have known this and that. He's been learning everything as he goes. He's been living his experience. He's the spokesperson not because he inherited it but because he knows most of everything. He knows what Selena thought, who Selena was, her likes and dislikes. Abraham has lived the whole thing from A to Z."

The Quintanilla family was not the Brady Bunch but a real family, fraught with frailties. They'd become targets of *la envidia* because they were successful, the thing they had scraped, sacrificed, and worked so hard for in the first place. Abraham was the reason Selena learned Spanish. He was the reason she developed such a degree of vocal control; he insisted she was a child prodigy, but in truth, she became the complete entertainer through practice, hard work, and sacrifice. If Abraham hadn't pushed, cajoled, hounded, and harangued Selena and her siblings, they might have never survived as musicians. Sure, he could be a bull, but it was for a reason. You had to be a hardass in a macho business such as this. The job description of manager was to act as pit bull for the artist. Being father as well was torture. He was fighting for Selena every single day, getting down and dirty in a business riddled with machismo, where too often booze, drugs, and women became as important as the music. He had to ignore the whispers of sexual innuendo from the audience, the promoters, and other musicians. It was bad enough in general, but they were talking about his precious daughter.

Abraham tried to be the buffer. He kept his kids out of the business aspect and focused on music while he did the dirty work, never letting the problems he encountered on a daily basis become his family's problems. If he seemed possessive, on a massive ego trip, smitten with megalomania, or simply came off like an oaf, or a *viejo salvaje*, or old savage, as one relative scathingly referred to him, he was doing what he had set out to do when he was a musician himself. Music was like a religion to him. He wasn't fighting because he was a troublemaker, he was fighting for his convictions. Laura Canales had wished aloud she'd had someone like Abraham to posture, bluff, fight, and intimidate so that no one would mess with her.

To many, that alone was heroic.

Now, press representatives requesting interviews were asked to submit a list of written questions in advance. When *Newsweek* sent a photographer to Corpus Christi to take a picture of Abraham in front of Q Productions, Abraham presented the photographer with a release that would grant all copyrights of the photograph to Abraham after it ran in the magazine. *Newsweek* declined to sign.

The saddest part of all was that the daughter who'd helped Abraham realize his dream wasn't there to enjoy it with him.

In the same week that *Dreaming of You* was released, the Texas Talent Musicians Association, the group that puts on the Tejano Music Awards, organized a meeting, the purpose of which was to promote membership of Tejano music businesses in the National Association of Recording Arts and Sciences. With enough members, there would be a sufficient voting bloc to lobby for a Tejano category in the music industry's Grammy Awards competition, replacing the existing Mexican/American category. Vicki Carr, a middle-of-the-road pop singer, had won this category, beating Selena. Other nominees included Vicente Fernandez, an international singer from Mexico, and Ramón Ayala, who was known as a *norteño* artist, not a Tejano one. In fact, the only two true Tejano acts to win Grammys in the Mexican/American category had been Selena, in 1994, and Little Joe, two years earlier.

The concept of a separate Tejano category immediately stirred up controversy among Tejano industry players. Some said the nature of the music transcended such a narrowly defined category; would an act have to be well-versed in polkas to qualify? Henry Gonzáles of Voltage Discos in Houston reflected that position, telling Thelma

Garza of the San Antonio *Express-News*, "If we try to get the Grammys to give us a Tejano category, we're limiting ourselves. We're separating ourselves from the Latino market, which is the original. If we separate ourselves we're going to stay that way, and we're going to be a small market."

"There's confusion because when it comes to the Tejano Music Awards, they've got *conjunto* split into two categories: progressive conjunto and *conjunto tradicional*," said Freddie Martínez, Jr. "When you think of *conjunto tradicional*, you're thinking about a four-piece conjunto with bass, drums, *bajo sexto*, and accordion. The early guys like Tony de la Rosa, Flaco Jimenez, and Valerio Longoria play with four pieces, but then so do Jaime y los Chamacos, only in a very modern, flashy fashion. What the TMA terms 'progressive conjunto' incorporates the accordion but also features keyboards and saxophones, like Emilio Navaira, Roberto Pulido, and David Lee Garza do."

The big bands like Selena y los Dinos and La Mafia were subject to a backlash for reaching out to a larger audience. "You hear a lot of that, 'They're not the same band anymore.' 'They're trying to appeal to the northern Mexico audience.' 'They forgot their true roots,' " Freddie Martínez, Jr., said. "Obviously, from the band's standpoint, from the record company's standpoint, they're selling more records, they're drawing more people, and getting more airplay doing this. They've sort of evolved. Even though you want to keep your original fans—you don't want to turn them off—the bottom line is sales."

Sure, a band could earn a handsome income working the circuit of gigs in San Antonio, Corpus, Houston, and points in between. But what was wrong with wanting more? Other entertainers aspired to higher goals, why shouldn't Tejano bands?

There were signs that the old ways were no longer enough to hold an audience. Paid admissions were down. Large nightclubs, whose owners controlled the liquor receipts, had taken over from the old dance halls and had scaled down the fat guarantees that had been common only a few years earlier. CDs and cassettes lacking the name *Selena* on it weren't selling. The label feeding frenzy, with its big signing bonuses, was over. Whether the blame lay with supergroups like Mazz and La Mafia, who commanded a high ticket price for special-event concerts, or the proliferation of videos and discos, Tejano was becoming more and more like the mainstream general market. At the same time, the regional sound was expanding to northern Mexico, to other corners of the Latin world, to other parts of the United States, and it was constantly reinventing itself.

The Corpus radio scene was typical of Tejano's changing image. All but one of the dozen Tejano-format stations were locally owned, an exception to the rule in broadcasting. Maybe it was the small size of the market, ranked 119th nationally, or the relatively cheap cost to get into it, but C.C. had the highest concentration of Hispanic-owned stations in the United States.

The labels pushed the music into the big leagues, but a sense of family nonetheless prevailed. Bands still tended to be managed by friends or relatives, there was still the attitude that agents, managers, and promotion people shouldn't be making as much money as the artist. The independent labels had an unwanted wake-up call. To compete, they had to spend the dollars that the majors were spreading around for advances, recording sessions, videos, and other marketing tools. "All the things that you have to sit down and consider now, you didn't have to worry about a few years ago," said Freddie Martínez, Jr. "You've got a big investment in just recording costs, production costs, and so forth. Then distribution costs. And you can't expect to get paid for at least sixty to ninety days, if you're lucky. If you can't hold out long enough, then this is the wrong business for you."

That begged the question of just what Tejano really was. A music pegged to the romance of the language, evoked by men in bow ties and shiny brocade tuxedos playing saxophones, trumpets, and trombones, swaying in time to a slow, dreamy rhythm? A modern pop sound every bit as commercial as the English language it emulated? A regional sound about to explode, or one so bent on assimilating it was destined to disappear? It was all that and more. That's what happened when you emulated the gringos' world while embracing bits and pieces of the *mundo de México*.

Those qualities assured a ready-made audience wherever there were communities of Texas-Mexicans. Puerto Rican and Cuban salsa, *cumbias* from Colombia, *son jarocho* music from Vera Cruz, *banda* from the Mexican interior, soca from all over the Caribbean, and Brazilian samba all emphasized percussion as a necessary ingredient of any song. The Tejano sound stressed romantic vocals and a sentimental, almost arrhythmic melody, elements that separated it from the rest of Latin music, forever inhibiting the crossover possibilities. Tejanos, it turns out, were just as idiosyncratic and peculiar to Latin-Americans as Anglo-Texans were to other Anglo-Americans.

"A lot of musicians are rediscovering where their music came from," music writer Vilma Maldonado said. "They want to know who they are and they want to present it to the world—not just to Texas. They want to show them what they have and what they've had all along. So they're bringing back all the oldies, all these classic songs, and just adding their particular influences, new sounds or whatever they were listening to while they were growing up.

"Look at La Mafia doing the Beatles song 'Let It Be.' That's not traditional in Mexico, but they're doing it because they want to introduce it to the rest of the world, show the rest of the world they could do it too, in their own style. We assimilate, you know? We adapt. We take a little bit from this culture, we take a little bit from that culture. But we don't lose our own culture."

Maldonado anticipated a roots movement. "Now it's time to go back to basics. Conjunto was the cantina music and that's what a lot of these bands are going back to, their parents' and their great-grandparents' music, bringing it back to life."

José Behar encouraged his bands to reach for a bigger international audience through cumbias and other wide-ranging sounds. An even newer generation of Tejano acts, including La Tropa F, the Hometown Boys, Michael Salgado, Intocables, Los Palominos, and Jaime y los Chamacos, were now urging their fans to go retro, back to the Tejano basics of accordions and polkas. Their stage dress may have been fancier, the equipment more powerful, but it still came down to music. And for Tejanos, music isn't music if you can't make circles around the dance floor.

The real triumph of Selena's artistry was not in crossing over to the English-language general market but in establishing herself as a Spanish-language mainstay first. To reach that goal, the little L. J. girl had to learn her parents' culture and the native tongue that was its essence. Making it as a pop star who sang in English was almost an afterthought.

A common chord had been sounded by all those who knew Selena: she had no idea how big she was. She treated everyone she came in contact with as a friend and an equal. At the same time, she possessed an instinct that allowed her to hone in on those people who played key roles in her career, making them all feel like family. Whether this openness was a result of training, of not having a life outside of entertainment, or a genetic disposition, she had the charisma and demeanor that other entertainers strive their entire careers to attain.

Fama, a magazine from Mexico, articulated the outpouring of emotion with the cover headline: "Selena, a Latin Goddess; an Angel Whom Heaven Reclaimed; Her Images and Her Fragrance Is Still Present."

In San Salvador, the program *Teletón* started one of its segments with a minute of *aplausos* for Selena's past participation in raising money for handicapped children. "Selena had a contract of love with us," said the show's M.C., Antonio Lemus Simón. "But now she has that contract with God."

Albert Huerta listed the attributes of Selena: "She was a very personable individual and very sincere, very down-to-earth, very humble. She was punctual, she was gracious. When she was interviewed, she always said the right thing. She was young, but she was very mature. She stood in a class by herself."

The same sentiment was voiced by practically every person whose path she crossed. Selena was a very special person, the paragon of the modern Latina, everyone's sister, daughter, and lover.

"I have this feeling she served a very important purpose in her short period of time here," said Al Aguilar. "She was like a messenger, an angel that came down here and touched all of these lives and said all these great things."

Her death served as a reminder to all Tejanos, all Mexican-Americans, all Latins and Hispanics, that theirs is a beautiful culture with a beautiful language, one that may be poor in capital wealth but rich in family values. If nothing else, there was that pride. And that pride was based in a belief system that had yet to pay off for most Mexicanos.

"People are doing things with their lives thanks to Selena, going on to college, couples who were divorcing reconciling," A.B. said, confirming her memory was a positive force.

Timing was possibly the most important factor in creating the Selena myth. At the time of her death, she still lived next door to her parents. She hadn't made the English crossover yet, she was still true to her *cultura*. To the public learning about her for the first time, there was pride in her sense of family values, her givingness, her ability to connect with both kids and adults. But Selena paid a price for that image.

There's a Mexican saying, *Por cada mal viene un bien*, For every bad thing, something good comes. The image of Selena eclipsed the actual person. In retrospect, her life had been exemplary, especially in light of the difficulties she endured: an overbearing stage dad and the loss of simple things like friendship and romance, which were part of a childhood she was denied. That was then. After her death, her perfection as a role model took on a life of its own.

In McAllen, eight-year-old Mandy Cano, a recent Selena convert, danced and lip-synched to Selena's CDs in front of her mirror, pulling her hair back in a tight ponytail, plucking her eyebrows to a thin line, tinting her lips a heavy red, and angering her fifteen-year-old sister, Jody, by raiding her drawers in search of bras that resembled Selena's bustiers and halters. For Mandy it was a form of playing dress-up.

For other girls who lived in the Rio Grande Valley, being Selena was serious business. Look-alike contests were sprouting around the Valley like mushrooms after a rain, drawing young girls decked out in tight pants, halter tops, and heavy makeup like Selena's and supported by parents wanting to be like Abraham. Alma Loya of Primera was proud to point out that her ten-year-old daughter, Lilly, did not require additional padding to emulate Selena's derriere. "She has the behind." Not surprisingly, the competitions were fueling incidences of *envidia*. Accusations of stage-hogging, stolen song lists, and rigged results tainted the events. "It's rude," nine-year-old Becky Meza of Primera told Fernando Del Valle of the *Valley Morning Star*. Meza's father, Joe, was so put off by the experience he pulled Becky out of the copycat competition circuit that had become a cottage industry in the Valley.

"Kids looked up to her, even teenagers, as far as education, staying in school," observed Vilma Maldonado of the McAllen *Monitor*. "Even though she had to drop out of school and took correspondence courses, people looked to her to stay in school and stay off drugs. It's true that she was so pure and so clean. And it's true also that what you saw onstage is what you got offstage. People just saw her as everything they wanted to be—the beauty, the down-to-earth type personality, always smiling, everything that a Mexican woman should have been, should be.

"She made us proud to be Mexican-American. She let other cultures know, other countries know that we are worth it, that we have something to offer, that we have qualities in our people, that there's nothing wrong with mixing English and Spanish when you speak, or mixing in some Spanish when you sing. She made it okay for us to be who we are and be accepted as we are. She was just the person that every Mexican-American wants to be. Through her music, she was able to say what she felt, to express herself. And I'm not sure she could do that off-stage. She was more at peace and happiest when she was singing."

So, evidently, was twelve-year-old Jennifer Peña. On September 20, the syndicated television news program *Hard Copy* ran a segment about Abraham's most recent discovery, whose pert appearance and perky countenance had been drawing comparisons to Selena for several years. Her forthcoming album, recorded under the auspices of Q Productions at Q Zone Studios in Corpus Christi, was already being anticipated by fans, who were flooding record stores with requests, according to the segment.

The precocious Peña did a pretty credible Selena, down to the spangled jewelry and bright red lipstick she adorned herself with, and she knew how to say all the right things, parroting the party line that no one could replace Selena, though Jennifer's moves, stage presence, and vocal inflections indicated she was trying as hard as she could to refute that notion.

On Sunday, September 24, Peña performed at Mateo Camargo Park in San Antonio, accompanied by Abraham, who made his appearance at the show emerging from a car surrounded by an entourage worthy of Elvis Presley. Peña, it was revealed after the show, was Abraham's choice to play the role of Selena in the farewell tour the following spring. His ideal Selena was the twelve-year-old *chica*, not the full-grown woman who was as strong-willed and independent as he was.

The artistry of all the young girls could easily be challenged. The impact could not. The very idea of being

Tejano, rather than just Mexican-American, Chicano, Mexican, or Hispanic, separated the people living in the Lone Star State from their cultural cousins elsewhere in the nation, stereotyping them as a fiercely independent bunch, just as Anglo-Texans were regarded as different by other Anglo-Americans. No other Latin culture exhibited such a split personality, which was no doubt inspired by the proximity to the border. Being Tejano meant an appreciation for old-country family values and traditions and an equal zeal for pure American pop. Selena was the paragon for this. She led by example, learning her language and heritage, living next door to her folks, a poster girl for nineties values—an independent businesswoman who was strong yet feminine. You could have it both ways, she announced. You could wear sexy clothes and still be a virtuous good girl from the barrio.

Selena's chart success with "I Could Fall in Love," the first single off *Dreaming of You*, and the followup, "Dreaming of You," finished the long quest of the little girl that began by singing "Feelings" at Papa Gayo's. In fifteen years, she had made the transition from all-American girl to Tejano queen to international Spanish diva and back to the Top 40 on her own terms (and the terms of her father). By holding her voice down to a level barely above speaking volume while doing perfectly crafted pop, Selena defined the radio sound she grew up with. The circle was complete.

The debate will never cease as to what could have been. If she had continued her career crossover. If she had continued her commercial endorsements. If she had carried her concept for her boutiques and her design house to fruition and expanded into Mexico, as she had hoped to do. If she and Chris had moved to their palatial estate south of town, out of the shadows of her parents, and created their own family, complete with kids, chickens, peacocks and horses. Dreams like that are the stuff of legends.

9
The Judgment

BEFORE THE SAD STORY COULD conclude, before the legend could flourish, there had to be closure. And before there could be closure, there was a final formality called the American criminal-justice system. Throughout most of the summer, the case of the *State of Texas* versus *Yolanda Saldivar* had been a minor irritant in the midst of the posthumous outbreak of Selenamania. Every week or two brought hints of potentially dark and volatile sparks to come. One such sizzler was in the August 22 edition of the tabloid the *Globe*, luridly headlined, "Accused Killer's Kinky Confession: Selena Died after Lesbian Love Quarrel." It appeared right next to other celebrity-obsessed screamers: "Kevin Costner Romancing Joan Lunden: *Waterworld* Hunk Sweeps Beauty off Her Feet" and "New Scandal: Sexy Di Caught with Married Hunk!"

The trial had the potential to answer questions burning in the public's mind. Why did Yolanda do it? Was the act fueled by envy, jealousy, hate, revenge, or desperation? Was it *la envidia*? Was it unrequited love? Suicide was a selfish act, but killing the object of one's obsession was even more so. Was she Selena's best friend, or her worst enemy? Was she finally acting out the feelings she had voiced for Selena before she went to work for her, that deep down inside, she hated her?

Who was the gun meant for? Did Yolanda buy it to kill herself, since the world she'd built for herself was in the process of crashing down around her? Was the gun meant for Selena? Or did Yolanda buy it to shoot the person who'd come between her and Selena? Was her obsession actually Abraham?

Whatever the motive, means, and opportunity, Yolanda Saldivar had the benefit of the kind of legal representation that a person of her stature and station in life normally couldn't afford. "Most defendants in a shooting like that would get a Volkswagen for a court-appointed attorney," a veteran Nueces County courtroom observer said. "She got a Cadillac." Richard "Racehorse" Haynes, arguably the best criminal defense attorney in Texas, agreed. "If Yolanda had fifty million in cash, she couldn't have gotten a better lawyer."

Douglas Tinker was an able defender, all right; the most capable criminal defense lawyer in Corpus, as a matter of fact. "As great and beloved a singer as Selena was, that's how great and beloved a lawyer Doug Tinker is," said Robert Hirschorn, a Galveston attorney and nationally known jury-selection consultant. "The jury will be enthralled by one of the players, and it's going to be a man who looks like Santa Claus. Do you know anyone who doesn't like Santa Claus?"

Besides bearing an uncanny resemblance to Saint Nick, the jovial Tinker knew how to argue a case. He put juries at ease by carrying his research materials into court in the forms of a Big Chief writing tablet and a cigar box. He spoke the language of regular folks. He argued persuasively. His salt-of-the-earth image was advertised by the softball team he sponsored: on the front of the team's T-shirts was a cartoon drawing of Tinker, barefoot and tipsy, sitting atop two boxes of beer and saying, "Don't bother me when I'm working on a case." The back of the shirt was emblazoned with the motto "If

Tinker Can't Get You Off, You're Probably Guilty."

One wall of his office, in an old residential two-story house on the southern edge of downtown, was covered with framed newspaper clippings about his work. He had hung the clips after visiting a friend, San Antonio defense attorney Gerald Goldstein, who had his walls covered with his greatest cases. "It attracts money," Goldstein told him. Though Tinker hadn't updated his wall in several years, the summary of thirty-two years' worth of South Texas lawyering, more experience than the entire prosecution team, was impressive, justifying both the plaque from the Texas State Bar declaring him Outstanding Criminal Defense Lawyer of the Year for 1995, and the unofficial nickname Tinker the Stinker.

His wall was a veritable gallery of the locally famous and infamous: George Parr, the last of the South Texas *patrónes*, who controlled Duval County with a paternal benevolence and an iron fist, sentenced to five years in prison for income-tax evasion. Joe Treviño, acquitted on charges of killing his daughter's boyfriend on the grounds of self-defense. The alleged high-dollar contract killer for a rich oil man, who beat a murder rap. A man found in a field with a dead woman and blood on his hands, gave a confession, and was still found not guilty. Jeffrey Johnson, accused of stabbing a neighbor with a hatchet (case dismissed). The two Calallen boys who supposedly shot and murdered a deputy constable trying to arrest them for malicious mischief (not guilty in two capital murder cases). Elisabeth Jeanne Jones, acquitted of charges that she killed her police officer husband.

That last one was a strange one. "The D.A. who got the indictment dismissed it after he decided there'd been a mistake. But a new prosecutor reindicted her. She was found not guilty. The district attorney was on the upside. History will record he was right, then he lost the next election."

He looked over the yellow clippings approvingly, but with self-effacement. "All the ones I lost, I never put up." In one such instance, one of the few occasions he accepted an out-of-town client, he represented Brad Branch, a follower of Waco messiah David Koresh. "Dick DeGuerin was calling other lawyers in Texas while Koresh and his followers were still under siege, and I said no. Then, after the fire, I got another call from DeGuerin. The first indictment had five people, and one of them called him to recommend a lawyer. I went and visited him and he got my juices up. So I took the case."

The outcome for Branch could have been worse, since he'd admitted in court that he fired on federal agents. As it was, he got forty years for manslaughter and was acquitted of murder and conspiracy-to-murder charges. Tinker's line of defense centered on who fired the first shot, the feds or Branch. "I think law enforcement skated clear in the ATF raid."

Tinker didn't particularly need to represent Yolanda Saldivar. He was sixty-one, on the cusp of retirement if he so desired. By taking her on as a client, he left little doubt that if the opportunity presented itself, he would have defended the accused slayer of Snow White. Tinker was born in Van Nuys, California, and moved around Texas with his father, who followed the oilfields for Shell. He graduated from high school in Edna, the same small town where Selena's paternal grandmother had been born, and earned his law degree at the University of Texas, in 1963. He went to work at the court of criminal appeals in Austin, then hired on as assistant district attorney for Nueces County from 1964 to 1968. After briefly working for a local law firm headed by Guy Allison, he set up his own shop, in 1981, as the only full-time criminal defense lawyer in Corpus.

The work had immediate and long-term impact on Tinker, both personally and professionally. "The accused is always the underdog and I liked that part. Oddly enough, I wasn't as idealistic when I started as I've become. Criminal defense attorneys are the only protection a citizen has against government and law enforcement. As the years go by, we're losing the protections we've had and it's getting worse. Prosecutors twist the law to make illegal searches legal. Judges are trying to please the public, especially the judges who are elected to their positions. They don't care about the accused. Criminal defense lawyers are the only group in America to protect the rights of citizens."

Yolanda Saldivar came into his life two days after Selena was slain. "The judge had already tried to get some other lawyer. One who didn't want to do it had two kids in public school in a predominantly Hispanic part of town. I don't have kids, but I was reluctant. One of the lawyers who works in the office was angry with me. He said they were going to burn down the house [office]. For days, he took home his computer every night, saying he didn't want to lose all his data because of a fire or vandals.

"When I agreed to take on the case, I thought to myself, 'My God, what have I done?' "

He found out when the threats started coming in, though he scoffed at them. "I got a few calls, but really not as many as some people expected. I've gotten a few letters. I went to a wedding at the Officers' Club at the Naval Air Station and somebody came up to me and said, 'Tinker, I thought you would have lost weight by now.' I asked why and he said, 'Because you can't go eat Mexican food anymore.' " Tinker was bemused when two professional bodyguards showed up at his office, résumés in hand. "I told them I couldn't pay them on the twenty-five dollars per day I'm getting."

Several friends in law enforcement offered him a bulletproof vest. He declined the offer. "Hell, if somebody is going to shoot you, they are going to shoot you. And I'm not apprehensive. I think the general public knows that somebody has to represent Yolanda. And I happen to be the one."

At Tinker's request, Westergren appointed a second lawyer for the defense, Arnold García, the fifty-seven-year-old former county and district attorney in nearby Alice, who has been practicing law for thirty-two years. Tinker took occasional refuge sailing the Laguna Madre, Corpus Christi Bay, and the Gulf of Mexico in his forty-foot sailboat, *Esprit Libre*, a pastime which enhanced his

Ernest Hemingway image. "You know, they say a sailor should have a boat that's a foot long for every year on him, but I stopped a while back." He laughed. "I used to want a Fiberglas sailboat, then a bigger one, then a bigger one, then one with a flush toilet. Man, if I had one of them, I'd have it made."

Carlos Valdez, district attorney of the 105th Judicial District, made the Selena case a mission. He wanted justice and full punishment. Anything less was not enough. This wasn't about some technicality in police work; this was about good and evil. Yolanda Saldivar was a murderer and had to pay the price. Valdez was an extremely popular prosecutor finishing his first term in office. He had grown up poor in the Molina neighborhood, about three blocks from the Quintanillas, and had photographs hanging in his office of a row of homes there and of an outhouse to remind him of his humble roots. "We didn't have indoor plumbing until sixth grade," he said. "I always want to remember that." Handsomely bookish and nattily attired with a close-clipped Skeezix haircut, the former county attorney for Nueces County had all the markings of a man of ambition with a big political future ahead of him. But Valdez insisted he was interested in no office other than the D.A.'s. He had never tried a felony before his election in 1992, but he compensated for his inexperience in the courtroom with his people skills. For instance, he was the only principal attorney in the trial who conducted his press conferences in English and Spanish. "I had been made aware that this case, to the Spanish media in this country and the whole hemisphere, was much, much bigger than the O.J. case," Valdez said. He also wisely delegated many nuts-and-bolts duties in court to his chief prosecutor, Mark Skurka.

Skurka was a garrulous man with unfashionable aviator's glasses, the upswept hair of an evangelist, and a girth that made Tinker look svelte. In his eight years with the D.A.'s office, he had prosecuted fifteen murder cases, including nine with capital murder charges, more than any other single prosecutor there. He had won one case against Tinker and lost another. Elissa Sterling was the prosecution's legal scholar and a paragon of motherly virtues, wearing her hair in a single braid and dressing modestly, barely showing her second trimester of pregnancy. Sterling had been with the district attorney's office for a year, having moved to Corpus Christi from Denver with her husband, who was in the navy. She became part of the team when the case was assigned to Westergren's court. Although she'd never prosecuted a murder, her expertise with legal precedents was a valuable asset.

Although Valdez felt confident about arguing his case, there were some bumps ahead on the highway. "I knew all along we had several problems," he said. He had a good idea that Tinker would use the accident defense after the first court-appointed defense attorney came to the D.A.'s office in search of Sergeant Paul Rivera's notes. Saldivar had told Tinker from the start that the shooting had been an accident. Valdez also recognized that Tinker was a formidable opponent who'd make them work to make their case. As Mark Skurka cynically noted, "Doug's clients don't have accidents, they have *terrible, tragic* accidents."

Tinker was effective enough to intimidate Abraham long before the trial. "He's trying to drag our family through the mud," Abraham told John Morthland, writing for *Entertainment Weekly*. "He's fishing around. He doesn't have a case. He wants my tax papers—what does that have to do with her killing my daughter? He's requested criminal records—what criminal records? He's trying to harass me; I don't know what he's trying to do. I wish we were over that so we could put it behind us. The woman killed my daughter, I already know exactly, step by step. I been doing some Columbo work and I know exactly what she done. She killed my daughter and she's gonna have to pay for it. That's something that God says: You do something bad, you gonna have to pay for it. I don't make the rules. I know this guy Tinker is trying to create an illusion, he's gonna try to smear us, he's gonna try to put the blame somewhere else. But at the end of the day, I know that justice will be served.''

Tinker's first victory was a Pyrrhic one. On July 20, he successfully convinced Judge Mike Westergren of the 214th District Court to lower Saldivar's bail. The amount, nonetheless, was still high—$200,000—and a clearly dissatisfied Tinker said his client would remain in jail. The second victory was more decisive. A little more than two weeks after the Selena album-release buzz, another set of lights, cameras, and action began to focus on the Quintanillas and Corpus. On the morning of Friday, August 4, the page-one headline of the *Caller-Times* read ''Saldivar Security to Be Tight,'' with a rundown of the prosecution and defense players, as the paper described the lawyers. Accordingly, a battery of television cameras jammed around the security gate on the ground floor of the Nueces County courthouse at 901 Leopard Street at 8 A.M., thirty minutes before the hearing was scheduled to begin, with their companion satellite trucks parked outside. From the scrutiny of the security-check personnel to the jostling of media hounds, it appeared to be the start of South Texas's Trial of the Century.

But Judge Westergren was merely holding a pretrial hearing to consider ten motions by the defense. The motions included a request to suppress the statement in which Saldivar admitted shooting Selena; a request for contracts between Selena and Q Productions; a request for investigations and audits by taxing agencies concerning Abraham and his businesses; a request for records from prosecutors for twenty-six items, including those regarding the treatment Saldivar received at Doctors Regional Medical Center on March 31; and medical records pertaining to liposuction surgery Selena allegedly had had before her death.

The most significant motion raised was the one to move the trial to another part of the state, citing potentially prejudicial publicity in Corpus Christi. Judge Westergren formally opened the pretrial proceedings by asking

Tinker if he'd like to make an opening statement.

"Ah, I might as well," Tinker responded deliberately in his soft, gravelly Walter Brennan voice. He didn't pussyfoot around to giving the basis of why they were all gathered there on the ninth floor that day. "There's never been a case in recent times in this county in which there's been greater publicity than this," he said. The public had witnessed Saldivar's arrest live on television. Selena had been honored in a way no single person had ever been before in the city. Local sentiment was overwhelmingly against Yolanda.

"In my office, there has been concern for the welfare of my client," Tinker said. "There would be less danger to me, my family, to my office, if this case was moved to another county. I will tell the court that if this case was in another county, I would be much safer."

District Attorney Valdez, the people's attorney, was soft-spoken but direct, countering that the issue wasn't publicity, but the kind of publicity. "We should not be punished with the way the publicity has been represented. It deals with other things that surround the case, but doesn't deal with the case specifically." Corpus Christi could handle the glare of the spotlight. "Your honor, O.J. Simpson can get a fair trial in L.A., Susan Smith can get a fair trial in Union, South Carolina. Yolanda Saldivar can get a fair trial in Nueces County."

A dozen witnesses, including various defense attorneys and former prosecutors, were called to the stand to give their opinion that Saldivar could not get a fair trial in the city. Former state district judge René Haas said the likelihood was about the same as "little green men coming down from Mars." Ann Coover, an attorney and court mediator, compared the impact of Selena's death in Corpus to the assassination of President John F. Kennedy. "But this case has gotten more, longer, than Kennedy's. I think this woman has been tried in the press. I live near Seaside Memorial Park and I've seen the parade of cars to [Selena's] gravesite. I've never seen anything like it. Yes, I think she pulled the trigger, but I don't know if she was guilty of the crime because I don't know what the defense is going to be.''

Luis Alonso Muñoz, the statesmanlike general manager of KUNO, was called to report on his Spanish-language radio talk show, "Opiniones," where the topic the previous week was "Can twelve impartial jurors be seated in Nueces County?" He received twenty-two calls in one hour. Seventeen said no, Muñoz reported. "It wasn't a scientific poll. Two that said yes mentioned how many years they thought she'd get. One said no, but she could get a fair trial if an Anglo was the prosecutor. Another said no, but if there were twelve women, it would be fair. One said an all-Anglo jury would do something different. Another said if twelve people from Molina were the jury, it would be different.''

The hearings continued on Monday, August 7. Abraham made an appearance, mostly to register scorn and disgust over his seat assignment in the row directly in front of the one seating relatives of Yolanda Saldivar. Refusing to sit down, he left the courtroom. By day's end, Tinker had been rebuffed in his quest for Abraham's business records, and Yolanda's confession had been introduced as evidence over Tinker's protests.

The records would prove that Yolanda was embezzling to cover for financial discrepancies Selena had with her father, Tinker argued.

Yolanda's confession to the killing was made without her saying anything about an accident, a Texas Ranger named Robert Garza said. He had observed Yolanda during her interview with Paul Rivera and Ray Rivera from behind a one-way mirror.

As Garza remembered it, "She said she pointed the pistol to her own head, and at that moment, Selena became fearful, became scared, and ran out of the room. In a gesture, she told Selena to close the door, and in a movement, she pointed the gun at Selena and the gun went off." Garza said Saldivar told police she had accidentally shot the singer; that conflicted with her written statement.

Garza told Rivera he "didn't feel comfortable with the way it was handled."

According to Garza, Rivera said he did not hear her say it was an accident. Rivera said she was trying to change it or twist it after she had already admitted it. He said he didn't deliberately leave it out. "What he told me was he knew enough about the case to know she wasn't being truthful," Garza said.

"He's wrong. The Texas Ranger doesn't know," Paul Rivera responded. "He wasn't even there. She never mentioned the word *accident*."

"If I thought it was an accident," District Attorney Valdez said, "I would dismiss the case."

The Ranger would be the key to Yolanda's claim that it was an accident. Tinker also sought to introduce the comments of police Sergeant John Houston, who spoke with Saldivar during the standoff in the Days Inn parking lot and later related, "Saldivar said, 'Her father hates me,' and 'Her father is responsible for this.' She said, 'He made me shoot her, he made me shoot her.' She kept saying that continuously."

On Tuesday, August 8, Judge Westergren ruled in favor of Tinker's client: the prospect of Yolanda Saldivar getting a fair trial in Corpus Christi was unlikely. "It needs to go," the judge said. "The real problem is the phenomena, and the confluence of the event [of Selena's death] in the hometown of this individual."

A sigh of relief was heard in many of the Anglo quarters of the city, especially among leaders concerned about the kind of publicity the trial would bring to the town. Mexicanos were none too pleased. Moving the trial implied they weren't fit to pass judgment. Valdez expressed that sentiment after the ruling came down. "[Tinker] wants this out of the Hispanic community. He thinks Hispanics don't have the sophistication to decide this case. It's a minor setback, but we will get over it. You can always change the location, but you can't change the truth." Tinker's motion to move the trial to a part of Texas with a smaller percentage of Hispanics in the general population was a "terrible indictment."

The next day, Westergren announced he'd settled on Houston. "It's the closest big city that would be acceptable." Tinker agreed. "I don't particularly like living in it. I don't particularly like driving in it, but I think Houston would be one of my choices. We didn't want something like here, where she's a local hero."

The pretrial low point for the D.A.'s office came when the *Caller-Times* ran the front-page headline "Tinker: We Can Prove It Was an Accident." The defense was winning the public relations war. "They were kicking our butt," complained Valdez. "In these high-profile cases, the public relations battle is important. What the media is feeding the public has a lot to do with it. We were building a house and the media looked at the foundation we laid and said, 'That's an ugly house.' We hadn't even started building. I had a blueprint in mind, but everything I read in the paper said we were putting together a weak case."

With three and a half million residents, the jury pool in Harris County was ten times as big as the one in Corpus. It was just a big ol' version of Corpus in many respects, a port city fifty miles inland from the Gulf of Mexico, some two hundred miles up the coast. From the defense's standpoint, it didn't hurt that Houston was once known as Murder City, U.S.A., where slayings of the most sensational variety were commonplace. From the prosecution's perspective, Houston was about as good as it would get. Almost one-fourth of the city was Hispanic, and Selena had one of her strongest fan bases there, sizable and influential enough to merit extensive coverage in the electronic and print media.

It was undisputedly the best crime city in Texas. You could tell by the way Harris County district attorney John Holmes welcomed the change of venue. "There is no chance of anybody not getting a fair trial in Harris County. I think Lee Harvey Oswald could get a fair trial in Harris County. We've got a jillion folks to choose from. So you can keep on truckin' until you get twelve fair ones.

I'm a white Texan, but I don't think I'd be any more harsh or any less harsh if [another white Texan] got killed."

Tinker felt he had a chance, at least. "We've got a run at this case. It's not a slam dunk. It's a defensible case, though there's a lot of things we don't have control over," he admitted. Those things he could control he was putting a spin on to the best of his ability. Once he'd gotten the change of venue, he focused on image. Throughout the pretrial hearing, Yolanda Saldivar remained rigid and emotionless in the courtroom, shoulders erect, eyes focused straight ahead, except for rare occasions when she leaned over to talk to García, a dolefully handsome man with a bald pate and a full mustache. She did not present a very sympathetic portrait. Defense attorneys were understandably concerned with how Saldivar was coming off and complained to the judge that what the public was seeing of Yolanda was "unflattering." The only opportunities cameramen and photographers had to record Yolanda was when she was being escorted in handcuffs from the jail to the court and back again. Westergren allowed the defense to arrange photo opportunities that presented Saldivar in a more positive light. One picture depicted her in a blue pants suit, looking out of a glass window on the ninth floor of the courthouse, her hands clasped in front of her, deftly concealing her handcuffs. Television stations now had stock footage of her looking up at the camera seated between García and Tinker, her short tight curls shiny.

It was the devil's bargain from the electronic media's point of view. "They threw us a bone, and we jumped at it," said Lilly Flores-Vela, a news anchor and reporter for KIII-TV. Flores-Vela went on to complain that Westergren's decision to keep cameras out of the courtroom was cramping her style. "How can you close the door to a proceeding that is very, very public?" she said in front of the Corpus Christi Press Club.

The attempt at media manipulation had mixed results. From the camera's eye, the specter of Yolanda Saldivar, her fatigued eyes staring somberly upward, still did not evince much sympathy.

On September 6, Judge Westergren heard from lawyers representing Court TV and the Univisión network, who wanted to televise the trial. As sound as their arguments were (the lawyers for Univisión filed a sixty-eight-page brief), they had the support of neither the prosecution nor the defense. In the hope of avoiding the taint of the O.J. Simpson trial, Westergren would not allow cameras in the courtroom. In deference to the taxpayers of Nueces County, he promised to run an expedient trial, hoping to seat jurors and hear testimony on the first day and limit the proceedings to no more than two weeks.

Less than two weeks before the trial was scheduled to begin, District Attorney Valdez announced that a grand jury would not hand down an embezzlement indictment against Saldivar until after she stood trial for Selena's murder. The decision was a wash. Tinker had said he'd ask for a delay in the murder trial if embezzlement charges were brought up beforehand. Now those charges would not influence the jury. However, embezzlement charges would have given the defense considerably greater access to various Quintanilla business records.

Shortly before the trial, Tinker and García were joined by Houston attorneys Fred Hagans and Patricia Saum. Many Houston lawyers had offered their services, but Tinker only took Hagans and Saum up on the offer. With his immaculately coiffed white hair and impeccable taste in suits, Hagans was the embodiment of the high-dollar Houston corporate attorney. He was a former partner of super litigator John O'Quinn, the second-richest lawyer in America, and was a specialist in personal injury lawsuits. Having expressed an interest in expanding his practice to defend clients accused of white-collar crime, Hagans was trying his first criminal case and invested considerable time and money for the experience, hiring a jury-selection expert, staging a mock trial, and offering the assistance of his co-counsel Saum, a striking, petite blonde.

The mock trial was held a week before the real one, in

a Houston high-rise outfitted with a courtroom complete with a judge's bench and jury box. It was common for attorneys in corporate lawsuits involving damages in the millions to stage mock trials, but criminal cases rarely had that luxury, given the twenty-thousand-dollar expense. The faux Saldivar trial indicated to Tinker that he had a chance. One-third of the mock jury voted to acquit. But their reaction to testimony concerning Sergeant Paul Rivera's handling of the confession troubled him. None on the jury was upset about the alleged lying cop. If they weren't bothered, would the real jury be? Would they buy the story that it was an accident?

El Caso de Selena, as it was advertised on billboards around Houston by one Spanish-language radio station, began on Monday, October 9, 1995. The first order of business in room 508 of the Harris County Courthouse was selecting twelve jurors and two alternates out of a pool of eighty-two men and seventy-three women. It was Nueces County district attorney Carlos Valdez's forty-first birthday. He wore a silver guardian angel that his wife had given him in his lapel. Yolanda Saldivar wore a beige plaid jacket and matching pants, with an ivory-colored ruffled blouse. "It looks like she lost a little weight—no makeup," observed Libby Averyt of the *Caller-Times*, one of three media representatives allowed to attend the closed hearing. "She talked a lot to investigator Tina Valenzuela."

About a third of the potential jurors had heard of Selena before her death; twenty-two said they had already formed an opinion regarding Yolanda's guilt. Tinker introduced Yolanda to each one in the courtroom. "We'd like you, throughout the trial, to look at her as the human being that she is." Saldivar said, "Good morning," and the jurors returned the greeting. Tinker then told the group, "The prosecution would like twelve highway patrolmen. I would like twelve people who believe a weapon can accidentally discharge when it's in the hands of someone else." Twenty jurors raised their hands and said they believed that was not possible. Valdez said, "In light of recent developments in this country, is anyone up here anti-police? If you are, that's not fair to me and I need to know that." One black woman raised her hand.

Shortly after the first day of jury selection concluded, Abraham called a press conference in the studios of El Dorado Communications, the parent of radio stations KQQK-FM and KXTJ-FM, two Tejano music stations that were the official hosts of the Quintanilla family during the trial. But two hours after the conference had been scheduled to start, Abraham still refused to come out until representatives from Univisión and Telemundo left the premises. He was upset with the two networks' coverage of Selena's probate, by their questions raised about his relationship with Chris, and by the reenactments of the murder staged on *Primer Impacto* the night before. "I feel like they have slandered my family," he later said. "My wife cried all night last night because of this."

Neither representative would leave, so after leading camera crews and reporters on a wild-goose chase from room to room, Abraham emerged shortly before nine. He talked briefly with a CNN reporter, saying, "I have never said that I hate her. I hate the act that she done. She killed my daughter." Spokesman Joe Villarreal then read a prepared statement reiterating that the family bore no ill will toward the defendant's family and was working to "follow through with Selena's dreams through the Selena Foundation, set up to support the education of future generations."

The *El Jucio en el Caso de Selena* special that aired live at nine that night on Univisión was hosted by Cristina Saralegui, the platinum-blond Barbara Walters of Spanish-language television, and featured live segments from Miami and Houston, *hermano en la calle* opinions from Nueva York, Miami, and Houston, a tour through a jail cell like Yolanda's and the courtroom, and reminiscences from the Barrio Boyzz and Martin Gómez, Selena's fashion designer, who said that without Abraham, "*Sin él*, I would have gone crazy."

El padre appeared on the show too, presenting a defiant and imposing image, wearing a black-and-white bebop-print sport shirt, scowling, with his arms folded across his chest, and exuding mystery from behind his tinted glasses. With his glowering image projected on a giant multiscreen monitor at the Miami studio set, effectively dwarfing host Cristina and the studio audience, he looked like nothing so much as Jabba the Hut with sunglasses.

When one studio audience member in Miami asked him, "What if the jury says she's innocent?" Abraham invoked the O.J. Simpson wild card, citing the sensational trial that had concluded in Los Angeles the week before with Simpson being found innocent of murdering his wife and her friend.

"Well, that's not gonna bring her back. Look what happened with O.J." After O.J., he was saying, anything can happen.

By the end of the second day, a jury of six men and six women had been empaneled, but only after Tinker had succeeded in getting prospective jurors to stand up individually, look Yolanda Saldivar in the eye, and say, "I don't believe Yolanda Saldivar is guilty unless the evidence is presented." At 6 P.M. Judge Westergren announced he would not bother selecting jury alternates. The process had dragged on long enough and he wanted to get the trial going. Nor did he feel it necessary to sequester the jury. They could go home every night, as long as they made an effort to avoid watching, hearing, or reading coverage of the trial.

During the selection process the Spanish-language media pestered the defense team about seating Hispanics. It was obvious the defense considered Latinos probable hard-liners in passing judgment on Saldivar. Once the jury was selected, Tinker turned the tables to complain to the press that the district attorney had used eight of eleven strikes to eliminate African-Americans as potential jurors, leaving only one fifty-eight-year-old housekeeper on the panel, along with four Hispanics and seven Anglos. On the heels of O.J. Simpson, African-Americans were perceived to be more suspicious of police work than other ethnic groups.

The actual case was presented on Wednesday, October 11, with considerable fanfare on the streets if not in the 228th District Court of Ted Poe, who had offered his courtroom to Westergren. The morning began with a lottery in front of the Family Law Center, near the courthouse. Although more than two thousand tickets were ready for distribution to hopefuls who wanted to attend the trial, there were more reporters on hand than prospective spectators. Still, those who did show up wanting to see the trial reflected Selena's fan base. They were of all ages, all walks of life, and almost all Hispanic. When the twenty-five lucky winners were announced, some screamed as if they had won a cash lottery, reacting for the benefit of a barrage of cameras.

The Preston Street and San Jacinto Street sides of the courthouse were surrounded by rows of television remote studios and satellite trucks, which were cordoned off from the public. The sidewalk on San Jacinto Street by the main entrance had barricades on both sides, one to protect the television crews and the other to restrain the growing number of Selena fans who showed up holding signs and wearing Selena T-shirts and other expressions of their faith and feelings.

On the media side of the San Jacinto Street barricades, grungy men balanced heavy cameras on their shoulders while surrounding perfectly coiffed and well-attired on-air talent standing amid the tangle of wires and cables. They represented a jumble of call letters and magazine and newspaper titles, including KRLD/TSN, KQQK, KEYH, KHOU, KLVL, XEWA, the *Caller-Times*, Houston *Chronicle*, San Antonio *Express-News*, Austin *American-Statesman*, Dallas *Morning News*, Associated Press, Reuter's, CNN, Court TV, and ABC radio news, KTRK, KXAN, KMEX, KPRC, KTMD, KGBT, KMOL, KENS, KXLN, KGBT, KRGV, *Hard Copy, Inside Edition*, Univisión, Telemundo, NBC, ABC, CBS, FOX, and Notimex.

One reporter, Miguel Martínez, telephoned daily live reports to Radio Cora in his native Peru.

Always ready to provide a quote or a visual was the Greek chorus of Selena's fans, standing across the sidewalk behind their barricades, constant reminders of why everyone was here. Since they were but a few yards away from one line of television trucks, they were a handy resource. If one desired to be on television or in the newspaper, all he had to do was stand behind the barricade, hold up a sign, and wait.

All of which led Mark Koelbel of KRIS-TV in Corpus Christi to pose the question, "[Is] the media covering a feeding frenzy or creating one itself?" The answer was, Both. Following the conclusion of the O.J. trial and shortly before the Bosnian war atrocities tribunal opened in Den Haag, the high-profile nature of the trial was a natural for media coverage, despite the ban on cameras in the courtroom. To trial-watchers living south of a line stretching between Corpus and San Antonio all the way to Tierra del Fuego, the Houston trial was in fact a far, far bigger deal than the O.J. trial, because both the victim and the accused were Latinas. That dramatic twist alone sparked a heated ratings battle between the Univisión and Telemundo Spanish-language networks, both of which devoted at least ninety minutes' worth of coverage daily, augmented by coverage from their respective Houston affiliates, KXLN and KTMD.

The *Caller-Times* provided the most comprehensive print coverage. The paper's two reporters on the scene, Libby Averyt and Eric Brown, were given about two hundred column inches a day, compared to around twenty column inches that other major Texas daily newspapers devoted to the trial.

In contrast to the circus on the street, the fifth floor was an island of calm. The 182-person-capacity court was less than full since many media reps with passes had opted to listen to the audio in the press room, from where they could file stories. Harris County courts administrator Jack Thompson and his assistant Janet Warner had vowed from the beginning there would be no breach of security inside the plain fifties-vintage institutional brick building, nor outbursts or disturbances from the crowd on the street. The well-worn, high-ceilinged courtroom with the framed State of Texas flag centered behind the judge's bench showed signs of wear and tear. Graffiti decorated some of the back rows of wooden gallery benches, hard as Baptist church pews. A working clock did the job of the broken original above it. Grease spots stained the back wall of the jury box, where thousands of heads had rested, pondering the fate of the accused. But Thompson and Warner kept their promise. Court was quiet and reverential.

The accused stared ahead blankly and looked drawn, quiet, and unable to hurt a flea much less pull the trigger of a murder weapon. She was surrounded by five sheriff's deputies stationed within arm's reach. Waiting on standby behind a door by the judge's bench were several SWAT team members. Deputies stood sentry at the courtroom doors. Police on horseback and bicycles were conspicuous at every intersection around the courthouse, and police on bicycles cruised the sidewalks. All visitors passed through security checks upon entering the courthouse building. Only those with passes were allowed inside a cordoned-off area on the fifth floor, where everyone entering the courtroom was subjected to a patdown and search. Bomb-sniffing dogs sniffed the seats.

The families of the accused and the victim sat in the first side rows, behind the defense attorneys' table and the prosecuting attorneys' table, respectively. Though both families shared the same humble roots, they were clearly of different economic and social strata. The Quintanillas were cut plenty of slack, were escorted in and out of the courtroom through a side entrance, and had brought along their own spokesman and hired a publicist. The Saldivars had to make their entrance and exit in front of the cameras waiting outside the courtroom door like everyone else, as well as endure threats and other expressions of hate from angry fans.

Although various relatives came and went, the two constants on the victim's side of the courtroom were Vangie

Quintanilla, A.B.'s wife—easily the most stylishly dressed regular in court, sporting a smart, close-cropped hairdo colored a light tint not found in nature—and Billy Arriaga, Suzette's handsome, square-jawed husband. The one Saldivar who attended the entire trial was Juanita, Yolanda's frail, gray-haired mother, wrapped in a sweater, the living embodiment of the *pobrecita abuelita*.

Spectators were seated on the side rows behind the families. Courtroom sketch artists occupied the first two rows of the middle section. Media representatives sat behind them.

The trial began with several objections raised by Tinker, including having any witness sitting in the courtroom, specifically the husband, father, and sister of the deceased; and having the audio feed being broadcast to anyone other than media. To test the audio, Tinker offered to sing "Green Green Grass of Home," and Valdez objected.

Yolanda stood up and pled "Not guilty" in a clear though small voice, then opening arguments were presented by the immaculate Valdez, looking like "a guy who's going places" as one pundit in the media section described him, and Tinker, portraying somebody's grandpa in his half-moon reading glasses. To counter that folksiness, Valdez brought a weathered satchel affixed with a "Valdez for District Attorney" bumper sticker.

Standing close in front of the jury, Valdez was almost upbeat in his opening statement, telling them with chipper enthusiasm, "We're about ready to embark—right after I sit down we start calling witnesses—on a journey together to seek justice. Now, what I'm doing in the opening argument is not really an argument but a road map of our journey. On March thirty-first of this year, the evidence will show you, Selena Quintanilla Perez was killed in a senseless and cowardly act of violence."

He stressed that the murder case he was trying "doesn't happen in a vacuum. There's certain things that lead up to it. We're going to show you some of the events that led up to the killing." He deflected anticipated defense strategy by admitting "There were not any witnesses to this shooting" and added that "there may be some inconsistencies to the story, because that's the way cases are." But he also noted it was not the prosecution's job to present a motive. "As I told you, this is not a terribly complicated case. It comes down to a simple act of violence."

Doug Tinker stood at a distance from the jury box. Easily the most experienced and entertaining lawyer in the court when it came to asking questions and getting the right answers, he spoke in a casual manner with a booming oratory developed before microphones became standard in courtrooms. He countered the prosecution's opening by painting Abraham as a controlling presence. "He lived vicariously through her." The kids, he said, "were unable to escape his control." Yolanda Saldivar had been threatened by Abraham for trying to help Selena start up operations of her fashion design house and her boutiques in Monterrey, Mexico, Tinker said. "It was an escape. Abraham never approved of these businesses. Evidence will show Abraham Quintanilla started making efforts to break them up. He accused her of being a lesbian, which was not true. The evidence will show there was a conflict in January. The evidence will show that Abraham Quintanilla threatened Yolanda physically."

Tinker portrayed his client as fearing for her life, trying to stay away from Abraham while secretly meeting with Selena. She had hired a lawyer to draft a letter saying she quit, but Selena had begged her to stay. He established a timeline: on March 6, after a confrontation in Corpus Christi, she left her apartment. She bought a gun on March 11 for protection, picked up the gun March 26, and went to Mexico, where her vehicle was followed. On March 30, Yolanda explained to Selena she'd been injured in Mexico. Selena took Yolanda to the hospital to check out her injuries on the morning of March 31. Returning from the hospital to the Days Inn, where Yolanda had rented a room, Selena dropped the records on the bed. She was upset and distressed. Selena made a motion toward the door, Yolanda picked up the gun and put it to her head, trying to kill herself, then waved the gun around, and it fired. Yolanda got in her truck looking for her.

During the next nine hours, while Yolanda sat in the truck with the weapon pointed at her own temple, the Corpus Christi police department's hostage negotiating team, led by Larry Young (whom Tinker described as a hero), talked to Yolanda. She said repeatedly, "I didn't mean to shoot her, the gun went off." Yolanda learned of Selena's death on the radio and continued to say, "I didn't do it, it was an accident." Audiotapes that would be introduced in the trial would confirm that, Tinker said.

The other major aspect of the defense strategy was challenging the case work of Sergeant Paul Rivera, one of the two officers who took Yolanda's confession. Rivera had a picture of Selena in his office and a relative who had been in the Army with Abraham, Tinker said. The confession Rivera obtained without a lawyer present was neither videotaped nor audiotaped. Instead, Rivera took notes, had a secretary type them up, and then shredded his notes, per department policy. But Robert Garza, the Texas Ranger who observed the confession, said, "I heard her say it was an accident."

"You're gonna know it was not intentional," Tinker told the jury.

The first witnesses the prosecution brought on were Abraham, Chris, and Suzette. Abraham removed his flashy pinky rings before taking the stand, and spoke calmly of a happy family band. Selena dropped out of junior high to take correspondence classes at the recommendation of the superintendent of schools, Abraham said softly. Abraham, Selena, A.B., and Suzette split everything up four ways rather than work under contracts. The whole family traveled together, including wife Marcella and their dog, in an old Ford van that pulled a trailer Abraham had built himself. Valdez's questions portrayed them as the embodiment of the rags-to-riches American dream. At one point, answering a string of rapid-fire questions from Valdez, he denied ever threatening Yolanda, calling her a lesbian, slashing her tires, raping her, having sex with her, or stabbing her with a knife. He kept his nose out of Selena's businesses, he said. He did admit confronting Yolanda in the presence of Suzette and Selena on March 9, 1995, after being told she had embezzled more than thirty thousand dollars from the fan club. "I showed her some documents that we had found," Abraham testified. "I told her I was going to go to police and proceed to make investigations of the embezzlement." On the following day, after his brother Eddie called, he kicked Yolanda out of the offices of Q Productions where Selena ran her design house operations.

In the first surprise of the trial, Tinker said he would not cross-examine Abraham, though he reserved the right to do so later; this kept Abraham out of the courtroom since he was still a potential witness.

Chris, speaking directly to the jury, told of Selena firing Yolanda the day after the confrontation on March 9, although she wasn't formally terminated because Yolanda had bank statements and records they needed for tax purposes, and because she had established connections that were crucial for starting up Selena's fashion businesses in Mexico.

Suzette contradicted Chris's testimony, saying that Yolanda was still employed on the morning of March 31. She also said that during the March 9 meeting, "I pointed to Yolanda in her face and told her she was a liar and a thief. I knew she was lying."

Tinker reserved the right to cross-examine Chris and Suzette later in the trial, too, keeping them out of court along with Abraham. Three days into the trial, A.B. was subpoenaed, too, not coincidentally after glaring in court at Yolanda and attorney Fred Hagans.

After the father, the husband, and the sister of Selena testified, Valdez called up Mike McDonald and Kyle Voss, two employees from A Place to Shoot, the gun range and shop where Yolanda purchased her pistol. McDonald related how Yolanda had told him she was a home nurse caring for terminally ill patients and that a relative of one of those patients had threatened her. He showed her a Taurus 85 .38-caliber five-shot double-action revolver, on which she placed a one-hundred-dollar deposit. Two days later, after she cleared criminal background checks, she returned to pick up the gun, paying the balance of $130. But two days after that, on March 15, she returned to A Place to Shoot and wanted a refund on the gun because, she said, her father had given her a .22 pistol. On March 26, the day before she left for Mexico, she returned to the gun shop and repurchased the weapon.

Kyle Voss, the president of the gun shop's corporation, conducted the repurchase transaction, and concluded the first day of testimony with a bizarre encounter with defense attorney Tinker, who cross-examined both McDonald and Voss. When Tinker pressed Voss for details on a time line, Voss asked if he could refer to notes on a piece of paper he'd pulled out of his pocket. The paper he'd scribbled on was an article clipped from the San Antonio *Express-News* that profiled Tinker. It caught Tinker's eye, and he walked up next to Voss and leaned over his shoulder, asking him to read the notes into testimony, over the protests of a red-faced Skurka. Most of the notes were derogatory remarks about Tinker scribbled on the picture accompanying the article: "suspenders to keep fat ass from showing," and "cheapass watch, wrist too fat for a classy watch," "protruding belly. Is it a boy or a girl," and "ambulance chaser," next to attorney Gerry Goldstein in the picture's background. Voss apologized again and again. Tinker accepted the apology with a benevolent grin. He'd made his point, managing to get both gun-shop employees to admit that guns do misfire, judging from the bullet holes on the walls and ceilings of the gun range.

Tinker, in the highest-profile trial of his career, was enjoying himself, retiring afterward to Buster's Drinkery, a little dive a block from the courthouse frequented by defense lawyers, taking with him his wife, sister, mother-in-law, and staff, and leaving Fred Hagans to talk to the press and express surprise that the prosecution had called such emotional witnesses as the family so early in the trial. Hagans even raised doubts that the defense would need to cross-examine them later in the trial. He did note that despite Abraham's denials of threats, the defense would present evidence to the contrary. He also questioned how the confession of Yolanda was obtained, noting that the police methodology of taking notes, typing a statement, then shredding the notes was questionable. "They didn't videotape, they didn't audiotape."

Valdez still seemed upbeat in his meeting with the press at the end of the day, repeating, "The state is trying to prove a simple case of murder, that's what we've been saying all along." He did express frustration that, under the laws of the state of Texas, "[The defense] knows everything we're going to do, and we don't know what they're going to do." Valdez's lower lip jutted out prominently after that last statement. He was feeling the pressure, evidence or no evidence. From the start, Judge Westergren cut Valdez little slack ("When I'm speaking, I'm the only one to be speaking," he advised him on the first day of court), which was also how he treated the defense's Fred Hagans. He was somewhat looser with Skurka, with whom he had previous experience in his court, and Tinker, a longtime colleague.

If there was one major difference between this trial and most others, it was that people cared. This case drew a crowd. Mark Skurka was caught off guard several times. "You make your argument or finish your questions and you turn around and see all these faces looking at you."

Out on the sidewalk, fans were gathering. One vociferous lady who won a lottery ticket to the trial one day, Eloisa Puente, was unmoved by what she'd seen in court. "We want justice. Now!" she shouted to several video cameras pointed in her direction while holding up a poster of Selena. "This isn't California, this is Houston. This isn't the fifties, this is the nineties. We don't want her behind bars. We want her in the electric chair."

Max Vargas, a truck driver from Lubbock, and his girlfriend, Gloria Macías—both wearing Selena T-shirts—

took vacation time to drive five hundred miles to watch the proceedings. They'd gone to Corpus for the funeral and had returned four times over the summer. Vargas was dubious about what was going on inside. "The defense is trying to get her off," he acknowledged. "If she didn't mean to shoot her, she shouldn't have had a gun. She had the gun."

The usually lifeless streets of downtown Houston were alive and full of color. Ice cream vendors stationed themselves on corners next to the mounted police and did a land-office business selling frozen treats from their carts. Fans brought their posters, handmade effigies of Yolanda, and paintings. One man handed out sheets of two original compositions he'd written about Selena. Three members of the García family held handmade photomontages and posters of Selena. Mother María's carried the message: "Yolanda, you didn't only take Selena away, you took part of our hearts." A small group of women banded together to shout for justice, though at first they couldn't decide whether the proper Spanish pronunciation was "jew-stee-see-ah" or "who-stee-see-ah."

At four o'clock, crowds started gathering on the sidewalk across Preston Street to get a glimpse of the daily broadcast of *Primer Impacto*, the Univisión network's hugely popular news show, hosted by the comely María Celeste Arraras, the media star of the trial. The doe-eyed, henna-haired Arraras, a Diane Sawyer type with significantly higher sex appeal, was a familiar face to Spanish audiences in the United States and fifteen foreign countries; she had a reputation for asking the tough questions. Unlike the majority of Spanish-language media at the trial, *Primer Impacto* strived to present both sides of the case by focusing on Saldivar and her family as well as the Quintanillas. Arraras's celebrity was ratified by the number of fans who congregated across from the studio tent where she delivered her daily four P.M. report and wherever she went in Houston. Arraras obliged them by waving to her admirers, patting her fanny with a wink in response to wolf whistles, and signing autographs.

Attorneys familiar with the case and Texas law were in great demand as courtroom analysts, among them Harris County prosecutor Johnny Sutton and Houston defense attorney Kent Schaeffer. The most insightful commentary came from Jorge Rangel, working for both *Primer Impacto* and the *Caller-Times*. The former Corpus Christi district judge knew both Texas law and the players involved, offering a perspective no one else could.

On the fourth day of the trial, Yolanda seemed more chipper. That morning, prosecutors brought in two nurses who explained what happened when Selena took Yolanda to Doctors Regional Medical Center, claiming she'd been raped, only to have the examination results convince Selena that Yolanda had fabricated the whole story. They left the hospital less than a half hour before the shooting. In the afternoon, the testimony of Trinidad Espinoza, Norma Martínez, Sandra Avalos, Rosalinda Gonzales, and Rubén DeLeon—all employees of the Days Inn—provided damning eyewitness accounts that effectively neutralized the defense's claim that the shooting was an accident. They all said they had heard the sound of gunfire and Selena's cries of "Help, help!" and saw Yolanda chasing Selena out the door into the courtyard, her arm raised with the gun still pointed at her, then walk calmly back to her room.

Espinoza's account was too much for Marcella and she had to be escorted from court. The next day, she was admitted to the coronary unit of St. Joseph's Hospital for overnight observation. She didn't appear in court again until Tuesday of the third week, when closing arguments for the trial were made.

Tinker aggressively cross-examined Norma Martínez, noting she had embellished her account since she'd given a written statement in April. He noted that Martínez mentioned nothing in the earlier written statement about hearing Yolanda say "bitch" while chasing Selena out the door, as she had now, testimony that caused Yolanda Saldivar to lower her head in the courtroom. He also found it odd that she had initially described the four-foot nine-inch Saldivar as being medium height and having blond hair with black roots showing.

"Are you nervous because I'm picking on you?" Tinker asked Martínez, who nodded tentatively.

Martínez stuck to her story and said she hadn't said anything about the word *bitch* before because it was a bad word. (Then again, Martínez didn't say anything about her own prior conviction for theft, either.)

Other witnesses confirmed that Selena bled to death, that her heart had stopped beating by the time she arrived at the hospital and all efforts to save her were fruitless. The issue of Abraham telling doctors that Selena would not approve of blood transfusions because of the family's belief in the Jehovah's Witness faith proved to be a moot point, since blood had already been transfused to no avail. Richard Fredrickson, the fire department paramedic who treated Selena at the motel lobby, testified about finding the egg-shaped gold-and-diamond ring clutched in Selena's hand.

At day's end, Tinker reported he'd received a death threat. Two days later, Valdez said he'd received one, too.

The most potentially explosive evidence in the trial was five hours' worth of taped conversations between Yolanda sitting in the motel parking lot with a gun to her head and Larry Young and Isaac Valencia of the Corpus Christi police department's hostage negotiation team. The dialogue revealed a distraught, panicky Saldivar on the edge, wailing, crying, hollering, and saying things that may or may not have been true.

"I don't want to live anymore because of what I did. Her family caused me lots of trouble. Her father hated her. Her father is responsible for this. He made me shoot her. He made me shoot her. The father was coming between us." Abraham was out to get her, she claimed. "I kept telling people about Abraham but no one would listen. No matter what I tell them, they don't listen to me. This man was so evil to me. My father even warned me about him. My father said I should get out before I get trapped." She also claimed Abraham raped her. "He stuck a knife in my vagina and he raped me a month and a half ago. He raped me in the apartment. He told me not to tell anyone or he would kill me.

"I did something very bad. I have disgraced my family."

The defense cited the tapes to show Yolanda was telling the truth. The prosecution used the tapes to support their belief that Yolanda was lying and didn't say it was an accident until negotiator Larry Young suggested so several times. They also pointed out that she blamed everyone but herself and rarely called Selena by name.

The special phone line used by the hostage negotiation team had one technical flaw. It picked up the signal from the KSIX-AM transmitter, located near the motel parking lot. Negotiators kept asking Yolanda to turn off the radio in the truck, which she insisted she had done. It was through this interference on the phone line from the news-talk station that Yolanda learned Selena was dead, at which point she became even more hysterical. At various moments in the background during the tense negotiations, the voice of Milo Hamilton could be heard calling an exhibition baseball game between the Houston Astros and the Texas Rangers, as well as the familiar melody of the "Theme from M*A*S*H (Suicide Is Painless)."

There were less tense moments: when Yolanda saw Young after talking to him and realized he was black; and when Young, trying to appeal to Yolanda's religious background, told her that if she came out, "the Virgin of Guadalupe will be with you."

"You can't be Catholic," Yolanda responded. She might have been distraught, but she wasn't stupid.

One thirty-minute stretch consisted of little else but Yolanda repeating the mantra, "Where's Larry?," punctuated by back-up negotiator Isaac Valencia's persistent "Yolanda" and occasionally interspersed by a mysterious and extremely irritating electronic buzz. The bizarre audio experience was memorable enough to inspire "Where's Larry?" T-shirts and laminated tags that were being hawked around the courthouse within a day.

If there was any advantage gained by the defense after Yolanda's hysterics and Larry Young's suggestion that the shooting was an accident were heard, it was the sight of Yolanda quietly crying as the courtroom was filled with the eerie sound of her sobs and moans recorded during the standoff. It was a pathetic show, but jurors could plainly see that the cold-blooded murderer, this monster who was supposedly evil incarnate, was also very much a human being.

The prosecution rested at the end of the eighth day of the trial, having called thirty-three witnesses to the stand. Their last witness, Corpus police firearms examiner Ed McKinstry, was cross-examined by Patricia Saum to better show jurors how a delicate woman might have handled or mishandled the murder weapon.

That afternoon at Buster's Drinkery, Tinker's eyes twinkled as the conversation shifted to the trial. "What if we called it here? How do you think it'd play?" he asked rhetorically.

Everyone around the table laughed. It was hard to tell whether or not he was kidding. Would the defense rest without calling a witness? If nothing else, Tinker always kept everyone guessing.

The following day, the defense opened by recalling Rubén DeLeon, the Days Inn marketing director, to determine that Shawna Vela was not in a position to have seen or heard Selena as she ran into the lobby, refuting her "Lock the door. She'll shoot me again" comment. Motel maid Gloria Magaña testified she heard the gunshot coming out of room 158 but that Trinidad Espinoza and Norma Martínez could not have seen Yolanda chasing Selena out of the room because their lines of sight were blocked. Another new witness was Marilyn Greer, Selena's seventh-grade reading teacher, who said Selena could have attended almost any four-year college on a scholarship had not Abraham pulled her out of school to concentrate on a music career. Then came Paul Rivera. Tinker chipped away at the hostile witness, who testified he'd known about the hostage tapes since April though he didn't attempt to gain access to them, and admitted he'd given Tinker a Selena T-shirt at the behest of Abraham Quintanilla. Finally, Barbara Schultz, the general manager of the Days Inn who made the first 911 call when Selena ran into the lobby, testified that Shawna Vela must have been mistaken about hearing Selena say, "Lock the door. She'll shoot me again!" Vela had a history of stretching the truth, said Schultz, the wife of a Corpus cop.

Immediately after lunch, Tinker asked the court to consider allowing the questioning of Yolanda to be limited to the parking lot standoff. Westergren denied the motion, and the defense rested. Abraham would not be cross-examined by the defense; the lesbian accusations, the alleged rape, the power struggle over Selena, and all the other fireworks promised in Tinker's opening statements went out with a fizzle. Did Tinker see something in the jurors that told him he could rest his case? He kept saying how much he liked the jury, especially the three big Anglo men in the back, one of whom had an affection for bowling shirts, another an ex-Marine with a tattoo on his forearm who could have been mistaken for football legend Terry Bradshaw. Or did he think he'd put a wedge in the prosecution's evidence? The answer was a little of both. "About halfway through the prosecution's case, I realized we were either gonna get everything we could or get trounced," Tinker said. It was going to be all or nothing.

Westergren dismissed the jury, the accused, and everyone else, informing the court they could stay for the bull session of legalese that would follow. The judge removed his robe, stepped down to sit directly in front of the defense and prosecution, and listened, with the microphones turned off, to each side's argument on whether or not the judge should instruct the jury to consider a lesser charge than murder in the first degree. Tinker told Westergren the defense requested that he instruct the jury to consider only murder in the first degree, a charge with a maximum penalty of life in prison. Either Yolanda was guilty of murder or she wasn't. The night before, on *Primer Im-*

pacto, legal analyst Jorge Rangel said that Tinker was playing poker. Now he was pushing all his chips to the center of the table.

At the beginning of the trial and as recently as two days earlier, Valdez said the prosecution would not consider asking the judge for a lesser included (which would give the jury the option of finding her guilty of a lesser charge), but with Tinker brazenly gambling, Valdez suddenly waffled, saying he wanted to think about it over the weekend. He'd never live it down if Yolanda was acquitted. He had to get some kind of conviction. But Selena's family, her fans, and almost the entire Hispanic population of Corpus wanted to see justice done. Twenty years in prison, much less probation, was not enough, not if good was to triumph over evil.

When court reconvened on Monday, Valdez and Tinker were still trying to stare each other down, both reiterating that they didn't want Westergren to instruct the jury to consider a lesser included. Westergren asked them more than once if they were sure about their decisions. A lesser included charge might be the best way out of an untenable situation. The lawyers were still trying to one-up each other before the closing arguments began. Where the prosecution normally opened and closed, the defense stating its case in between, Valdez waived the prosecution's right to open, choosing to restrict his remarks to the final closing, following the defense.

Hagans began by tenaciously hammering on the inconsistencies in the motel employees' eyewitness accounts and going after Paul Rivera, accusing him of trying to make a case at the expense of justice. Whenever Hagans took the floor during the course of the trial, he lived up to his high-dollar-lawyer image by cross-examining aggressively, leading witnesses with the phrase, "Wouldn't you agree . . ." Tinker followed, making an impromptu recitation of the accident theory, attacking the sloppy police work, and apologizing to the jury for his rambling style because "sometimes my mind is like a pinball." He made some good points but never completely tied the loose ends together. If Valdez had been underwhelming, Tinker had been overhyped.

Skurka began the prosecution's closing statements by affixing a picture of Selena to a wall in the jury box and speaking to it. Frustrated by parrying with attorneys on the other side who were either flamboyant and famous or wore expensive suits, he appealed to the jury's down-home sensibilities by telling them, "I'm just a country lawyer from Corpus Christi," over the defense's objection, then describing the defense's claim of an accident as "hogwash." It was the old Squid Defense, as he had often said before in Nueces County courts: trying to confuse the predator with a cloud of black ink.

If doubts had been raised, they were not considered reasonable by the jury. It took less than two hours for them to find Yolanda Saldívar guilty of murder.

"You might not want to sit down next to us," Douglas Tinker wearily rasped one hour later, holding on to a glass of Chardonnay. "It's been a while since I've won one." With his shirtsleeves rolled up and suit pants pulled above the knees, he sighed and leaned against the back of the booth by the door at Buster's Drinkery. The boys at the next table were engrossed in their usual game of gin rummy, while immediately outside the bar a demonstration was taking place like none ever seen before around this part of downtown Houston. Horns were honking, music blaring, and crowds filled the sidewalks, waving signs and cheering wildly as if a great national victory had been won. There was literally dancing in the streets.

Tinker, slouched low in the booth, and Arnold García, looking more grizzled than ever as he glumly sat across the table and stared blankly at a can of Coors Light while a Marlboro Light 100 burned between two fingers, had plenty to contemplate. They'd gambled and lost. They had decided not to ask the judge to instruct the jury to consider a lesser charge, such as voluntary manslaughter, which would have meant a shorter sentence. They had rested their case before calling up Abraham, whom they had portrayed in opening arguments as the controlling stage dad and manager, a marked contrast to the man who removed his flashy pinky rings before taking the witness stand and answered the prosecution's questions by calmly speaking of puppy dogs and one big happy family. Nor did they put their own client on the stand.

"Yolanda says she wants to testify during the punishment phase," Tinker told García, who shook his head adamantly. "You don't want to do that." The hostage negotiation tapes spoke volumes for her. Besides, the prosecution would have torn her up. Tinker nodded in agreement. "Hindsight," he muttered to himself.

With Diez y Seis going on a few footsteps away, there wasn't a better place than Buster's for Tinker and García to take refuge. The regulars knew too well how their brethren from Corpus were feeling at the moment. Many of them had been on the short side of similar verdicts. So they tried to salve wounds with offers to buy a round. The sound of horns honking grew more persistent. More than once, Tinker had spoken of going out in a blaze of bullets, like Zapata.

"They saw us walk in. They know we're here," he said to García with mild irritation. The response on the street clearly rattled him. It underscored the realization that Yolanda Saldivar was a marked woman for the rest of her life, no matter where she was. "We take the threats of the Mexican Mafia very seriously," Tinker said, referring to the dominant prison gang in the Texas penal system. That's why he told the jury it was his prayer to escort Yolanda home at the end of the trial. García begged to differ. In many respects, Yolanda was better off in prison.

When the newsreader on the six o'clock news touted coverage of "the trial of Selena," Tinker talked back to the tube, sputtering, "The Selena trial? What about the Yolanda Saldivar trial?" It had been a long day, and watching the youthful visage of District Attorney Carlos Valdez appearing on the screen, stating, "As I said earlier, we're coming to Houston to find justice and I think we found it today," didn't make it any easier.

The honking outside continued. Tinker nodded to García. "I guess we have time for another round." He was buying this time, for everyone in the bar. As barkeep Candis Lockard brought out fresh drinks and the boys at the next table continued their card game, a smile creased Tinker's worn face.

"Well, at least this reduces our chances of getting shot."

By the time the guilty verdict had been handed down, the Selena fan contingent had grown to several hundred strong and had become considerably more savvy. During the noon recesses and at the end of court each day, the fans gathered with television reporters around spectators who'd attended the trial, listening to their comments about what they'd seen and heard in court. Some regulars had become celebrities in their own right, such as the aptly named Shorty, who wore a doo rag under his ball cap, shades, baggy shorts, and high tops, bobbing and weaving to "Como la Flor" playing on the boom box he carried (police officers knew him by another name, under which he had frequently been booked in the Harris County jail). Jaime René Cevallos handed out business cards identifying himself as a candidate for mayor of New York City in 1997.

The media-chorus interaction was epitomized by a live report by Irma Garza to viewers of KGBT-TV in the Rio Grande Valley one afternoon. While Garza recounted the events of the day, a songwriter from Dallas named Nelson Alberto Cruz sidled up a few feet behind her on the other side of a police barricade and began singing his original composition "El Ultimo Adiós a Selena" at the top of his bellowing voice while gesturing dramatically to the framed photo of Selena someone held next to him. Three guitarists and a maracas shaker played an accompaniment.

Two days after the guilty verdict was handed down, the elusive Dr. Ricardo Martínez appeared on *Primer Impacto*. Introduced as a well-known Monterrey plastic surgeon, the ponytailed doctor said he was Selena's friend, confidant, doctor, and financial adviser. Both the prosecution and defense had sought him out, but his deposition, taken by phone, was never introduced into the court record. In court, defense attorney Tinker said the purpose of their meeting was to have liposuction surgery done on Selena and Suzette, but Martínez did not talk about specifics, citing the confidentiality of the doctor-client relationship.

Martínez did say that there had been problems between Selena and Abraham and that Abraham had always been opposed to Selena's opening a business in Mexico, he said.

Finally, Martínez said that he had never trusted Yolanda and that Selena was feeling apprehensive about Yolanda and about her family disapproving of her friendship with her. The doctor said this friendship was the result of Selena's isolation. She trusted Yolanda too much, he said, as a friend and a business associate. Selena had no male or female friends because the demands of the music business didn't permit much time to develop relationships. Her dream to be a successful fashion designer was her outlet, he said. Music came second. She was tired of life on the road and felt worn out.

The sentencing phase began on Tuesday afternoon of the third week of the trial. Under Texas law, both the prosecution and defense could call up witnesses, and cross-examine them, to vouch for or testify against the guilty party's character. Valdez, clearly feeling his oats, called a number of witnesses, including a forgery investigator, an accountant, and several beauty suppliers who spoke about incidents that led to the embezzlement charges that Valdez said he would present to the Nueces County grand jury after the murder trial ended. To a person, they portrayed Yolanda as a book-juggling, double-invoicing, hot-check-writing thief. Tinker objected loudly enough that Westergren testily agreed to hear the eight witnesses without the presence of the jury. By day's end, the judge decided to allow the jury to hear the same eight witnesses testify on the following day, although he warned the prosecution they were skating on thin ice. By introducing embezzlement accusations before Saldivar had been formally charged, Valdez was inviting an appelate court ruling that could jeopardize the guilty verdict.

Overnight, Valdez had a change of heart, after he and Skurka took a long walk around Greenway Plaza near their hotel, smoking cigars. The next day the prosecution called only Dr. Faustino Gómez, a San Antonio dermatologist for whom Saldivar had worked from 1980 to 1983. Without the jury present, Gómez told of monies that were embezzled by Saldivar and how the discrepancy was settled out of court through his insurance company. In the jury's presence, Dr. Gómez testified only that in his opinion, Yolanda Saldivar was not a law-abiding citizen.

The defense called nine witnesses in less than two hours to testify about Saldivar's good character, the last being her father, Frank. Frank Saldivar was the most tenured headwaiter in San Antonio, having served diners at Jacala restaurant for forty years. He and his wife of forty-seven years raised seven children on his modest income, trying to instill the values in them that they held dearest. The munchkin-size man attended the first day of the trial and could not return since he was a potential witness for the defense until the sentencing phase, when he spent his sixty-ninth birthday on the witness stand imploring the jurors to have mercy on the woman he called "our baby girl." He asked the jury to raise their hands if they believed in God. Before Valdez could object, more than half answered in the affirmative. "I hope some of ya'll have sons and daughters and you believe in God," Saldivar then told them. "We have lost two lives."

Closing arguments for the sentencing phase took less than an hour. Tinker thanked the jury and made his case for probation, pointing out his client had no prior criminal record. "I'm here to say I believe in you," he said, adding, "That doesn't mean I take back anything I said during the guilt phase of the trial." He asked them to be fair. "You know that Yolanda Saldivar has already suffered. You heard that anguish in her voice. She has suffered greatly. You know from the tape she is horribly remorse-

ful about her conduct on March 31." He attempted to read
a note that Saldivar had written before the judge sustained
the prosecution's objection. It was just as well, since it
said: "No one suffered more over Selena's death than I
have," a statement that any of the Quintanillas might have
disputed.

Skurka once again taped a picture of a smiling Selena on
the wall of the jury box, as he had during the closing remarks of the guilt phase, and spoke of the path they'd all
embarked upon together and how it was coming to a close.
He recalled Selena's last moments, "as she ran screaming
for help, trying to escape the woman running after her with
a gun in her hand. I think of that path and what a horrible
way to die. We're not here to reward Yolanda Saldivar for
what she did. We're here to punish Yolanda Saldivar for
what she did. She blamed everybody else except herself.
You should punish her with a life sentence. You should
give her what she took—life."

Valdez thanked the jury, and reminded them that on the
other side of the courtroom were "several excellent lawyers and one murderer." He implored the jury not to forget "the beautiful voice, the golden voice that brought
joy to millions of people. I'm asking you to write a verdict
we can live with. I'm asking you for life." The brief wrap
was perhaps his finest presentation of the trial.

Westergren sent the jury into deliberation at 1:12 P.M.
while Yolanda bowed her head and moved her lips si-
lently in a prayer.

While the jury deliberated behind closed doors, the
mood in the courtroom turned informal and almost jovial.
The end was in sight. Attorneys visited with spectators.
The sheriff's deputies ceased patting down media when
they entered the courtroom. Autograph fever, born of
boredom, was in the air. A bailiff approached Yolanda
Saldivar and whipped out a court pass, asking her to sign
it. Pretty soon, Westergren and Valdez were signing
their signatures too. The Saldivar family sought out
the scribbles of several reporters. Tinker posed for the
sketch artists and quipped, "If the jury never comes back,

if they rode off into the sunset, it'd be fine with me."

The din grew so loud that a bailiff had to shout, "Quiet in the courtroom!" Judge Westergren, talking to two young lawyers in the gallery, sheepishly raised his hand and said, "I'm afraid it was me." Two spectators dozed off in the back corner. So, briefly, did Abraham Quintanilla, sitting alone in the family seating section. This was hardly the stuff of a Trial of the Century.

In the late afternoon the jury sent Westergren a note telling him they were deadlocked and asking him if they could go home and sleep on it. He asked them to continue deliberating and arranged for them to be sequestered in a hotel overnight.

At 2:23 P.M. on the second day of deliberation, a buzzer sounded in the courtroom, signaling the jury had determined a sentence. The long deliberation, observers guessed, was in the defense's favor, suggesting a moral victory snatched from the jaws of defeat if the sentence was anything less than life. Both Tinker and García were upbeat. "That guardian angel that found the Texas Ranger and the hostage tapes for Yolanda had fallen asleep during the verdict," García said. "I think she may have just woken up." Maybe Yolanda would get probation, as Tinker had argued to the jury she should. Valdez was worried about a hung jury. Even if it was over the sentence, and not guilt, if there was no resolution, "We'd have to start all over again," he said.

Fifteen minutes later, as the Quintanillas joined hands and said a prayer, Westergren read the sentence: Life in prison. Juror Charles Arnold, a tall, strapping man with silver hair, one of the men Tinker kept saying he liked so much, had held out for a twenty-to-forty-year sentence before giving in. That would have been more than enough time to do penance and still give Saldivar a chance to rehabilitate herself, Arnold said afterward.

Valdez saluted the jury on their way out and Yolanda quietly sobbed while being shielded by investigator Tina Valenzuela before hugging her mother and father good-bye. The Quintanillas were quietly escorted past the railing to thank the jury, who extended their condolences. Valdez was hugged by three jurors. Tinker rated no better than a handshake.

A festive mood erupted on the streets again. Although the crowds were slightly smaller, they made more noise, chanted louder, and honked more incessantly. Making the victory all the sweeter was the appearance of Carlos Valdez. After holding his final conference with the press pool, he walked around the corner to the courthouse entrance to engage the Selena chorus that had gathered every day behind police barricades since the trial began. To shouts of *"Arriba, Valdez!"* and *"Viva, Fiscal!"* he smiled, shook hands, signed autographs, and kissed babies, looking for all the world like a presidential candidate on the stump. He also spoke to the fans in Spanish, telling them to be calm and to go home. "The devastation of two families is no reason to celebrate," he said. Clearly relieved and beaming like a little kid, Valdez finally had finished the job he had set out to do seven months earlier. "I may not have sold my case to the media," said Valdez, who had been depicted by the press as "flashy," "dapper," and "stylish" early in the trial and "underwhelming" and "wooden" toward its conclusion. "But the twelve most important people in the courtroom believed us."

That night, the three prosecutors had their own celebration, letting vegetarian Elissa Sterling select the Khyber Indian restaurant for dinner. "The best thing about this case was spending all this time talking to each other," Sterling said. "We never get to do that in Corpus, where there's ten things going on at once." After letting Sterling off at their hotel, Valdez and Skurka went to the Half-Price Books store near Rice University and browsed for an hour and a half. "Nobody talked to us about the trial," Valdez observed.

Tinker announced he would appeal the case. He still believed his client. "I met Yolanda Saldivar right after I got appointed," he related afterward. "It took her a while to be comfortable with me, but after a while she knew I'd do what I could. I knew nothing about the case. There's not one thing she told me then that didn't turn out to be true. She told me about the accident. She told me what the negotiators said. The more that happened, the more I believed this was an unintentional shooting.'' When last seen leaving the courthouse, Tinker was still being hounded by Selena fans. They didn't want his head, though. They wanted his autograph.

As murder trials go, the one in Houston had little to do with the O.J. Simpson trial in Los Angeles other than that it involved homicide and a celebrity. Nonetheless, the O.J. comparison frequently came up in the national (read: Anglo) media, while the Chicano community embraced the concept too, albeit their trial had an even better story line. In fact, once the trial began, the fear started spreading through the barrios of Houston, San Antonio, and Corpus that the Saldivar trial was a little too much like the O.J. trial, meaning Yolanda might get off due to police officer Paul Rivera's questionable handling of the confession. *Un pinche pendejo*, one lousy cop. People on the street were nervous that a procedural error was going to mess everything up.

Tinker assessed his own closing statements as ''ineffective,'' but he was already working at a disadvantage after the prosecution called witnesses that the defense had wanted and admitted to the jury in advance that there had been inconsistencies. ''We showed the jury what the problems were before Doug could use them to his advantage,'' Valdez said. In the end, the most powerful effect of the O.J. trial was perhaps the most subtle and indirect. After Simpson walked away from the court a free man, almost every single person called for jury duty anywhere in America over the following weeks had the opportunity to contemplate what they would have done if they'd been sitting in judgment in Los Angeles. The Houston jury hearing the case of the *State of Texas* versus *Saldivar* was composed of people who'd decided that they weren't going to let a technicality get in the way of the evidence as it had done with O.J. They never bought the accident story.

The defense raised many questions during the trial but, after all was said and done, never answered most of them. Were the boutiques really skating on thin financial ice? Why was the band so cash-poor in early 1995? Was the mysterious Dr. Martínez merely an investor in Selena's Mexican fashion ventures, or more than a business associate or friend? Did Selena have a bag packed, ready to run off to Mexico, as Yolanda had indicated to the defense team? Arnold García claimed they still had the packed bag. Yolanda had also concocted the story that she'd walked into the apartment in Monterrey that Dr. Martínez allegedly kept for Selena, only to find the doctor engaging in sex with his nurse. When Yolanda informed Selena, according to this scenario, Selena blamed the messenger: Yolanda was messing around with Martínez. Thus the rape story was fabricated: Selena and Yolanda ripped Yolanda's clothes before going to the hospital so that Yolanda could prove to Selena that there was no presence of semen and that she didn't have sex with Martínez.

Or at least that was the way Yolanda saw it. That didn't answer Yolanda's accusation that Abraham raped her. On the hostage negotiation tapes, Saldivar said, "He raped me. He stuck a knife in my vagina." Nor did it address other inconsistencies. Rather, her accusation and subsequent lack of explanation of what she meant to say merely shored up the prosecution's claim that Yolanda was a pathological liar.

If there was a mistake, it was the family's long goodbye to Yolanda. Once her misdeeds came to light, her firing was dragged out over a three-week period. Chris Perez testified on the witness stand that Selena fired Yolanda on March 10. Suzette Arriaga testified Selena was about to fire Yolanda on March 30, which was corroborated by boutique nail tech Celia Solís. Having all that time to contemplate being cut off from the person she described as "my best friend" and "the only friend I ever had" could have been enough to drive Yolanda Saldivar over the edge and make her shoot Selena in the heat of the moment. Whether or not the firing of the weapon was an accident or intentional, having her world crash was too much for Yolanda to stand. As she said to Larry Young hours after she did the deed, "I had a problem with her and I just got to end it."

Much had been said over the summer about the trial sullying the image of Selena. At the start of the trial, Douglas Tinker declared, "Selena Quintanilla Perez is dead. There's nothing I can do about that. But regardless of what you've heard, nothing about this trial is going to reflect badly on Selena Quintanilla Perez. When this trial is done, her reputation is going to be as clean as it was before her death." And it was, despite the questions posed by the defense, the stories generated in the tabloid press, and the innate human desire to gossip about the famous and infamous. Selena really was the all-American girl with the kind of values people dream for their children. For that reason alone, she continued to give many people hope who had no reason to hope before. Her star shone brighter than ever. *Puro corazón.*

At the Seaside Memorial Park, the crowds thinned out enough to remove the orange storm fencing from around the black marble marker. The mesquite tree behind the marker appeared healthy and growing despite the carvings in its bark. The city of Corpus Christi honored Selena by renaming the Bayfront Auditorium and dedicating to her a statue and a gazebo pavilion on the bayfront seawall. The pilgrims who continued to come to pay homage had several places in the city to pause and reflect. There was also talk of building a Tejano Hall of Fame in the old county courthouse.

Selena's father continued to be almost as fascinating a study as his daughter. Depending on his mood and demeanor, he was the grieving father or the hustling band manager. Not one to shy from the spotlight, he spoke his mind, although his boorish behavior could have frightened Yolanda Saldivar, giving basis to her claims that he was the catalyst behind Selena's death. The press covering the trial tolerated Quintanilla's less than pleasant demeanor because he was good copy, guaranteed to boost ratings and readership. The media needed him as much as he needed the media and each would accommodate the other, with reservations. Even better, as a former musician and stage father, he'd been preparing himself to be in the public eye almost all his life. If he played his cards right, there was considerably more ahead of him than just a career developing and recording young acts through Q Productions. He was absolutely correct in his claim that he was the best person to protect and conserve Selena's image. Whether he could do so with a semblance of the dignity and humility that made his daughter the role model she was remained to be seen.

The Quintanilla family emerged from the long ordeal stronger and tighter than ever. The bullying tactics of Abraham may have tempered sympathetic feelings toward the grieving family, but bluster aside, he and Marcella did raise a daughter who didn't drink, didn't smoke, and was the only major Tejano star not to endorse a beer brand. They had been good parents who instilled the values in Selena that made people look up to her. After the guilty verdict was announced, they declined to comment to the press pool at the courthouse, preferring to engage media one-on-one on their own terms and conditions, conducting press conferences at the studios of the official radio stations hosting the Quintanillas during the trial. Marcella expressed the sadness of knowing that no matter how things had turned out, her daughter was still gone. A.B. joined his father in attacking the defense lawyers for running the family's reputations through the mud ("They got off easy," Doug Tinker responded) and dismissing various unauthorized books, articles, and reports as lies. It all made for good copy.

A 900 number had been set up to telephone a message of condolence to the Quintanillas for only $3.99 a call. In addition to the Selena movie, the planned Selena y Los Dinos farewell tour, and other Selena memorial projects,

Abraham concentrated on activities at Q Productions, building a roster of young talent for his custom label distributed by Capitol-EMI, including the twelve-year-old singing sensation Jennifer Peña, who many said could be the next Selena. Suzette managed the boutiques and oversaw Selena merchandising. A.B. Quintanilla III was one of the most in-demand Latin producers in the United States.

Chris Perez was looking for a new place too, effectively rendering the three homes on Bloomington Street one big empty nest. Perez still appeared devastated by the loss of his wife, always on the verge of tears, though the aristocratic young man with the ponytail was a slight, delicate figure to begin with. In court, with his arm around Marcella and being comforted by Suzette, he seemed as much a Quintanilla as anyone. He struggled to get on with his life and indicated at San Antonio's Hard Rock Café that he wanted to continue playing guitar, focusing on rock music. He answered critics who questioned the handling of the probate will by telling San Antonio columnist Carlos Guerra, "I didn't have a lawyer, just like Selena didn't have a lawyer. We didn't need a lawyer because this is family. And why should I worry about losing something? I have already lost what I always wanted. I would trade everything I had if I could have her back."

On November 14, two weeks after the trial ended, Yolanda Saldivar finally spoke publicly. María Celeste Arraras, the host of *Primer Impacto*, had dogged Saldivar since the shooting, writing her more than forty letters. Her persistence paid off when Saldivar agreed to an interview in the Nueces County jail on November 9. Arraras began the hour-long one-on-one explaining that her program and network had not paid Yolanda for the interview, nor had Yolanda made specific demands regarding questions or content.

Yolanda dressed for the interview in a red jacket with marching-band buttons, her permed hair glistening. She appeared calm, though her eyes were teary on several occasions. Over the course of the interview, which was conducted in Spanish, she portrayed herself as Selena's confidante in what amounted to a mother-daughter relationship. She was telling her side of the story because Selena had come to her in a dream and asked her to tell the world the secret she had shared with her.

She called Selena *m'ija*, my daughter. "She was like a child to me," she said, and suggested that Selena looked up to her like a parent, calling her Mom or Mama, never referring to her as Yolanda. The only people who cared for Selena, Saldivar said, were Dr. Ricardo Martínez, in Monterrey, and herself. Selena's family, she said, loved Selena only for her money.

She denied romantic involvement with Selena and said that Martin Gómez and Abraham Quintanilla, Jr., were responsible for spreading the rumor that she was a lesbian. She demonstrated her movements during their last moments in the motel room, showing how she picked up the gun and held it to her head, and how it allegedly went off as she motioned toward the door. But Arraras tripped her up on several points. Asked why she didn't put down the pistol after the weapon discharged, Yolanda said she held it because she didn't want anyone else to harm Selena. She said she didn't even realize she had wounded her until several hours later. Explaining how the gun went off while she was motioning toward the door, Yolanda first said she had wanted Selena to close the door, then later said she had wanted Selena to open the door. She also claimed to Arraras that she was the first to call 911 to get emergency help, although there is no record of that call.

The jury in her trial was biased, she said, but her conscience was clear.

"God knows it was an accident." She asked Marcella Quintanilla to forgive her, and said she had tried to tell her about Selena's secret back in January but Marcella never returned her call.

At the end of the program, Arraras reached the same conclusion many observers had after the trial ended: there were more questions now than ever before. Ultimately, the interview did Yolanda little good. Her comments were self-serving, her comportment pathetic: a serious martyr complex rife with *penitente* religious references. Although she spoke several times of Selena's secret, Yolanda made it through the entire hour without providing any details. The mystery would not be solved. She would have plenty of time to contemplate when to reveal it.

The secret she hinted at was Selena's diary, which Yolanda had supposedly retrieved from Mexico before going to Corpus that fateful March evening. According to Yolanda, Selena wasn't looking for the bank records when she left the motel room on Thursday night. Selena didn't dump the contents of the satchel on the bed of the motel room in search of canceled checks moments before she died, either. She wanted her diary, which Yolanda was withholding from her. Selena wanted the book in which she had expressed her innermost thoughts. Or so went the scenario Yolanda had mapped out.

In early December, Abraham appeared on *Primer Impacto* to tell his side of the story to Arraras. Yolanda, he said, killed Selena purely for malicious reasons. It was the fifth time she had tried to lure Selena to her death, he said, and after Yolanda killed Selena, she had intended to shoot him at the recording studio. Yolanda's dark side would emerge at her embezzlement trial, he said, although the Nueces County grand jury had not handed down an indictment on those charges.

Selena's death and legacy galvanized the Hispanic community in Texas in a way that no movement, including La Raza Unida, nor any person, including César Chávez, had ever accomplished. A sense of pride welled up in the barrios of this state that had never been felt before, evidenced by *ofrendas* to Selena, like the elaborate one with the Whataburger bag (Selena's favorite fast food hamburger) at Casa Ramírez in the Heights of Houston for the Day of the Dead celebration on November 1.

Texas Hispanics could no longer be ignored. If nothing else, their economic clout was undeniable. *People* magazine announced the startup of a Spanish-language edition, following the phenomenal sales of three Selena covers in four months. *El Premio Mayor*, the popular new Mexican *telenovela* produced by Emilio Larossa, was rife with Selena references. Sasha, the famous *telenovela* star, played a pretty young girl with a serious Selena hang-up, evidenced by the Selena pictures on her wall and the Selena music playing in the background.

In light of that, the verdict and the sentence were for the best. It shored up trust in a legal system that has come under increasingly close and critical scrutiny. It proved to Texas's largest minority group that not all experiences with the law are negative; that criminal justice, flawed as it might be, really does work. In Houston, at least this one time, no tricky lawyer claiming an accident nor any rogue cop was going to divert attention from the fact that Yolanda Saldivar murdered Selena Quintanilla Perez. Even Ranger Garza could not shake them with doubt, though one observer cynically noted it was a historic moment, marking the first time a Texas Ranger spoke out in defense of a Mexican-American.

Following the trial, the League of United Latin American Citizens mounted a campaign to urge Hispanics to seek jury duty. Now that they had seen up close how the system worked, perhaps they'd be more inclined to participate in the process. Frances Gemma, an older woman who attended some of the trial and demonstrated on the sidewalk, said it was the first time she'd ever been in a courtroom. "I saw that justice was gonna be done," she said. "There was justice in Houston. Otherwise, I think they were gonna break every window around here."

The defense raised some valid issues about how police investigations are conducted. Overall, the Corpus Christi police department deserved high marks for the manner in which they handled the shooting and the standoff with Saldivar. But given the evidence, some changes were clearly called for. If the department could afford video cameras to record DUI and DWI suspects, they could afford video or audio recorders for interviewing murder suspects. If they didn't shred their notes on other cases, then why did they for murder cases?

The issue of lead hostage negotiator Larry Young telling Saldivar that her lawyer Richard Garza would be waiting for her when she gave up, only to have her waive her rights when no attorney was present at the police station, called for clarifying the role of a negotiator during similar standoffs. District Attorney Valdez said that just because a negotiator promises somebody the moon doesn't mean that they'll give them the moon when they get out. On the other hand, FBI hostage negotiation guidelines strictly require negotiators not to say anything that isn't true.

The street celebrations around the courthouse evoked mixed feelings. Overall, the mood was festive and lively enough to prompt the two women who usually stood by the entrance with their graphic pictures of aborted babies to take a break for a few days. But there was something disturbing about the mob-like shouts of *"Cul-pa-ble, cul-pa-ble"* and *"Cien años, cien años"* echoing through the concrete canyons; signs such as the caricature of Yolanda in the middle of a target with the words *La marrana*— the sow—written underneath; and the "Kill Yolanda" message painted in white shoe polish on the windshield of a Toyota. At least others showed some imagination, such as the one that paraphrased a line from the crossover country hit "It's Not the End of the World" by Selena's old labelmate and duet partner Emilio Navaira: "There can never be enough justice for Selena, but it's a damn good start."

But amidst the jubilation was a contrasting sense of *luto*, or mourning, once one of the underpinnings of Mexican culture. The tears on the faces of many fans, especially older women, confirmed that *luto* still had relevance in this community. For them, Selena had already evolved from a pop star into an icon of grief, a symbol of how harsh, unjust, and hurtful death can be, especially when it takes someone so young, promising, and full of life. Even when there was no pain or personal tragedy of their own to lament, they would always have Selena's loss to mourn. The healing process would never really end. The hurt would never go away. It was small wonder that Selena was now immortalized in more street murals than Mexican revolutionaries Pancho Villa and Emiliano Zapata, and was almost as popular as the Virgin of Guadalupe. But it still didn't change the realization that everyone wished they had no reason to be there. Truman Bradshaw of Fort Worth, the only Anglo fan of Selena's who showed up regularly in the spectator seating section, reckoned the sentencing was almost a moot point. "Whether it was an accident or no accident, there's no winner." Finally, though, there was closure.

In life, Selena was a superstar, an entertainer who transcended her particular field to enjoy a popularity unprecedented for a singer who specialized in a regional style of music. In death, she became the first tragic heroine in the Latin world since Frida Kahlo, the tortured wife of Mexican artist Diego Rivera who became more revered after her passing than during her life. When she performed, Selena made people happy by making them feel good with music, a basic tenet she shared with her father. Her posthumous image no longer served to soothe the savage beast within but instead was a touchstone for salvation, hope, and redemption; hence the Selena shrines, the Selena votive candles, and the Selena veneration throughout the Latin world.

The pop crossover songs were almost beside the point. The music that defined her spirituality were the songs of hurt and pain and emotion, such as "Tú, Sólo Tú," which stayed on the Latin charts long after the English songs faded from heavy rotation, and "Como la Flor," a song in which she bids farewell to her love, accepting loss with a liberating sense of resignation.

Her pain was everyone's pain, and through her suffering could be tolerated and accepted. Through her, knowing what she went through to get to the position of prominence she achieved in her brief time on earth, healing was possible.

Oddly enough, it was her father, the self-appointed guardian of her image, who fought the worship of his daughter most vociferously while he scrambled to control the exploitation of all things Selena. At the heart of the cognitive dissonance was his ambiguity about professed faith and living faith. Being a follower of the Jehovah's Witness sect, he was torn about fully immersing himself in the faith because of the business he and his family were in. The World's Fastest-Growing Religion, as the Witnesses called themselves, would not accept them as they were. Was now the time to commit?

Abraham's family were not Witnesses, he emphasized to reporters on several occasions. His parents were. "We're studying," he said. "With what has happened to my daughter, I believe in the Jehovah's Witness faith, but I'm not a practicing member," Abraham told John Morthland, reporting for *Entertainment Weekly*. "I have done some very serious thinking and I am gonna try to line up my life with God. Not fanatically, but with the knowledge, understanding . . . I believe in the Resurrection, and I want to be there when Selena's resurrected to receive her back."

Veneration was not part of his beliefs. "The Bible says that God is a jealous god, that he wants exclusive devotion from us, not to use idols," he told Morthland. "I can't control people's beliefs or ideology. I know what I believe, what Selena believed, and we're gonna try to please God. What people do, we can't control. I didn't speak out when Selena died but I didn't want people to receive her that way, as an idol rather than as a good-hearted, lovable person that cared for people."

The bewildered reaction underscored a lack of understanding all around. The Quintanillas, the Days Inn management, the funeral home, the entire city of Corpus Christi were in denial. This was South Texas, *ese*. Icons and icon worship were part of the territory, from the peyote shrine in Rio Grande City to the Don Pedro Jaramillo shrine near Falfurrias. Shrines of religious significance were found all over the region, with the thickest concentration in the Rio Grande Valley. The latest wave began back in 1983, when the image of Christ appeared on a *gordita*, a fat, grilled tortilla, in the bordertown of Hidalgo, south of McAllen in the Rio Grande Valley, and a shrine with candles and flowers was erected at the site. Downriver were other shrines—one in Brownsville, where the image of the Virgin Mary appeared on a cottonwood tree, another in Progreso, where the Virgin Mary's likeness was discovered on the floor of a shower stall at the E & E Mini Mart, a third in La Feria, where the Virgin Mary manifested herself on the frilly curtains of a window in the home of the Chávez family, and still another in Elsa, where, in 1993, Dario Mendoza found the image of the Virgin Mary on the side panel of his '81 Camaro. Shrines had been erected at all of the sites, attracting pilgrims from both sides of the border who hoped their encounter with the spiritual apparitions would have a profound effect on their lives and the lives of their loved ones.

Dr. Tony Zavaleta, a dean at the University of Texas at Brownsville and a scholar of folk religion, commented, "It seemed to me in the immediate hours and days after the murder of Selena that the energy that I was seeing, which was absolutely phenomenal, was combined with religious beliefs, folk religion, [the messages on] her fence there in Corpus Christi, the *corridos*. It just had to be that someone would channel her spirit. . . . It's just a matter of time. Whether it be in Corpus Christi, Los Angeles, or Weslaco, someone will bring down the spirit of Selena and will give *consejos*, or heal.

"If the faithful desire, they will come."

The faithful desired. They were coming. The answer was found in the land of Selena's ancestors, in a little town in northern Coahuila called Espinazo, on the highway between Monterrey and Monclova, some four hours by car from the Rio Grande. The entire community was a shrine to one of its own, the Niño Fidencio, a childlike, humble housekeeper whose healing powers sanctified him to true believers and subjected him to vilification by the Catholic Church. The story of El Niño has become the stuff of legend. He was in his late twenties when he became aware of his powers through a vision he had of some miners who had been injured in an accident. Then he saved a woman by performing a cesarean section on her although he had had no medical training. He removed tumors with shards of glass. He made lepers whole again. He also presented plays, concerts, and dances for entertainment, for he believed people should have fun in life, and there was pleasure in the arts.

When El Niño died in 1938, his family, like Selena's family, was overwhelmed by the devotion and faith expressed by pilgrims who came to the town where he lived and performed his miraculous healings. Rather than deny them access to the object of their devotion, the Niño's family and all of Espinazo accommodated them, opening their homes and other sites that the Niño had frequented. Celebrations were spontaneously organized around his birthday and saint's name day in March and October, drawing tens of thousands of the faithful from both sides of the border. The people came in search of cures, in search of hope, in search of solutions not found in the physical world. They stopped at the old tree where El Niño healed. They stopped at the tomb inside the family house. They stopped in the garden. They stopped on the hill where some said he had performed miracles. They wanted to walk in his steps and see, feel, and hear what he must have been like.

El Niño was the first mass-media–produced saint. At the time his miracles were most prolific, the movie newsreel had come into popularity in Mexico, and cameramen from Mexico City descended on Espinazo to record his deeds on film which was then seen by millions of moviegoers. With the fame came the controversy. The more well known El Niño became, the more vociferously he was attacked by priests and doctors. Death only made his spirit greater and more pervasive.

On the day the defense rested in *State of Texas* versus *Saldivar*, several thousand true believers had gathered some five hundred miles to the southwest for El Niño's fall festival. This observance was much like observances in previous years: the hopeful prayed to the Niño and to God for specific needs or general deliverance from evil. The one significant difference was the presence of Selena. For the first time in the fifty years of Nino Fidencio festivals, El Niño's image was outnumbered by another's. Likenesses of Selena were everywhere, appearing on dozens of T-shirts, worn by people of all ages and from all walks of life. Among the many petitions pilgrims made on behalf of their loved ones and themselves, there was a new question being asked by the faithful: Why was Selena taken from us to heaven so soon?

Selena was both a real person and a symbol, the poetic image of youth, beauty, wholesomeness, and family values, an inspiration to young people that they can be faithful to the old ways while embracing modern ideas. Her life ended in a tragedy that would forever be replayed in millions of minds, a senseless tale of betrayal by one who had loved her. Those circumstances are precisely why her image has become something greater and more influential than it ever could have been in life. The pilgrims were coming. The candle had been lit. As long as there were those who remembered, the flame would burn. Her spirit was alive. Through her, there was redemption for all. *Eternamente.*

Notes

References appear in chronological order within each chapter.

CHAPTER ONE

Paul Schuster Taylor. *An American-Mexican Frontier*. New York: Russell and Russell, 1934, 1971.

Americo Paredes. *With a Pistol in His Hand, with a Pistol in His Hand: A Border Ballad and Its Hero*. Austin: University of Texas Press, 1951.

"Mexican-Americans," Corpus Christi *Caller-Times*, May 25, 1976.

Bill Walraven, "Heritage of City's Mexican-Americans Is Long and Hard," Corpus Christi *Caller-Times*, February 7, 1983.

Joe Nick Patoski, "Polka Picante," *Texas Monthly*, January 1986.

Spencer Pearson, "Who Named the Bay," Corpus Christi *Caller-Times*, September 25, 1988.

Ron George, "Villarreal Meets Kinney," Corpus Christi *Caller-Times*, September 25, 1988.

Eugenia Reynolds Briscoe. *City by the Sea*. New York: Vantage Press, 1985.

Mike Chávez, "The Dinos, Now and Then," Corpus Christi *La Voz Latina de KUNO*, March 1991.

José Antonio Burciaga. *Drink Cultura: Chicanismo*, Santa Barbara, California: Capra Press, 1993.

José E. Limón. *Dancing with the Devil: Society and Cultural Politics in Mexican-American South Texas*. Madison, Wisconsin: University of Wisconsin Press, 1994.

Helen Simons and Cathryn A. Hoyt. *Hispanic Texas: A Historical Guide*. Austin: University of Texas Press, 1992.

Karen Lister, "Selena's Dreams," Corpus Christi *Caller-Times*, July 16, 1995.

Doug Hancock, interview, July 30, 1995.

Freddy Fender, interview, August 2, 1995.

Manuel Dávila, Jr., interview, August 3, 1995.

Freddie Martínez, Jr., interview, August 12, 1995.

Nano Ramírez, interview, August 23, 1995.

Freddie Martínez, Sr., interview, August 26, 1995.

Adrian Treviño, interview, January 15, 1996.

CHAPTER TWO

Advertisement, Brazosport *Facts*, October 3, 1980.

"Self-Improvement Course Successfully Completes Session," Brazorian *News*, December 24, 1980.

Selena, interview with Joseph Harmes, October 1992.

Vicente Carranza, "Selena," *La Voz Latina*, May 1995.

Johnny Herrera, "The Music Scene," *La Voz Latina*, May 1995.

Annie Pérez, interview, July 2, 1995.

Louie Matula, interview, July 3, 1995.

Pat Diehl, interview, July 3, 1995.

Primo Ledesma, interview, July 12 and August 19, 1995.

Carmen Read, interview, July 13, 1995.

Rena Dearman, interview, July 13, 1995.

Karen Lister, "Selena's Dreams," Corpus Christi *Caller-Times*, July 16, 1995.

Primo Ledesma, interview, August 19, 1995.

Armando Treviño, interview, August 19, 1995.

Nina McGlashen, interview, August 19, 1995.

Judy Peacock, interview, August 19, 1995.

Yolanda Flores, interview, August 20, 1995.

Alex Espinoza, interview, August 26, 1995.

Sam Flores, interview, August 26 and September 9, 1995.

Harold Lindloff, interview, August 27, 1995.

Santos Serda, Sr., interview, September 7, 1995.

Dr. Rod Cannon, interview, September 14, 1995.

Linda Pegoda, interview, September 14, 1995.

Bobby Reed, interview, September 15, 1995.

Meredith Lynn Cappel, interview, September 22, 1995.

Candy O'Conner, interview, September 27, 1995.

Selena special, Telemundo television network, broadcast September 28, 1995.

CHAPTER THREE

"City Second in Latin-Anglo Segregation," Associated Press, Corpus Christi *Caller-Times*, July 26, 1966.

Anne Dodson, "Truan Says Latin Drop-Out Rate Unjust to Society," Corpus Christi *Caller-Times*, December 15, 1970.

Ray Caballero, "Sleeping Giant Has Bad Case of Apathy at Election Time," Corpus Christi *Caller-Times*, May 24, 1976.

Mary Alice Davis, "Mexican-American Representation in Office Still Low," Corpus Christi *Caller-Times*, May 25, 1976.

Jay Jorden, "Accusing Fingers Point at Hispanic Leaders," Corpus Christi *Caller-Times*, April 23, 1981.

Loretta Macías, "Hispanic Custom Steeped in Tradition and Faith," San Angelo *Standard-Times*, August 28, 1985.

Leandro Rivera, "Selena y los Dinos Make Sudden Impact on Tejano Music," *Tejano Entertainer*, June 1986.

Ramon Hernandez, "Teenage Tejano Singer Already an Award-Winner," San Antonio *Express-News*, April 23, 1987.

Dave Ferman, " 'Madrecita' Holds Special Place in Hispanic Family," Corpus Christi *Caller-Times*, May 8, 1988.

Rosemary Barnes, "Breaking Through," Corpus Christi *Caller-Times*, December 29, 1988.

Ramon Hernandez, "Selena's Life Is Scheduled Around Concert Schedule," San Antonio *Express-News*, March 2, 1989.

Vincent Rodríguez, Jr., "Mature Selena Sees Success," Corpus Christi *Caller-Times*, April 9, 1989.

"First Album Is in the Works," Corpus Christi *Caller-Times*, *Vista* magazine, June 4, 1989.

Vincent Rodríguez, Jr., "Tejano Music Awards Caravan of Stars Will Stop in Coliseum," Corpus Christi *Caller-Times*, July 20, 1989.

Ray Caballero, "Jury Wheel Figure Talks on Civil Rights," Corpus Christi *Caller-Times*, March 27, 1991.

Selena, interview with Joseph Harmes, October 1992.

"Rising Star," *People* magazine commemorative issue, Spring 1995.

Ramon Hernandez, interview, July 25, 1995.

Rubén García, interview, July 30, 1995.

Joanna Powell, "Selena: Her Family Shares Their Private Grief," *Good Housekeeping*, August 1995.

Freddie Martínez, Jr., interview, August 15, 1995.

Laura Canales, interview, August 18, 1995.

Freddie Martínez, Sr., interview, August 24, 1995.

Greg Barrios, interview, September 5, 1995.

Marilyn Greer, interview, September 6, 1995.

Ernest Garza, interview, September 15, 1995.

Rubén Cubillos, interview, September 18, 1995.

Selena special, Telemundo network, September 28, 1995.

CHAPTER FOUR

Ramiro Burr, "Young Tejano Star Ready to Shine," San Antonio *Light*, February 25, 1990.

"Local Girl Makes Good," Corpus Christi *Caller-Times*, March 10, 1990.

Ramon Hernandez, "Selena on a Winning Streak," San Antonio *Express-News*, December 28, 1990.

"Selena Wows Fulmore Junior High Students," San Antonio *La Prensa*, March 1, 1991.

"Gold Record to Be Awarded to Local Singer," Corpus Christi *Caller-Times*, October 26, 1991.

Scott Williams, "Tejano Gold: Selena Quintanilla Sings Songs of Success," Corpus Christi *Caller-Times*, November 1, 1991.

Ramiro Burr, "Selena Slides into Houston Date," San Antonio *Insider*, December 15, 1991.

Tim Brooks and Earle Marsh. *The Complete Directory to Prime Time TV Shows, 1946—Present*. New York: Ballantine, 1992.

Ben Tavera King, "What Is *Tejano*? Don't Ask *Webster*," San Antonio *Express-News*, October 25, 1992.

Ramiro Burr, "Latin Music Had a Big Year in '93," San Antonio *Express-News*, December 26, 1992.

Joe Nick Patoski, "Sound of *Musica*," *Texas Monthly*, January 1993.

René Cabrera, "Selena Tapes New Album at Coliseum," Corpus Christi *Caller-Times*, February 5, 1993.

Dan Calderon, "Fans See Selena Album Recorded," Corpus Christi *Caller-Times*, February 8, 1993.

John Lannert, "SBK Signs Latin Star Selena to Worldwide Deal," *Billboard*, November 20, 1993.

"Selena Riding *la Onda* to the Top," *Revista Alegre*, February 1994.

Ramiro Burr, interview, September 15 and 29, 1995.

Selena special, Telemundo network, September 28, 1995.

Cristina special, Univisión network, October 9, 1995.

René Cabrera, "Selena: Her Music," *La Voz Latina*, May 1995.

David Wright, "Selena's Wedding Secret," *National Enquirer*, December 12, 1995.

CHAPTER FIVE

Jerry Bergman. *Jehovah's Witnesses and Kindred Groups*. Brooklyn, N.Y.: 1984.

M. James Penton. *Apocalypse Delayed: The Story of Jehovah's Witnesses*. Toronto: University of Toronto Press, 1985.

Watchtower Bible and Tract Society. *Yearbook of Jehovah's Witnesses*.

Watchtower Bible and Tract Society. *Knowledge That Leads to Everlasting Life*.

Jim Beal, Jr., "Selena Wins a Grammy for 'Live' Recording," San Antonio *Express-News*, March 2, 1994.

Ramiro Burr, "Entertainers Navaira, Selena Scoop Up Multiple Honors," San Antonio *Express-News*, March 14, 1994.

Matt Flores, "Selena Expected to Jam Berry Fete," San Antonio *Express-News*, April 9, 1994.

Ramiro Burr, "La Mafia, Selena Top New Releases," San Antonio *Express-News*, April 17, 1994.

Ramiro Burr, "Texas Performers Nab *Billboard* Awards," San Antonio *Express-News*, May 22, 1994.

Ramiro Burr, "Miguel, La Mafia, Selena Honored," San Antonio *Express-News*, May 22, 1994.

Karen Snelling, "Mosquito Festival Concert Homecoming for Singer," Brazosport *Facts*, July 29, 1994.

Ramiro Burr, "Tex-Mex Market Gains Industry Stature," San Antonio *Express-News*, August 28, 1994.

"Coca-Cola Goes Tejano with the Introduction of the Selena Commemorative Contour bottle," Corpus Christi *Tejano Review*, November 30, 1994.

Ramiro Burr, "Selena Still the Fashion in Tejano Music," San Antonio *Express-News*, December 2, 1994.

Rose Mary Budge, "Tejano Concert Star Selena Huge Success—As Is Her Gomez-designed Women's Line," San Antonio *Express-News*, December 4, 1994.

Ramiro Burr, "Energetic Selena Works Music Magic," San Antonio *Express-News*, December 5, 1995.

Ramiro Burr, "1994 Saw Continued Boom in Latin-music Sales," San Antonio *Express-News*, December 18, 1995.

Ramiro Burr, "Selena y los Dinos Will Headline the Free 'Teach the Children' Festival Saturday and Sunday at Market Square," San Antonio *Express-News*, January 15, 1995.

Ramiro Burr, "Selena Takes 6 Honors to Dominate Tejano Music Awards," San Antonio *Express-News*, February 12, 1995.

Ramiro Burr, "Singer Wants Apology for Award Mix-up," San Antonio *Express-News*, February 14, 1995.

Cindy Ramos, "Spurs, Selena Join in Dome for Stay in School JAMboree," San Antonio *Express-News*, March 19, 1995.

Rick Mitchell, "Mi Corazón, My Love," Houston *Chronicle*, April 2, 1995.

Cindy Tumiel and Kym Fox, "Saldivar Said to Have Once Hated Selena," San Antonio *Express-News*, April 9, 1995.

Enrique Lepetegui, "A Crossover Dream Halted Prematurely, Tragically; Some Ambitious Plans Were Under Way to Bring Selena to Mainstream U.S. Audience," Los Angeles *Times*, April 8, 1995.

Tejano Notes, the newsletter of the Texas Talent Music Association, June 1995.

Cynthia Sanz and Betty Cortina, "As Fans Pay Tribute to a Fallen Star, Chris Perez Mourns the Woman He Loved," *People* magazine, July 10, 1995.

José Hernández, interview, June 1, 1995.

Cameron Randle, interview, June 1, 1995.

Freddy Fender, interview, August 2, 1995.

Manuel Dávila, interview, August 3, 1995.

Casey Monahan, interview, August 7, 1995.

Freddie Martínez, Jr., interview, August 15, 1995.

Peter Watrous, "Selena's Legacy," *New York Times*, August 21, 1995.

Albert Huerta, interview, August 25, 1995.

Vilma Maldonado, interview, August 29, 1995.

Greg Barrios, interview, September 3, 1995.

Danny Noyola, interview, September 21, 1995.

Selena special edition, *Fama* magazine, September 1995.

Selena special, Telemundo network, September 28, 1995.

Cristina special, Univisión network, October 9, 1995.

René Cabrera, "Selena: Her Music," *La Voz Latina*, May 1995.

Dr. Ricardo Martínez, interview, *Primer Impacto*, Univisión network, October 25, 1995.

Yolanda Saldivar, interview, *Primer Impacto*, Univisión network, November 14, 1995.

CHAPTER SIX

"Fans Shocked by Fatal Attack on Selena," Brazosport *Facts*, April 1, 1995.

Michael Q. Sullivan, "Selena Fans Remember Her Through Prayer, Praise," Brazosport *Facts*, April 2, 1995.

Jesse Katz, "For Barrio, Selena's Death Strikes a Poignant Chord," Los Angeles *Times*, April 2, 1995.

Frank B. Williams and Enrique Lopetegui, "Mourning Selena," Los Angeles *Times*, April 3, 1995.

Ron George, "Selena was Seeking Spiritual Meaning," Corpus Christi *Caller-Times*, April 3, 1995.

Eric Brown, "Saldivar Pleads Not Guilty," Corpus Christi *Caller-Times*, April 7, 1995.

Ron George, "Mass to Be Celebrated for Selena," Corpus Christi *Caller-Times*, April 14, 1995.

Valeria Godines, "Mass Celebrates Selena's Birth, Life," Corpus Christi *Caller-Times*, April 17, 1995.

Ricky Dávila and Albert Dávila, Jr., interview, June 20, 1995.

Josh Lemieux, "Saldivar Claims Selena's Father 'Came Between Us,' " Associated Press, August 10, 1995.

Joanna Powell, "Selena: Her Family Shares Their Private Grief," *Good Housekeeping*, August 1995.

CHAPTER SEVEN

"Family Bids Tearful Farewell to Singing Star Selena," Brazosport *Facts*, April 4, 1995.

Vivienne Heines, "Husband Recalls Life with Selena," Corpus Christi *Caller-Times*, April 4, 1995.

Editorial, "Remembering Selena," Brazosport *Facts*, April 6, 1995.

"Reader Recalls Little Selena: A Girl Who Shared and Cared," Brazosport *Facts*, April 6, 1995.

Editorial, "Just Ignore Him," Brazosport *Facts*.

Eric Brown, "Saldivar Pleads Not Guilty," Corpus Christi *Caller-Times*, April 7, 1995.

Josh Lemieux, "Selena's Death Stirs Deep Emotions in Young Hearts," Associated Press, April 10, 1995.

"Remembering Selena," Hondo *Anvil-Herald*, April 13, 1995.

Ron George, "Mass to Be Celebrated for Selena," Corpus Christi *Caller-Times*, April 14, 1995.

Valeria Godines, "Mass Celebrates Selena's Birth, Life," Corpus Christi *Caller-Times*, April 17, 1995.

Diane Richbourg, "Selena Album Scheduled to Be Released in July," Corpus Christi *Caller-Times*, April 20, 1995.

Jeff Classen, "Internet Entry Promoting Selena Foundation Concert," Corpus Christi *Caller-Times*, April 25, 1995.

Letters to the Editor, Brazosport *Facts*, May 9, 1995.

Valeria Godines, "Quintanilla Unveils Anti-Gun Campaign," Corpus Christi *Caller-Times*, May 5, 1995.

Karen Brooks, "Saldivar Cheated Selena," Corpus Christi *Caller-Times*, May 13, 1995.

Mary Batts Estrada, "Tejano Music—Hot 'N Spicy," *Vista* magazine, May 1995.

Ramiro Burr, "Twin Awards Programs Spread Honor and Confusion," Houston *Chronicle*, June 11, 1995.

Robert Dominguez, "Selena Still Selling Strong," New York *Daily News*, June 30, 1995.

Ramiro Burr, "A Pop Culture Milestone," *Hispanic Business* magazine, July 1995.

"Selena Can't Be Considered for Walk of Fame for Five Years," Associated Press, July 7, 1995.

Cynthia Sanz and Betty Cortina, "Haunted by Grief, Her Family Takes Comfort in Her Musical Legacy," and "As Fans Pay Tribute to a Fallen Star, Chris Perez Mourns the Woman He Loved," *People* magazine, July 10, 1995.

Josh Lemieux, "Bootleggers Already Putting Out New Selena Release," Associated Press, July 12, 1995.

Rubén García, interview, July 30, 1995.

Manual Dávila, Jr., interview, August 1, 1995.

Tina Valenzuela, interview, August 24, 1995.

David Bennett, "Selena's Worth at Death Said to Be $163,000," San Antonio *Express-News*, September 26, 1995.

Josh Lemieux, "Selena's English Song Soars," Associated Press, June 17, 1995.

Robert Dominguez, "Selena Still Selling Strong," New York *Daily News*, June 30, 1995.

Christopher John Farley, "Old Rock, New Life," *Time* magazine, July 10, 1995.

Ramiro Burr, "Selena's CD Tipped to Create History," San Antonio *Express-News*, July 16, 1995.

Karen Lister, "Selena's Dreams," Corpus Christi *Caller-Times*, July 16, 1995.

Fernando González, "Crossover: An Obsolete Idea for Latinos?," Miami *Herald*, July 16, 1995.

Roger Catlin, "Selena's Album: A Tribute to What Would Have Been," Hartford *Courant*, July 16, 1995.

Salvatore Caputo, "Selena's Success Generated Ethnic Pride," Arizona *Republic*, July 16, 1995.

Cary Darling, "Hype Machine Cranks into High Gear for Release of Selena's New Album Tuesday," Orange County *Register*, July 17, 1995.

Mario Tarradell, "New Album Celebrates the Late Selena, But Only Hints at What She Could Have Become," Dallas *Morning News*, July 17, 1995.

David Zimmerman, "Selena's Bilingual 'Dream' Hits Stores," *USA Today*, July 18, 1995.

Kelley Shannon, "Fans Line Up to Buy Selena Album 'Dreaming of You,' " Associated Press, July 18, 1995.

Ramiro Burr, "Dream Come True" and "Selena Crosses Over to Pop," San Antonio *Express-News*, July 18, 1995.

Pamela Ward, "Slain Singer's Fans Snap Up New CD," Austin *American Statesman*, July 18, 1995.

Vilma Maldonado, "Music Stores Brace for Selena CD Crush," McAllen *Monitor*, July 18, 1995.

Ramiro Burr, "Selena CD Sales High But Not Overwhelming," San Antonio *Express-News*, July 19, 1995.

Pamela Ward, "Selena Fans Make New CD a Commodity *Muy Caliente*," Austin *American Statesman*, July 19, 1995.

Jeanne Jakle, "Vanessa Williams Lands Hispanic Role," San Antonio *Express-News*, July 20, 1995.

Thelma Garza, "Tejano Vies for Category at Grammys," San Antonio *Express-News*, July 20, 1995.

Vilma Maldonado, "Selena Release a Smash Hit," McAllen *Monitor*, July 22, 1995.

"Selena Case Suspect Staying Behind Bars," Associated Press, Austin *American Statesman*, July 22, 1995.

Peter Watrous, "Selena: Inklings of What Might Have Been," *New York Times*, July 30, 1995.

John Morthland, "The Selling of Selena," *Entertainment Weekly*, August 18, 1995.

Jean Seligmann with Tim Padgett, "Diva Duel: Who Plays Selena?," *Time* magazine, August 28, 1995.

CHAPTER EIGHT

Richard Zelade, interview, June 5, 1995.

Ricky Dávila and Albert Dávila, Jr., interviews, June 20, 1995.

Karen Lister, "In Death, As in Life, Selena Continues to Attract Devoted Fans," Corpus Christi *Caller-Times*, July 16, 1995.

Claudia Perry, "Selena's New Album May Realize Her Crossover Dream," San Jose *Mercury News*, July 18, 1995.

Jane Sumner, "Selena Look-alike," Dallas *Morning News*, July 28, 1995.

Al Aguilar, interview, August 2, 1995.

Albert Huerta, interview, August 12, 1995.

"Stern Show Returns to TCI Cable," "Conquering Stereotypes," Corpus Christi *Caller-Times*, August 12, 1995.

Cristina, Univisión network, August 21, 1995.

Olga Flores, "Bilingualism Is Knowledge, Not Ignorance," Austin *American Statesman*, September 1, 1995.

Selena special edition, *Fama* magazine, September 1995.

David Uhler, "Selena Babies," San Antonio *Express-News*, September 4, 1995.

Bill Angelini, interview, September 8, 1995.

Julie Watson, "Visions of Virgin Mary Abound in the Valley," McAllen *Monitor*, September 3, 1995.

Ron George, "Selena's Band to Make One Last Tour for Fans," Corpus Christi *Caller-Times*, September 14, 1995.

Fernando Del Valle, "Look-alike Contests Intensify," *Valley Morning Star*, Austin *American Statesman*, September 21, 1995.

Ron Rosenbaum, "Elvis, Healer," *New York Times Magazine*, September 24, 1995.

Lauraine Miller, "Crowds Drawn to Selena," Dallas

Morning News, October 6, 1995.
Enterese, Edición de Colección Selena, Univisión net-
work, October 9, 1995.
Selena special, Telemundo network, September 28, 1995.

CHAPTER NINE

Libby Averyt and Eric Brown, "Man of the People,"
Corpus Christi *Caller-Times*, May 7, 1995.
Suzanne Gamboa, "On Eve of Trial, Selena's Fame Still
Grows," Austin *American Statesman*, October 8, 1995.
Patty Reinert, "Potential Jurors Say Minds Set," Houston
Chronicle, October 10, 1995.
Dr. Ricardo Martínez, interview, *Primer Impacto*, Univi-
sión network, October 25, 1995.
Yolanda Saldivar, interview, *Primer Impacto*, Univisión
network, November 14, 1995.
Eric Brown, "Saldivar Security to Be Tight," Corpus
Christi *Caller-Times*, August 4, 1995.
Matt Flores, "Judge to Rule on Saldivar Venue," San
Antonio *Express-News*, August 8, 1995.
Josh Lemieux, "Defense Tries to Block Saldivar's Al-
leged Confession," Associated Press, August 8, 1995.
Eric Brown, "Confession Questioned; Judge Rules to
Move Murder Trial," Corpus Christi *Caller-Times*, Au-
gust 9, 1995.
Matt Flores, "Saldivar Trial to Be Moved from Corpus,"
San Antonio *Express-News*, August 9, 1995.
Josh Lemieux, "Saldivar Defense Attacks Police Han-
dling of Statement," Associated Press, August 9, 1995.
Libby Averyt, "Confession Questioned, Officers Disagree
on If Saldivar Said 'Accident,' " Corpus Christi *Caller-
Times*, August 9, 1994.
Eric Brown, "Tinker: We Can Prove Accident," Corpus
Christi *Caller-Times*, August 10, 1995.
Libby Averyt, "Prosecution, Defense Paint Different Pic-
tures," Corpus Christi *Caller-Times*, August 13, 1995.
Christine Laue, "Judge Describes Emotions in Selena

Case," Corpus Christi *Caller-Times*, August 18, 1995.

Patty Reinert, "Defense Repaints Picture of Events in Selena Case," Houston *Chronicle*, August 20, 1995.

Tom Kuncl, "Accused Killers' Kinky Confession: Selena Died after Lesbian Love Quarrel," *Globe*, August 22, 1995.

"Networks Denied Live Coverage of Selena Trial," Associated Press, Austin *American Statesman*, September 7, 1995.

Michelle Koidin, "Houston Economy Outgrows Oil Industry," Associated Press, Austin *American Statesman*, September 28, 1995.

"Embezzlement Indictment Against Saldivar Delayed," Associated Press, Austin *American Statesman*, September 30, 1995.

David Bennett, "Saldivar's Defender Tops in Field," San Antonio *Express-News*, September 10, 1995.

Dick J. Reavis. *Ashes of Waco*. New York: Simon and Schuster, 1995.

Cristina special, Univisión network, October 9, 1995.

Carlos Guerra, "Selena's Widower's Future Unclear," San Antonio *Express-News*, October 6, 1995.

Discography

45 RPM SINGLES

1978   The earliest known recording was a tape made of the seven-year-old Selena by Johnny Herrera on a portable cassette recorder at his House of Music record shop in Corpus Christi. The songs were sixties vintage English-language pop oldies and two songs in Spanish: "Con Esta Copa," written by Herrera, and "Que."

The Quintanilla children, performing as Southern Pearl, recorded a demo pressed as a 45 single at Sugar Hill Studios in Houston.

1980   "Tomorrow's Rains Fell Today (In the Twilight of My Sorrow)," a country-western version of "Si Quieres Verme Llorar," written by Johnny Herrera, was recorded on a two-inch master at Hacienda Recording Studios in Corpus Christi but never released.

1981 "Feelings" (Dime), recorded during a talent contest in Lake Jackson on a cassette recorder.

1982 "Sueños Dulces" (Patsy Cline's "Sweet Dreams" sung in Spanish), backed with "Me Necesitabas" (Anne Murray's "You Needed Me" sung in Spanish). Freddie Pressed but not released

"A Hundred Pounds of Clay," sung in Spanish Freddie Pressed but not released

1983 "No Puedo Estar sin Ti" backed with "Se Acabó el Amor" Freddie FR-451

"Ya Se Va" backed with "Tres Veces No" Freddie FR-593

"Encontré el Amor" backed with "Soy Feliz" Cara CA-216

"Se Me Hace" backed with "Estoy Contingo" Cara CA-226

1984 "Dejame Volar" backed with "La Tracalera" Cara CA-238

"Escríbeme" backed with "Aunque No Salga el Sol" Cara CA-247

1985 "Oh, Mamá" backed with "Un Primer Amor" Cara CA-282

1986 "Dame un Beso" backed with "Con Esta Copa" GP-302

"A Million to One" backed with "Muñquito de Trapo" GP-304

"Yo Te Dare" backed with "Acuerdate de Mi" GP-313

1987 "La Bamba" backed with "Tu No Sabes" GP-317

1988 "Terco Corazón" backed with "Quiero" GP-322

"Yo Fui Aquella" backed with "Como Quisiera" RP-1006

"Contigo Quiero Estar" (promotional copy) Capital-EMI PH-19328

1990 "Baile Esta Cumbia" backed with "La Carcacha" (promotional copy) EMI-700 1141

"Ya Vez" backed with "La Tracalera" Capitol-EMI HA-19430

CD SINGLES

1992 "Quiero" (Mexico promotional copy) EMI-78 956 129

1993 "Dondequiera que Estés" w/the Barrio Boyzz (promotional copy) EMI Latin DPRO-79043

1994 "Amor Prohibido" (promotional copy) EMI DPRO-79199

"Bidi Bidi Bom Bom" (promotional copy) EMI Latin DPRO-42835

"No Me Queda Más" (promotional copy) EMI Latin DPRO-42904

"Fotos y Recuerdos" backed with "Tesoro" by Graciela Beltran (promotional copy)   EMI Latin DPRO-42939

1995   "Tú, Sólo Tú" backed with "I Could Fall in Love" (promotional copy)   EMI Latin DPRO-42975

"Techno Cumbia" backed with   EMI Latin DPRO-10618

"El Toro Relajo"   EMI Latin DPRO-10642

CASSETTES

1984   *Selena y los Dinos*   Freddie FR-1294
"Ya Se Va," "Cruzare la Montaña," "Se Acabó Aquel Amor," "Ya Lo Se que Tú Te Vas," "Parece que Va Llover," "Tres Veces No," "Give Me One Chance," "Tú Solamente Tú," "Lo Tanto que Te Quiero," "Call Me"

1985   *The New Girl in Town*   Cara

1986   *Texas Class—Patsy, Laura, Selina [sic] Zandra* Freddie LP-1486

1995   Tejano Music Awards. Celebrando La Quinceañera (with "Bidi Bidi Bom Bom")   General Mills promotional

LP ALBUMS

1984   15 Hits the New Generation—Various Artists Freddie LP-1296
(includes "Ya Se Va" and "Tú Solamente Tú")

1986   *Alpha*   GP LP-1002
"Dame un Beso," "Con Esta Copa," "Soy Amiga," "Corazoncito," "Sentimientos," "Pero Como Te A'ido Pa que Me Sirve la Vida," "Pensando en Tí," "El Tejano," "Dame un Amor"

Muñequito de Trapo   GP C-1005
"Brindis de Amor," "A Million to One," "El Ramalazo," "La Mirada," "Rama Caida," "Diferentes," "Muñequito de Trapo," "Cuando Despierto," "Enamorada de Tí," "El Circo"

1987   *And the Winner Is . . .*   GP LP-1009
"Acuerdate de Mi," "Tú No Sabes," "La Bamba," "Tres Dias," "Yo Te Dare," "Te Amo Sólo a Tí," "Cuando Nadie Te Quiera," "Corazón Abandonado," "Salta la Ranita," "Ven a Verme"

1988   *Preciosa*   RP LP-8801
"Terco Corazón," "Cien Años," "Siempre," "Quiero," "Sabes," "Quiero Estar Contigo," "Como Te Quiero," "Yo Fui Aquella," "Como Quisiera," "Cariño Mío"

Dulce Amor   RP LP-8803
"Dulce Amor," "Que," "Tú Solamente Tú," "Always Mine," "Costumbres," "Dime," "No Llores Mas Corazon," "La Puerta Se Cerro," "Cariño, Cariño Mío," "Quisiera Darte"

1989   *Selena y los Dinos*   Capitol-EMI H1E42144
"Tú Eres," "Sukiyaki," "Contigo Quiero Estar," "Besitos," "Amame, Quiereme," "Tengo Ganas de Llorar," "My Love," "Quiero Ser," "Mentiras," "No Te Vayas"

1990   *Personal Best*   CBS RRL-80323
"Terco Corazón," "Siempre," "Quiero," "Qui-

ero Estar Contigo," "Como Te Quiero," "Cariño Mio," "Dulce Amor," "Yo Fui Aquella," "Dime," "No Llores Mas Corazón," "Quisiera Darte"

16 Super Exitos Originales Capitol-EMI H1E42299 "Estoy Contigo," "Sentimientos," "Acuerdate de Mi," "Tú No Sabes," "Costumbres," "Siempre," "Dame un Beso," "Yo Fui Aquella," "Cariño, Cariño Mío," "Dulce Amor," "Quiero Estar Contigo," "Terco Corazón," "Dime," "Ya Se_Va," "Cien Años," "Quiero"

14 Super Exitos/14 Super Estrellas Capitol-EMI H1F42346
(includes "Sukiyaki")

Tejano All Stars Capitol-EMI H1F42348
(includes "Contigo Quiero Estar" and "Mentiras")

Ven Conmigo Capitol-EMI H1E42359

CDS

1989 Selena y los Dinos Capitol-EMI H2Y42144
"Tú Eres," "Sukiyaki," "Contigo Quiero Estar," "Besitos," "Amame, Quiereme," "Tengo Ganas de Llorar," "My Love," "Quiero Ser," "Mentiras," "No Te Vayas"

1991 *Tejano All Stars, Volume One* Manny MCD-3010
(includes "Yo Fui Aquella")

Tejano All Stars, Volume Two Manny MCD-3015
(includes "Dulce Amor")

1992　Alvaro Torres: *Nada Se Compara Contigo* (duet on "Buenos Amigos") Capitol-EMI H2Y42537

Entre a Mi Mundo Capitol-EMI H242635
"Si La Quieres," "Como la Flor," "Yo Te Sigo Queriendo," "Qué Creías," "Las Cadenas," "Vuelve a Mi," "La Carcacha," "Siempre Estoy Pensando en Ti," "Missing My Baby," "Amame"

Baila Esta Cumbia (Mexico release) EMI 216 799052 2
"Baila Esta Cumbia," "Cariño, Cariño Mío," "Como la Flor," "Terco Corazon," "Ya Ves," "Quiero Ser," "Contigo Quiero Estar," "La Carcacha," "Ven Conmigo," "Yo Te Amo," "Besitos," "Siempre"

Tejano All Stars EMI Latin H2 72438 29050 2 1
(includes "Tú Robaste Mi Corazón")

Tejano All Stars, Volume Three EMI Latin H2 07777 42702
(includes "Yo Te Amo" and "La Tracalera")

Tejano Music Sweepers EMI Latin H2 07777 42717 2 1
(includes "Yo Me Voy" and "Ya Ves")

Entertainers of the Year: Selena-Emilio EMI Latin H2 07777 42754 2 2
"Como la Flor," "Buenos Amigos," "Yo Me Voy," "Siempre Estoy Pensando en Tí," "Ven Conmigo," "Amame"

1993　*Tejano All Stars, Volume Four* EMI Latin H2 07777 42752 4 8
(includes "La Carcacha" and "Las Cadenas")

Quiero (Mexico release)   EMI 0 77778 95612 9
"Siempre Estoy Pensando en Tí," "No Debes Jugar," "Yo Me Voy," "Las Cadenas," "Qué Creías," "Yo Te Sigo Queriendo," "La Llamada," "Si La Quieres," "Tú Robaste Mi Corazón," "Quiero"

Seleña Live   EMI Latin H4 07777 42770 4 4
"Como la Flor," "Baila Esta Cumbia," "Amame," "Siempre Estoy," "Pensando en Tí," "Ven Conmigo," "Perdoname," "Qué Creías," "Si la Quieres," "Porque le Gusta Bailar Cumbia," "La Carcacha," "Besitos," "Ya Ves," "Las Cadenas," "Yo Te Amo," "No Debes Jugar," "Tú Robaste Mi Corazón," "La Llamada"

Encuentro de Super Grupos   EMI Latin H2 07777 42787 2 0
(includes "Qué Creías")

The Tejano Explosion   EMI Latin H2 07777 42821 2 3
(includes "Si la Quieres," "Como la Flor," "Cuantas Veces")

Ayer y Hoy   EMI Latin H2 07777 42854 2 1
(includes "No Debes Jugar," "Ya Ves," "Si la Quieres")

Mis Mejores Canciones/17 Super Exitos   EMI Latin H2 72438 27190 2 1
"Como la Flor," "Mentiras," "Qué Creías," "Besitos," "Yo Fui Aquella" "Despues de Enero," "Vuelve a Mi," "No Quiero Saber," "Costumbres," "Tengo Ganas de Llorar," "Baila Esta Cumbia," "Yo Me Voy," "La Carcacha," "Tú Eres," "Sukiyaki," "Estoy Contigo," "La Tracalera"

Tejano All Stars Volume Five EMI Latin H4
7243 28050 4 5
(includes "Tú Robaste Mi Corazón")

Tejano All Stars Fonovisa TMCD 3034
(includes "Como la Flor," "La Carcacha,"
"Baita Esta Cumbia," and "Qué Creías")

1994 *Amor Prohibido* EMI Latin H2 72438 28803 2
5
"Amor Prohibido," "No Me Queda Más,"
"Cobarde," "Fotos y Recuerdos" *"El Chico Dep
Apartamento 512,"* "Bidi Bidi Bom Bom,"
"Techno Cumbia," "Tus Desprecios," "Si una
Vez," "Ya No"

12 Super Exitos EMI Latin H2 30907
"Si una Vez," "La Llamada," "No Debes Ju-
gar," "Las Cadenas," "Technocumbia," "Tú
Robaste Mi Corazón," "Bidi Bidi Bom Bom,"
"No Quiero Saber," "La Carcacha," "Missing
My Baby," "Como la Flor," "Qué Creías"

Super Exitazos/Tejano Hits Volume Two Freddie
FRCD 1642
(includes "Ya Se Va" and "Tú Solamente Tú")

Tejano Super Powerz Freddie FRCD 1682
(includes "Tú Solamente Tú")

Selena Cema S21 18104
"Como la Flor," "Si la Quieres," "Quiero,"
"Baila Esta Cumbia," "Yo Te Amo," "Qué
Creías," "Ya Ves," "Quiero Estar Contigo,"
"La Tracalera," "Besitos"

The 100,000 Club Series: Platinum Pack EMI
Latin H2 4275323

(includes "Baila Esta Cumbia," "La Carcacha," and "Qué Creías")

1995 *Mis Primeras Grabaciones* (reissue) Freddie FRCD 1294
"Ya Se Va," "Cruzare la Montaña," "Se Acabó Aquel Amor," "Ya Lo Se que Tu Te Vas," "Parece que Va Llover," "Tres Veces No," "Give Me One Chance," "Tú Solamente Tú," "Lo Tanto que Te Quiero," "Call Me"

Tejano Music Awards Winners EMI Latin H2 72438 33610 2 1
(includes "Bidi Bidi Bom Bom")

Las Reinas del Pueblo: Selena y Graciela Beltran EMI Latin H2 72438 32639 7 8
(includes "No Debes Llorar," "Bidi Bidi Bom Bom," "La Llamada," "Qué Creías," "La Carcacha"

Dreaming of You EMI Latin H2 72433 34123 2 7
"I Could Fall in Love," "Captive Heart," "I'm Getting Used to You," "God's Child (Baila Conmigo)," "Dreaming of You," "Missing My Baby," "Amor Prohibido," "Wherever You Are (Dondequiera que Estés)," "Technocumbia," "El Toro Relajo," "Como la Flor," "Tú, Sólo Tú," "Bidi Bidi Bom Bom"

1996 *The Songs of "West Side Story"* (Various Artists) RCA Victor 09026-62707-2
(includes "A Boy Like That")

Discography research by Ramon Hernandez, Hispanic American Celebrities Exhibit and Archives, Zoll Bandera Rd. #1707, San Antonio, Texas 78228.

Acknowledgments

A LTHOUGH THERE'S ONLY ONE BYLINE underneath the
title of this book, it could not have been written without the help of many others. Most important were Richard
Zelade, who shared his observations of growing up in Selena's hometown of Lake Jackson, and his wife, Diana
Ibarra López de la Fuente, who shared her observations
of growing up in Espinazo, Mexico, Niño Fidencio's
hometown; and David Bennett, for his knowledge and understanding of Corpus Christi and San Antonio and his
tenacious reporting for the San Antonio *Express-News*.
Ramon Hernandez provided invaluable insight into the
early days of Selena y los Dinos through his reminiscences, photographs, and by opening up his Hispanic-
American entertainment archives to me. Somehow,
someday, I hope his collection will find the permanent
home it deserves. Kathy Marcus was invaluable in putting
together the art.

Writer John Morthland was a sympathetic sounding
board and precious resource. Joseph T. Harmes gener-
ously shared his interview transcripts, observations, and
thoughts. Mary Margaret was the kind of research assistant every biographer hopes for. Melissa Heinz cranked

out transcriptions like clockwork. Abel Salas, David Courtney, and Andrew Goldman were instrumental in filling in the blanks. John Wheat made sure the accents were in the right places. David Anderson offered legal advice.

My colleagues in the info-gathering game, especially Carlos Guerra, Ginny Carol, Daisann McLane, Libby Averyt, Eric Brown, Patty Reinert, Thelma Garza, KWEX-TV, *Si* magazine, Ramiro Burr, and Maria Celeste Arraras, were generous in providing the details. David Flores helped me see the big picture. Johnny Herrera reaffirmed the beauty of being one's self. And Joe Villarreal helped make everything turn out for the best.

I'd also like to thank Gregory Curtis, my editor at *Texas Monthly,* for giving me the space to write three articles about Selena; and *Texas Monthly* editors David McCormick and Evan Smith, researcher Pat Booker, and copy editor Jane Dure. And to Casey Monaham, the director of the Texas Music Office of the Governor's Office, for all the guidance.

Finally, thanks to my own family for putting up with me, and to families everywhere.